Women in America

Women in America

A Guide to Books, 1963-1975

*With an Appendix
on Books Published 1976-1979*

BARBARA HABER

UNIVERSITY OF ILLINOIS PRESS

Urbana Chicago London

Illini Book Edition, 1981
By arrangement with G. K. Hall & Co.

Library of Congress Cataloging in Publication Data

Haber, Barbara.
  Women in America.

  (Illini books)
  An updated ed. of the author's 1978 work published
by G. K. Hall, Boston.
  Includes index.
  1. Women—United States—Bibliography. I. Title.
Z7964.U49H3 1981 [HQ1410] 016.3054'0973 80-28029
ISBN 0-252-00826-X (paper)

For Herb, Jon, and Nicky

Contents

Preface to the Paperback Edition

In preparing the update of *Women in America* for this paperback edition, I at first considered—and then immediately decided against—using the format of the original book. Faced with identifying significant books about American women written between 1976 and 1979, I found more than 200 titles that I felt ought to be included to document appropriately trends in the new work. It soon became apparent to me that my original format, which features long reviews of individual books, would not be feasible for an appendix that is necessarily limited in length. Rather than cut back the number of titles under consideration, I thought it more valuable to include them all and to shape them within the topical arrangements found in the original table of contents. Using the format of an extensive bibliographic essay seemed to me, therefore, a wise course.

As my work on this appendix was under way, I noticed a profound change in my point of view about the new books as compared with the way I had responded to material several years ago. That first time around I was intent on identifying what I had perceived to be "authentic female experience" from the masses of writing on American women that had appeared between 1963 and 1975. Looking back now, I realize that I had read those books with an isolated sense of discovering that women had perceptions and experiences that are unique and that I was intrigued with the ways in which authors recognized or failed to recognize this "truth."

In approaching books about American women written since 1975, I found that the unifying principle that had guided my commentary in the original book was no longer pertinent. The seeking out of evidence that reflects distinctive female experience is not an appropriate way to view current books. That is because authors now approach the subject of women with the collective assumption that sex is as basic and valid a category for analyzing human behavior as such traditionally viewed divisions as class, race, or national group. The substance of the new work is, for the most part, scholarly. From the standpoint of numerous disciplines authors are pushing out the frontiers of knowledge about women in their efforts to comprehend and explain the causes for and the manifestations of the unequal treatment of women in the society. The purpose of the essay that follows is to call attention to the range of subjects, the variety of ideas, and the development of methodology in the work at hand. The books are a testimony not only to the rapid development of scholarship centering on women, but to the diversity and quality of the work.

In keeping with the arrangement used in the original table of contents, the organization of this update is by topic rather than by discipline. Given the interdisciplinary nature of much of the work on women, an emphasis on subject matter more than on the academic niche of the author seemed valid and to the point. This format, however, is not without problems and necessitates some explanation for some of my decisions. Books on women's history, the discipline that has produced more studies than any other, are spread among several categories. The section, "History," contains general studies, anthologies, and biographies, while histories that deal with particular subjects such as "health" and "work" are placed within those headings. Likewise, books principally concerned with the subject of sex roles are in more than one place. For example, those concerned with the relationship between sex roles and the educational process are in "Education," while most of the others are in the section called "Sex Roles."

I made a departure from the original format by introducing the heading, "Lesbian/Feminism," to cover books on that subject instead of continuing to treat them within the topic "Sexuality." This change reflects the evolution of an important category of writing on women that must be understood within the terms defined by authors. It is, finally, the recognition of trends and themes that emerge from the material that is for me the real point of organizing this guide to the literature on women. My underlying hope is that readers will share with me an appreciation for the growing quality and continuing development of a field of study that is scarcely ten years old.

Barbara Haber
Cambridge, Massachusetts
October 1980

Introduction

My decision to compile an annotated bibliography of current books on American women grew out of my position as the Curator of Printed Books at Radcliffe College's Arthur and Elizabeth Schlesinger Library on the History of Women in America. The Schlesinger Library is a social history library that has been in existence for more than thirty years collecting not only books and other printed materials but also the personal papers of women and the records of women's organizations. I first came to the Library in 1968, just before the new feminism had emerged as a social movement; therefore, as the book selector, I oversaw the development of a collection which reflects the impact of the women's movement on both academic research and popular writing. In both these areas recently, books about American women have become so prolific that I felt that a general bibliography which documented the scope of the new feminism would be of value.

Because this guide covers so broad a range of material, I feel that it may serve an audience whose needs have not yet been met. I have in mind college teachers not familiar with recent literature on women's issues who would like to incorporate such material into introductory courses; librarians interested in building a core collection in women's studies; undergraduate students; and general readers who might welcome some guidance in structuring independent reading programs.

My principles of selection for this bibliography are the same as those that have shaped the Library's collection. They are principles that have evolved gradually.

Before 1968 the selection of books had not been a challenging problem because few contemporary books on American women were being written. That a special collection on women even existed was considered by some an anachronism, a sentimental holdover from the nineteenth-century suffrage movement. In fact, when new books on American women appeared, they often were histories of the suffrage movement or other reform activities in which women had participated, a reflection of the limited traditional definition of women's history. Other new books were, typically, the biographies of famous women or of the wives of famous men. As a general guideline for book selection in earlier days, the Library bought books that related to the acquisition of a manuscript collection. If, for example, a woman doctor donated her papers, the Library would more likely acquire materials to complement that acquisition. So, for the most part, the book collection had been considered the companion-piece of the manuscript collection.

The printed collection began to take on its own integrity in response to the impact the women's movement made first on periodicals, and later on books. Before 1968, the Library received either popular glossy magazines like *The Ladies' Home Journal, McCall's* and *Vogue,* or the official publications of women's organizations like the League of Women Voters, or government publications sent out by the Women's Bureau. Then periodicals of a new sort began to appear, their titles an augury of what was yet to come: *Off Our Backs, Ain't I a Woman, No More Fun and Games.* They were published by small groups of women whose feminism was sparked by the discrimination they had experienced in working with civil rights and anti-war groups.

By 1970 the new feminism was reflected in books. Anthologies like Robin Morgan's *Sisterhood is Powerful* and Mary Lou Thompson's *Voices of the New Feminism* contained reprints of some of the earlier feminist articles and offered new statements by women who were a part of the growing movement. Theoretical books appeared that year — *Sexual Politics* by Kate Millett and *The Dialectic of Sex* by Shulamith Firestone. These were followed by a barrage of books written by academic and popular writers who were expressing feminist concerns in works like psychologist Phyllis Chesler's *Women and Madness* and novelist Elizabeth Janeway's *Man's World, Woman's Place.*

It soon became clear to me that an aggressive book collecting policy for the Library had to be formulated, one that would assure a responsible documentation of the new women's movement. As a general guideline I have tried to anticipate what future scholars of the period would expect to find in a research library's collection on women. It seemed to me that they would be looking for evidence of how the movement influenced the direction of research in many fields and how it affected the lives of many women. This concern led me into areas that had never before been considered within the scope of the Library: art history and literary criticism written from a feminist point of view; studies in psychology, sociology and anthropology specifically relating to women; books on law or health, formerly of interest only to professionals, now the subjects of feminist analysis.

My aim in this bibliography has been to identify these recent books and to organize them into subject categories according to those issues that have naturally emerged from the writings. Writers are attempting to uncover women's history; to examine discrimination of a kind that has been institutionalized in education, the law, religion and employment. They question the very texture of women's daily lives — how society's notions about sex roles have effectively closed off options, and what the psychological cost of this has been for women.

Such themes as these were at the center of my concern as I examined the books included in this bibliography. In writing the annotations I was interested not only in the writers' insights into female experience but in the value of those insights to women in general. In order to convey my sense of the relevance of the writers' observations to women, I often had to go beyond the kind of objective description one usually finds in reference books. I had to respond to material and make evaluative comments for the sake of highlighting what I perceive to be authentic female experience.

Some books obviously lend themselves to this kind of analysis more readily than others. Therefore, I decided to include in each subject category some long annotations as well as brief ones. In analyzing two books that deal with the problems of sexism in the schools, for instance, I chose to write a long essay on Barbara Grizzutti Harrison's *Unlearning the Lie: Sexism in School,* a detailed account of a woman's involvement in an attempt to change her own children's school, and how she herself was changed by her experiences. I gave less space to *Sexism in School and Society* by Nancy Frazier and Myra Sadker, a fine book, but one that discusses similar problems on a relatively abstract level.

Inevitably, I found that my reviews of the biographies were the longest. I felt that the lives of such women as Isadora Duncan, Judy Garland and Sylvia Plath dramatically illustrated the conflicts that mark the lives of many women: the strain between their professional and private roles; their psychological dependencies; the nature of their relationships to men, to their mothers and sisters, and to their children. Biographies of women which fail to examine such fundamental questions, even though they may be about historically more important figures, are given brief attention in this guide.

Omitted from the guide are fiction, poetry, drama and juvenile literature; highly technical studies aimed at a limited professional audience; reference books; non-book material; reprints and books about women which do not relate to American life. Despite these omissions, there remains a huge body of works about American women, and I have had to limit my consideration to books published between 1963 and 1975. I use the publication date of Betty Friedan's *The Feminine Mystique* as a starting point because it is generally accepted as the first contemporary American book to attribute women's problems to a sex-biased society and not to personal failure. I use 1975 as a cut-off point for practical reasons. Given the limitations imposed by time and normal human energy, it was not possible for me to include the many books on American women that have appeared since then. Although I find myself disheartened by the thought that this guide could not include some excellent new books, I take comfort in the knowledge that it responds to a need that I have heard expressed for almost a decade. "Can you give me a list?" people would ask. Now at last I can.

Acknowledgments

I wish to thank the Harvard University Library for awarding me a fellowship provided by Charles and Mary Tanenbaum for Harvard librarians. I received the grant when this project was still in the planning stage, a time when such encouragement was much needed. I am also grateful to my colleagues at the Schlesinger Library who, as good listeners, helpful advisers and warm friends have contributed to this work and to the pleasure I regularly take in working at the Library. Finally, I thank Herb Haber, my husband, who edited, advised and cheered me on especially when this project was nearly completed, a time when such encouragement was most needed.

Abortion

No other issue concerning American women has raised more controversy than the question of abortion. It includes aspects of sex, religion, politics and even race in its scope, all subjects charged with passionately held beliefs. The enormous amount of literature on the subject expounds many different points of view, and varies from manuals of practical information to abstract treatises on morality. Most of the books deal with medical and legal aspects and some are principally concerned with social ethics. Occasionally writers are so preoccupied with sophisticated moral arguments and maintain a level of discussion so abstract that neither women nor the issue of women's rights are ever mentioned in their books.

When in 1973 the Supreme Court abolished restrictions on abortion for the first three months of a pregnancy, one might have expected that all of the discussion and complicated arguments which preceded that decision would be academic; however, the controversy is far from dead. There are still those — in the anti-abortion movement — who hope to bring about a constitutional amendment which would once again make abortion illegal in the United States. Thus, the issues discussed in many of these books have been kept alive, despite the Supreme Court ruling.

Callahan, Daniel. *Abortion: Law, Choice and Morality.* **New York: Macmillan, 1970. 524p.**

This is the single, most comprehensive survey of the abortion question ever to appear. Indeed, when the book first came out, one reviewer suggested that it gave more information about abortion than most readers wanted to know.

Callahan approaches his task by discussing the moral, medical, social and legal questions and considers ''an array of theories'' and a ''mass of data'' before setting forth policy recommendations. Never doctrinaire, Callahan presents and organizes material in the hope that the reader will understand the implications of such a serious question. Since the polemicists are one-sided in their views, Callahan felt that he should expand the boundaries of the arguments so that the reader can come to some coherent position on the moral legitimacy of

1

abortion. Callahan states his own view succinctly in the Walbert collection, *Abortion, Society & the Law*:

> My position is that abortion should be legally available on request up to the twelfth week of pregnancy; that abortion is morally justifiable under a variety of circumstances, but should always be undertaken reluctantly and with a strong sense of tragedy; and that the humane society would be one in which women were neither coerced to go through with pregnancies they do not want nor coerced by social, economic, or psychological circumstances into abortion. I cannot accept the position of those who would deny all respect to the fetus. Nor can I accept the position of those who hold that the right to life of the fetus is sufficient in all cases to override the right of women to choose an abortion. On the contrary, I accord the right of women to control their procreation a high status, as a crucial ingredient of the sanctity or dignity of life.

Hall, Robert E., ed. *Abortion in a Changing World.* **New York: Columbia University Press, 1970. 2 vols. 377 p. and 218 p.**

These volumes are the report of the proceedings of an international conference on abortion convened by the Association for the Study of Abortion in 1968. The participants were experts in five areas — ethical, medical, legal, social and economic — affecting abortion. The formal papers and panel discussions therefore placed the abortion problem in many contexts, and there were sharp differences of opinion among the speakers. As Hall saw it, "The primary purpose of the conference was not to debate or promote abortion law reform, not to incite controversy or achieve consensus, but rather to explore the field of abortion, to exchange knowledge about abortion, and to expose this knowledge to public view." In spite of this declared intention, the participants evaluated their data on abortion with an eye to suggesting how the reform laws should or should not be formulated. In their book, *The Abortion Controversy*, Betty Sarvis and Hyman Rodman refer to these volumes extensively in order to cite the major issues of the abortion controversy.

Sarvis, Betty and Hyman Rodman. *The Abortion Controversy.* **2nd edition. New York: Columbia University Press, 1974. 207p.**

Of all the books that have appeared on the subject of abortion, this is the most readable. It is a clearly written, well organized history of the controversy.

The debate became intensely emotional during the sixties and early seventies and ignited fiercely contrasting views among various groups. Feminists understand abortion to be a natural right for women, a choice which allows them control over their own lives and freedom from bearing unwanted children. Proponents of the right to adequate health care, a growing movement, consider inexpensive, safe abortion an important human right; this attitude is shared by those concerned with the "quality of life," the principle that children should be born not only healthy but wanted. On the other side is the "right to life" movement whose proponents believe that all life must be protected for its own sake, and that abortion should be illegal. At the same time, black power advocates have seen abortion as a form of genocide which, together with sterilization, can lead to the annihilation of third-world people.

Before 1960, much of the literature on abortion was directed to the professional community, but two events occurred in the 60's which changed that narrow interest — the thalidomide scare and the German measles epidemic of 1964. The fear of producing badly damaged babies shook the public, and a desire to loosen the restrictions on therapeutic abortion became a matter of immediate importance. As it happened, the American Law Institute had planned a 1962 revision of the Model Penal Code which contained a ready-made proposal for abortion reform; it became the model for proposed and enacted abortion legislation at the state level. The American Law Institute's position was that abortion should be permissable under certain circumstances and up to a certain period of gestation. The allowable circumstances were to be cases of rape, incest, fetal deformity and threats to the physical or mental health of the mother.

Before the passage of reform laws, legal abortions were available only to women whose lives were endangered by their pregnancy. The reform laws did not satisfy anybody. The pro-abortionists believed that abortion should be readily available without requiring special justification; the anti-abortionists felt that there were no justifications for abortion.

From 1969 to 1972 a phenomenal number of abortion cases were brought up before many levels of courts, including the Supreme Court. In one opinion, Justice Douglas wrote, ''The subject of abortions — like cases involving obscenity — is one of the most inflammatory ones to reach the Court. People instantly take sides and the public, from whom juries are drawn, makes up its mind one way or the other before the case is even argued.''

On January 22, 1977, basing its decision on the individual's right to privacy, the Court ruled that a state could not intervene in the abortion decision between a woman and her physician during the first three months of pregnancy. The Court's sweeping decision rendered all original and reform laws unconstitutional, and changed the legal position of the United States on abortion from one of the most restrictive to one of the most permissive in the world.

This book organizes the numerous and complicated issues that surround the abortion controversy. By offering historic context, the authors explain the 1973 Supreme Court decision as founded in the right of privacy between physician and patient and not on the right of women to control their own reproduction. Since the decision came at a time when feminists were organized to fight for abortion on demand, many assume that the Court was responding to the needs of women. It is more likely to assume that it was responding to the rights of physicians.

Schulder, Diana and Florynce Kennedy. *Abortion Rap*. New York: McGraw-Hill, 1971. 238p.

In January of 1970, a group of women and their six female attorneys pressed a suit in Federal Court against the State of New York challenging the constitutionality of the state's abortion laws which had been standing since 1828. Tired of having the abortion issue legislated by men, the women testified on their own behalf that abortion laws were unconstitutional, limiting women's right to privacy and their right not to bear children. Their aim was to have all anti-abortion laws repealed, not merely liberalized. The suit never was decided, but was declared moot because the New York State Legislature had voted to amend its state laws. Diane Schulder and Florynce Kennedy, two of the attorneys who presented the case, have edited some of the testimony for this book. About the whole experience they say, "it is not to be regarded as a dispassionate travelogue through the topography of New York abortion law repeal and reform. It is in no sense an effort to extend the myth of 'objectivity.' It should rather be viewed as a brief to be presented to a people's tribunal. We were and are advocates of the women's case."

And so they are, for what follows is nearly ninety pages of accounts of personal crises because of unwanted pregnancies. The women tell stories which are not lurid or sensational, but represent typical experiences and the possible choices that were available to women. Their first decision was either to go through with the pregnancy or else to abort. Those who carried their babies had to choose either to give them up or to keep them; those who chose to abort had to find a way to do it in relative safety. All of the women who carried their babies to term chose to give them up for adoption, but not before going through a series of humiliating experiences — being hidden away in homes with other pregnant women, working as mothers' helpers in the homes of strangers, going through the agony of giving away the child. Finding an abortionist led women on desperate hunts through cities in America for doctors who, they hoped, would not butcher them, and led others to Puerto Rico, London and Japan where safe abortions were available if one had money to get there. In all of these cases, a safe, inexpensive abortion is what the women really wanted. That possibility would have rescued them from the disruption of leaving school or work, to say nothing of the trauma associated with a surreptitious abortion.

In addition to presenting this testimony, Schulder and Kennedy give a brief history of the women's suit, discuss some legal aspects of the abortion issue, and summarize the views of doctors, social workers and theologians who break down what they see as some of the myths of the abortion issue.

Although the feminist point of view on abortion is an important issue in all of the women's liberation material, this is the only full-length book that deals with the subject exclusively from the point of view of the women involved.

* * *

Brody, Baruch. *Abortion and the Sanctity of Human Life: A Philosophical View.* **Cambridge, Mass.: MIT Press, 1975. 162p.**

Brody is a philosopher who reasons that "at some point between two and twelve weeks after conception, the fetus becomes a human being with all the rights to life ... belonging to such an entity. Thereafter ... it is wrong for the mother to abort the fetus, even if her life is threatened by its continued existence. More-over, there should be strict laws against abortion, although there may be good reasons for not treating abortions as ordinary homicides.''

Carmen, Arlene and Howard Moody. *Abortion Counseling and Social Change: From Illegal Act to Medical Practice.* Valley Forge: Judson Press, 1973. 122p.

The authors describe here the work of the Clergy Consultation Service on Abor-tion which helped women receive safe and inexpensive abortions in 1967, long before they were legal in the United States. Once the New York State abortion laws had been liberalized, clergy counselors worked to make sure that the medi-cal delivery system was adequately responding to the demand. This book, then, is a discussion of the difficulties involved in both changing laws and implement-ing them.

Cohen, Marshall, ed. *The Rights and Wrongs of Abortion: A Philosophy & Public Affairs Reader.* Princeton, New Jersey: Princeton University Press, 1974. 127p.

This book contains five philosophical debates on the abortion issue, each one generally centering on the question of when exactly the fetus becomes a person.

Hardin, Garrett. *Mandatory Motherhood: The True Meaning of "Right to Life."* Boston: Beacon Press, 1974. 136p.

Hardin, a biologist and a committed proponent of a woman's right to an abor-tion, counters the ''Right to Life'' arguments in this book. His major point is that motherhood should not be mandatory any more than abortion should be used as punishment.

Lader, Lawrence. *Abortion.* Indianapolis: Bobbs-Merrill, 1966. 212p.

As the result of his interest in Margaret Sanger and the issue of bearing un-wanted children, Lader became sympathetic to the rights of women to elect abortion. He wrote this book at a time when abortion had not yet become a social issue, and explained why he thought that laws restricting abortion should be abolished.

_____. *Abortion II: Making the Revolution.* Boston: Beacon Press, 1973. 242p.

In this, his second book on abortion, Lader describes his involvement in the abortion movement. After the publication of his first book in 1966, he found himself in the midst of the controversy which led ultimately to the repeal of abortion laws. Because he had written about skilled abortionists who were operating in this country, Lader began to receive letters and phone calls from women asking for referrals. What began casually developed into a time-consuming commitment for him as he continued to help more and more women. When the Clergy Consultation Service on Abortion began functioning in 1967, Lader felt that an important step had been taken, for the clergymen brought moral weight to the principle of abortion referral, something which Lader and other activists had lacked.

Lee, Nancy Howell. *The Search for an Abortionist.* **Chicago: University of Chicago Press, 1969. 207p.**

Nancy Lee is a sociologist who saw the possibilities of studying the communications networks among women who arranged their own illegal abortions. She prepared a questionnaire which was answered by 114 women who underwent abortion. They described their reasons, their reactions, and the ways in which they found an ''invisible'' service in a country in which abortion was illegal. Lee concludes that women were able to locate a previously unknown abortionist by questioning a relatively small group of friends and acquaintances.

Luker, Kristin. *Taking Chances: Abortion and the Decision Not to Contracept.* **Berkeley: University of California Press, 1975. 207p.**

In preparing this study the author analyzed medical records and conducted extensive interviews with a large sample of women who had undergone abortion. She discovered that eight out of ten women obtaining abortions had previously used contraceptives but stopped, consciously putting themselves in a risk-taking situation comparable to smoking or skiing. Her findings raise serious and disturbing questions and will have consequences for counselors at family planning centers who have previously supposed that unwanted pregnancies are, more often than not, the results of failed contraception.

Noonan, John T., ed. *The Morality of Abortion: Legal and Historical Perspectives.* **Cambridge, Mass.: Harvard University Press, 1970. 276 p.**

This anthology provides a comprehensive survey of anti-abortion arguments by men who base their philosophical positions on legal and historical sources. Noonan's apprehensions are stated in his introduction: ''At a time when abortion is the cry, when the orthodoxies of the hour make questioning of the postulates underlying its imminent acceptance impertinent, when the well-informed managers of the media know that abortion will sweep all before it, it is not too late to face the central issues.'' For Noonan and his contributors, the most central issue is the Western tradition of protection of innocent life.

Planned Parenthood of New York City. *Abortion: A Woman's Guide.* **New York: Abelard-Schuman, 1973. 145p.**

This book appeared shortly after the Supreme Court had legalized abortion in the United States. It is a guide for pregnant women who are considering abortion and offers information on the range of practical problems relevant to their situation: determining pregnancy; deciding about abortion; learning about types of abortion; and controlling fertility in the future.

Walbert, David F. and J. Douglas Butler, ed. *Abortion, Society, and the Law.* **Cleveland and London: The Press of Case Western Reserve University, 1973. 393p.**

The essays in this anthology are, for the most part, written by people who have been involved in the abortion controversy for a long time and who advocate liberalization of the laws. What makes this book different from other collections is that the discussions tend to be legalistic and raise questions that are still timely and, in some cases, not settled, e.g., the right of minors to have abortions without parental permission and of wives without husbands' consent; the constitutionality of residency and hospital requirements; the eligibility of women undergoing abortions for Medicaid benefits; and the certification of commercial referral agencies.

Black Women and Native American Women

It is noteworthy that recent books about black women are no longer entirely the work of white social scientists. They are now by black women describing their own experiences and expressing their own concerns about life in America. In their accounts certain themes recur: how some women have transcended the limitations of poverty and lack of opportunity to achieve success within terms they have struggled to define for themselves; why black women have been unable to identify with the aims of the women's movement; and the unresolved question of what kind of collective action can improve the position of black people in America.

Another general theme that is recognizable in many of these books is the difference in point of view between generations. While older black women put their trust in God to help them through adversity, younger women are putting their trust in themselves. If their work is evidence, they believe in the possibility of social change and face life with angry determination instead of resignation.

Books about other minority women are scarce. For the moment, books about Native American women are being written mainly by white men and women. The book, *Halfbreed,* by Maria Campbell is a rare exception. There is not as yet a body of literature written by Spanish-speaking women in the United States. One hopes and expects that this soon will change.

Angelou, Maya. *Gather Together in My Name.* **New York: Bantam, 1975. 181p.**

This book, the second in the autobiographical series this gifted black writer is producing, covers just two post-war years and ends when Angelou is nineteen years old. During this period she left the South to live in San Francisco, rejoined her mother, and faced the difficulties of adult life in an urban setting. She was outside of the influence of the strict grandmother who had raised her. As an unwed mother, though still a child herself, she faced the problems of earning a living during chaotic times, with little preparation for the task of making her

9

way in the world. Her mother, an old hand at surviving, told her daughter, ''Be the best of anything you get into. If you want to be a whore, it's your life. Be a damn good one. Don't chippy at anything. Anything worth having is worth working for.''

Angelou refers to this speech as her mother's version of Polonius' advice to Laertes in Shakespeare's *Hamlet,* a comparison which illustrates Angelou's witty penchant for describing gritty realities in sophisticated literary terms. And it is one effect of her style that the reader wonders how this particular young woman managed to develop her talents in spite of the heavy odds against her. Surrounded by whores, pimps, addicts and thieves, she sampled the life each had to offer, and one by one rejected them all in her search of her own survival.

In the midst of her harsh environment, she got caught up in the dreams that Hollywood fed most American girls who grew up in the 40's. She says, ''I wanted a man, any man, to give me a June Allyson screen-role life with sunken living room, and cashmere-sweater sets, and I, for one, obviously would have done anything to get that life.'' The same yearning that sent hordes of white American girls off to college or into safe marriages led Angelou into involvement with a pimp who set her up in a whore-house, at a trade she soon realized she was poor at. The next man she met, a heroin addict who dealt in stolen clothing, helped her to earn a living selling clothes. Narcotics intrigued her, but she promised her addict friend that she would stay away from drugs. At the end of the book, after returning to her mother's house, more street-wise, but still unclear about how to conduct her life, she says, ''I had no idea what I was going to make of my life, but I had given a promise and found my innocence. I swore I'd never lose it again.''

Angelou, Maya. *I Know Why the Caged Bird Sings.* **New York: Random House, 1970. 281p.**

Angelou is publishing her autobiography in a series of books and this first one is mainly about her girlhood in the South in the 1930's. She spent most of her early years in the country town of Stamps, Arkansas, where she was raised by her grandmother, the owner of a country store, a livelihood superior to that of most other black people in the community who picked cotton to survive. The atmosphere of the household was strict and religious, but it also provided unusual opportunities for education and the lifelong love of literature which shows through all of Angelou's work.

In relating the episodes which helped to form the adult she became, Angelou brings to life anecdotes that capture the nobility of her gtandmother and the rage Angelou felt when anyone tried to undermine that dignity. Poor white kids came to the store and taunted the grandmother, calling her disrespectful names and mimicking the way she stood and held her arms. Angelou describes being sick with fury over the injustice of a world that allowed this to happen. Another time, when Angelou was in agony from two decayed teeth, her grandmother took her to the only dentist in town, a white man to whom she had loaned money during hard times. He refused to help the suffering child and said he would ''just as soon stick his hand into the mouth of a dog than a nigger.'' Grandmother and child had to travel twenty-five miles to the nearest black dentist before Angelou could be relieved of her pain.

One of the most poignant scenes in the book is a description of Angelou's eighth-grade graduation from the school where she had achieved honors and recognition. In the midst of excitement and high hopes, the white administrator appeared and gave a disheartening speech about the servile jobs awaiting little black children who behave themselves. When the unwelcome guest left, the students saved the day by spontaneously rising and singing ''Lift Ev'ry Heart and Sing,'' a song informally known as the Black National Anthem.

Angelou's ability to bounce back from each spiritual affront she felt during her early years is the theme of this beautiful book. It is a common theme in literature, but books with strong and courageous black female protagonists are rare.

Cade, Toni, ed. *The Black Woman: An Anthology.* New York: New American Library, 1970. 256p.

About the relationship between black and white women, Toni Cade asks, ''how relevant are the truths, the experiences, the findings of white women to black women? Are women after all simply women? I don't know that our priorities are the same, that our concerns and methods are the same, or even similar enough so that we can afford to depend on this new field of experts (white, female).''

This anthology has grown out of Cade's impatience with what she feels to be the irrelevance of much feminist literature to the problems of black women. Considering all the work that needs to be done to organize black and other third world women, Cade sees this book as a beginning, a preliminary exposure of feelings and opinions of minority women. It contains poetry, stories, essays and memoirs, forms that seem to her the best way to reflect the preoccupations of the contemporary black woman in America.

Campbell, Maria. *Halfbreed,* New York: Saturday Review Press, 1973. 157p.

Maria Campbell, a western Canadian of mixed French, Scot and Cree blood, writes ''I want to tell you what it is like to be a Halfbreed woman ... about the joys and sorrows, the oppressing poverty, the frustrations and the dreams ... I am not bitter. I have passed that stage. I only want to say: This is what it was like, this is what it is still like.''

She describes the disadvantaged life of her people who are called ''halfpeople'' by full-blooded Natives and ''dirty breeds'' by the whites. Victims of such prejudice learn to despise themselves, and it is Maria Campbell's fight to accept herself which becomes the major theme of her book.

She was helped in her earlier years by her great-grandmother who told her, ''Go out there and find what you want and take it, but always remember who you are and why you want it.'' However, circumstances prevented Campbell from the luxury of self-discovery. When she was twelve her mother died, and the care of seven young brothers and sisters fell on her. Hoping to provide them a home, she entered a loveless marriage. Her husband deserted her and their child; the welfare department took away her young brothers and sisters; and she slipped into a life of prostitution, heroin addiction and alcoholism.

When she realized how debased she had become, she began to fight for her own salvation. She understood that her problems were symptoms of the mistreatment that affected all her people — hostility and negligence from those in power and the sense of defeat that comes from chronic deprivation. Maria Campbell rid herself of her addictions and found ways to work within federal agencies to help her people gain support and autonomy from the government.

While acutely aware of the damage to both Halfbreed men and women inflicted by a bigoted society, Campbell is especially sensitive to historic prejudice against women. She comments, ''The missionaries had impressed upon us the feeling that women were a source of evil. This belief, combined with the ancient Indian recognition of the power of women, is still holding back the progress of our people today.''

Davis, Angela. *Angela Davis: An Autobiography.* **New York: Random House, 1974. 400p.**

Angela Davis, just thirty when this book was published, believed it presumptuous to be writing an autobiography at her age. Her intention was not to glorify herself or to set herself apart from others, but to describe her growing sense of identity with all other oppressed people. Her book, therefore, is a political biography, a description of the experiences of her early life that formed her and the horrors of the political trial that almost destroyed her.

As a child growing up in segregated Birmingham during the late 1940's and early 50's, Davis became accustomed to functioning within a hostile environment. She questioned what she calls the ''Booker T. Washington syndrome,'' the notion that those who work hard will be rewarded, and that black people have to work harder for fewer rewards. ''It often struck me,'' she says, ''they were speaking of these obstacles as if they would always be there, part of the natural order of things, rather than the product of a system of racism, which could eventually overturn.'' Her refusal to accept this system found expression first in her education at home and abroad, and later in the political activities to which she has since devoted her life.

After her education, Davis began a teaching career in California. As a black intellectual who was also a communist, she was hated and feared, and eventually fired from UCLA where she taught philosophy. Her political activities were well charted by the authorities during the period when black power and student power were growing militant forces.

She was therefore already well-known in California before the time of her famous trial. After her arrest, Davis was held without bail and endured eighteen months of imprisonment before she was finally exonerated of the murder charges that had been brought against her. In describing this experience she understates her fears for herself. Characteristically, she generalizes from her own experience and expresses a passionate concern for all other political prisoners and disenfranchised people.

Grosvenor, Verta Mae. *Thursdays and Every Other Sunday Off: A Domestic Rap.* Garden City, New York: Doubleday, 1972. 156p.

At the beginning of her book, Verta Mae Grosvenor has a quotation by Andrew Johnson who said: ''I wish to God every head of a family in the United States had one slave to take the drudgery and menial service off his family.'' As things turned out, she points out, he got his wish, for black women have been performing arduous domestic chores in America longer than they care to remember.

Grosvenor comments on the patent absurdity of a class society where white people assume their superiority even though they may be less intelligent and responsible than their black domestics. Through the use of lively anecdotes, she provides evidence showing how black women have felt about the impossible situations they have been forced to endure: molested by white husbands; insulted by bratty children; overworked and underpaid by the women who hire them and who, as Grosvenor puts it, are off to their ''women's lib'' meeting while dumping the care of their homes and children onto the black women who work for them. She describes such episodes with a stylish wit that barely obscures her anger.

Guffy, Ossie. *Ossie: The Autobiography of a Black Woman.* New York: Norton, 1971. 224p.

Ossie Guffy says about herself, ''I'm a woman, I'm black, I'm a little under forty, and I'm more of black America than Ralph Bunche or Rap Brown or Harry Belafonte, because I'm one of the millions who ain't bright, militant, or talented. I got more children than I can rightly take care of, but I ain't got more than I can love.'' Few poor women write books, and the facts of Ossie Guffy's life speak more forcefully than the generalizations of many social analysts.

She was born in Cincinnati in 1931, the fourth of five children in a family that had been surviving the Depression because Guffy's father had a steady job. This security did not last; her father died when she was thirteen months old. Left penniless, her mother had to find a way to support her young family, and for a black women that way was to clean houses for white women. Guffy's mother left the children in the care of grandparents so that she could move into a live-in situation, seeing her children only on weekends. Since the grandmother went out to work each day, the care of the children was left to the grandfather whose drunken negligence led to the death of Guffy's sister when she got too close to a wood-burning fire. This pattern of family life — women doing domestic work, men finding no work at all — was typical for Guffy for most of her life as it is for many other black women.

By the time she was fifteen, her early sexual sophistication brought her into marriage and motherhood. Not able to cope with the responsibility of a growing family, her husband deserted her when Guffy was expecting her second child. After that, Guffy's life centered on her children and her need to find work in order to care for them. Although her relationships with men were brief, her friendships with women endured. She often relied on their help in giving her a place to live and caring for her children while she worked. By the time she met Clarence Guffy whom she married, she had five children, and together they had four more. They eventually moved to California where Clarence found work, and Ossie became involved in community organization.

Ossie Guffy's life is special in its ordinariness. She is one of many black women who have learned to survive within the milieu of poverty and lack of opportunity. Talented and educated black women like Maya Angelou and Angela Davis have other kinds of remarkable stories to tell. Ossie Guffy's life is about everyday coping.

Jackson, Mahalia with Evan McLeod Wylie. *Movin' On Up*. New York: Hawthorn, 1966. 212p.

Mahalia Jackson could have been any kind of popular singer she wanted to be. Friends particularly urged her to sing the blues, but she never wanted to sing anything but gospel songs. "Blues are the songs of despair," she explained in her book, "but gospel songs are the songs of hope. When you sing them you are delivered of your burden. You have a feeling that there is a cure for what's wrong. It always gives me joy to sing gospel songs ... I tell people that the person who sings only the blues is like someone in a deep pit yelling for help, and I'm simply not in that position."

Like other devout black women of her generation, Mahalia Jackson put her trust in God and heaven. Although she suffered gross insults from the white world even after she was established as a famous singer, her response was always to clothe herself in dignity and to face down the bigotry she met. She was routinely refused service in restaurants and gas stations as she toured the South. Instead of responding with hatred and contempt, Mahalia Jackson philosophized about the stupidity of bigotry and the hypocrisy of white people who entrust the care of their children to black people, but refuse to sit near them in restaurants.

Singing for people was her life, not political activism. At first her gospel singing was popular only with her own people, but she later became popular throughout America, Europe and even the Middle East. The pleasure she took in success seems to be pleasure in new experiences rather than in wealth or fame.

Her book reveals a philosophy of life shared by other black women of her generation who are comforted by religion, a point of view that was challenged by a younger generation of blacks in the 1960's.

Ladner, Joyce A. *Tomorrow's Tomorrow: The Black Woman*. Garden City, New York: Doubleday, 1971. 304p.

Joyce Ladner is a black sociologist who refuses to look at the poor black woman in America as a "social deviant." Her perception is that blacks experience a different social reality from whites in America — in effect, a different America. Her purpose in this book is to develop a new conceptual framework to encompass the autonomous system of values, behavior, attitudes, sentiments and beliefs of young black women.

A number of them and their families were interviewed by Ladner in a low-income neighborhood in St. Louis. She examined the texture of life for the average girl in the urban black community, questioning how she defined her roles and patterns of behavior and from whom she acquired her models. Ladner is particularly interested in seeing whether there is a significant disparity between the resources young black women have to accomplish their goals and aspirations and those resources available to typical white teenagers in American society.

Ladner concludes that institutional racism in this country has set the black community apart to such a degree that it is unreasonable to apply white values to the behavior of black people. Whites assume that upward mobility is available to everyone, whereas Ladner demonstrates that blacks do not share that assumption. Only exceptional black women have been able to move up and out of their restrictive contexts.

Ladner demonstrates that being black and female has been a double burden, one that explains the general unwillingness of black women to participate in the women's movement. Racism and sexism are both enemies, but in setting priorities, black women have often felt that it is not in their best interests to pit themselves against the black male. The myths and realities of the strong black female have been a burden to women desiring social equity for black men.

There is a parallel between Ladner's search for a new intellectual model to replace received and counterproductive interpretations of black culture and the search by feminist scholars for new definitions of the contributions of women. It is but one effect of cultural racism that such efforts are being carried out separately rather than simultaneously.

Lerner, Gerda. *Black Women in White America: A Documentary History.* **New York: Pantheon, 1972. 630p.**

Gerda Lerner spent four years locating documents of black women in libraries across the country. From the material she concludes that, ''The black woman's aim throughout her history in America has been for the survival of her family and of her race. While she has for many long periods been forced to socialize her children to a pretended acceptance of discriminatory patterns, she also had managed to imbue them with race pride and a desire for full equality.''

The documents Lerner presents cover the period between 1811 and 1971. The earliest deal with letters and receipts regarding the buying and selling of slaves, and the last piece in the book is a speech given by the modern civil rights worker, Fannie Lou Hamer, ''The Special Plight and the Role of Black Women.'' Lerner offers rich and varied evidence reflecting the progressive concerns of black women: sexual vulnerability to white men; difficulties of getting an education; problems of making a living; activities within the National Club

Movement; positions on race pride; and positions on womanhood. This book is, and will continue to be, of enormous value to scholars.

Moody, Anne. *Coming of Age in Mississippi.* **New York: Dial Press, 1968. 348p.**

Anne Moody came of age in the early 1960's in time to be involved in the Civil Rights Movement. Her earlier years were spent in rural Mississippi where, as the oldest of a large poor family, she was raised with limited expectations. Most of the black men she knew worked in the cotton fields and the women worked as domestics. At the age of nine, Moody followed the pattern of her mother's life by cleaning house for a white family. But unlike her mother, Moody developed feelings of resentment which set her apart from most of the people she knew. She never accepted the inferior status of her people, nor was she placated by the notion of heaven — the place where justice would prevail — which had sustained older generations of blacks. Instead, she looked at the world around her and "kept trying to learn the white folks' secret" which could explain why their lives held every advantage over black lives.

By the time Moody was in her teens, she stopped looking for rational explanations for racial injustice and began to understand that black people were in danger simply because they were black. Incidents of racial violence occurred with frightening regularity throughout the 1950's; some blacks in her community were murdered. Instead of making Moody more docile, these experiences radicalized her: "I was fifteen years old when I began to hate people. I hated the ... whites who were responsible for the countless murders ... but I also hated Negroes. I hated them for not standing up and doing something about the murders..."

In her fantasies, Moody imagined herself killing all of the white people in town, but realizing that she did not have it in her to kill, she began to escape within herself. She worked hard in school, finally winning a scholarship to Natchez College. The award made it possible for her to leave home permanently.

In college she met other young people who shared her sense of rage, and participated in the voter registration activities that SNCC organized. She writes, "I could feel myself beginning to change. For the first time I began to think something would be done about whites killing, beating, and misusing Negroes. I knew I was going to be a part of whatever happened."

Moody participated in the Woolworth lunchcounter sit-ins in Jackson, Mississippi, and spent several months working on voter registration for CORE in Canton, Mississippi.

The fear and intimidation which she observed in the black community made her realize that until her people had economic security, politically daring activities would be futile. Her fervently practical state of mind is illustrated by her reaction to Martin Luther King and the August 28, 1963 March on Washington: "I sat on the grass and listened to the speakers, to discover we had 'dreamers' instead of leaders leading us. Just about every one of them stood up there dreaming. Martin Luther King went on and on talking about his dream. I sat there thinking that in Canton we never had time to sleep, much less dream.''

Anne Moody's book reveals the sensibility of a young black woman whose rage set her apart from older generations. It is a story of pain, alienation, hope and doubt. Moody believed that, if anywhere, the power to change things was in people. But she is never sure change will occur, for in the last passage of the book, when listening to young blacks sing ''We Shall Overcome,'' she says, ''I wonder. I really wonder.''

Reid, Inez Smith. *"Together" Black Women.* **New York: The Third Press, 1975. 383p.**

Sponsored by The Black Women's Community Development Foundation, this study was designed to investigate the attitudes of black women activists about social issues in general and civil rights in particular. With the help of other black interviewers, Reid conducted taped interviews with black women throughout the country. The women were asked their opinions on topics as diverse as the women's liberation movement and the pre-Watergate Nixon.

It was immediately clear that the women objected to the term ''militant,'' feeling that it was a derogatory label imposed by threatened whites. The term ''together'' expressed to them the concept of people appropriately and responsibly concerned about the fate of their race.

Some of the findings of the study show that these black women felt their interests were diametrically opposed to those of the women's movement. Organizing against black men seemed to them wrong since black men were sharing the struggle against racism. The women also expressed disenchantment with party politics and with the idea that social reform led by white people was helpful. They expressed a willingness to embrace violence as the only viable solution to black oppression, but felt in a state of limbo as they awaited the next stage of the black struggle.

Reid's study is valuable as it deals with a group of women who would not casually offer their opinions to scholars. Her sensitivity to the concerns of her subjects allowed her to add an important book to the growing list of studies of black women.

Wells, Ida B. *Crusade for Justice.* **Chicago: University of Chicago Press, 1970. 434p.**

Ida B. Wells wrote her autobiography in the years before her death in 1931, but it was not published until 1970 when her daughter, Alfreda M. Duster, edited the work for the series ''Negro American Biographies and Autobiographies,'' edited by John Hope Franklin. The particular value of this book is that it covers a period of black history which has not been well-documented. In explaining the purpose of the book, Ida Wells said, ''It is ... for the young people who have so little of our race's history recorded that I am for the first time in my life writing about myself. I am all the more constrained to do this because there is such a lack of authentic race history of Reconstruction times written by the Negro himself.''

Born into slavery in Mississippi in the middle of the Civil War, Ida Wells had the benefit of an early education, and began a professional life as a school teacher. After the death of her parents, she moved to Memphis where she became an outspoken journalist, expressing her rage at the lynchings of black men in the South. She soon drew the attention of British leaders who became sympathetic to the cause of the American Negro.

Wells was invited to Great Britain where she began a series of lectures that further publicized the effects of racial injustice. In the meantime, she continued to appear in the Negro press at home where she reported her experiences abroad. This period in her life, before her marriage, was the time in which she fought most energetically for the rights of her people, and was respected and acclaimed for doing so.

After her marriage in 1895 to Ferdinand Lee Barnett, a Chicago journalist, Ida Wells settled in Chicago where she became a prominent civic leader. She was instrumental in founding the NAACP and the National Association of Colored Women's Clubs.

Ida Wells was an elegant and articulate woman. Her own conduct bordered on the Victorian, and she expected high standards of behavior from everyone. She says, ''Because white people forget Christianity and good breeding when dealing with those who belong to the darker races is no justification for this dark race to do the same.''

*　　*　　*

Albertson, Chris. *Bessie.* **New York: Stein and Day, 1972. 253p.**

Most people remember that the great blues singer, Bessie Smith, died a tragic death. The legend is that after a car accident in which she suffered a critical loss of blood, she was refused admission to a hospital because she was black. But as Albertson describes the facts, she was taken straight to a hospital for blacks by an ambulance that had been late in arriving and she died en route. As her biographer, Albertson's great strength is his knowledge of jazz, of the early history of the recording industry and of the exploitation of black musicians. His uncritical acceptance of accounts about Bessie Smith from a few living relatives is disappointing. He does not give a clear picture of what Bessie thought about herself or her times.

Brooks, Gwendolyn. *Report from Part One.* **Detroit: Broadside, 1972. 215p.**

Gwendolyn Brooks's autobiography is a strong expression of black pride. Her feelings are most apparent in the poetry which she includes and in her descriptions of her travels to Africa.

Carson, Josephine. *Silent Voices: The Southern Negro Woman Today.* **New York: Delacorte, 1969. 273p.**

The author moved throughout the South interviewing black women whose voices had been unheard during most of their history in this country. With the technique of a novelist, Carson weaves together vignettes of women of all ages and various occupations and communicates the feelings and attitudes they express about their lives.

Exum, Pat Crutchfield, ed. *Keeping the Faith: Writings by Contemporary Black American Women.* Greenwich, Conn.: Fawcett, 1974. 288p.

This anthology contains poetry, fiction and excerpts from autobiographies of such well known black women writers as Nikki Giovanni, Gwendolyn Brooks, Maya Angelou and Anne Moody as well as works by less familiar writers.

Gehm, Katherine. *Sarah Winnemucca: Most Extraordinary Woman of the Paiute Nation.* Phoenix: O'Sullivan Woodside, 1975. 196p.

Sarah Winnemucca was a Paiute princess who campaigned for justice for her people. In this fictionalized biography, Gehm employs imaginary dialogue to bring immediacy to Winnemucca's life. She became well known in the East through extensive lecture tours and through her book, *Life Among the Piutes: Their Wrongs and Claims* (1883). Elizabeth Peabody aided her in her effort to get aid for the Paiutes.

Holt, Rackham. *Mary McLeod Bethune: A Biography.* Garden City, New York: Doubleday, 1964. 306p.

Mary McLeod Bethune was a black woman who devoted her life to improving educational and social possibilities for black youth. She founded the Bethune-Cookman College in Daytona Beach, Florida, and took leadership in founding the National Council of Negro Women. This is a popular biography which lacks scholarly notes.

King, Coretta Scott. *My Life with Martin Luther King, Jr.* New York: Holt, Rinehart and Winston, 1969. 372p.

Coretta King was the wife of a great man. Now a widow, she still sees herself in relationship to Martin Luther King, Jr. In this work she focuses on the feelings of trust, optimism and religious conviction that were central to their marriage.

Landes, Ruth. *The Ojibwa Woman.* New York: Norton, 1971. 247p.

This ethnological field study investigates the relationships between men and women in Ojibwa culture of Western Ontario. It contains rich examples of village and tribal life and organizes the material around the life cycle crises, a device which shows how social patterns are related to male and female concepts of identity.

O'Meara, Walter. *Daughters of the Country: The Women of the Fur Traders and Mountain Men.* New York: Harcourt, Brace and World, 1968. 368p.

O'Meara researched journals, letters and other writings of white men whose activities in the fur trade in the first half of the 19th century brought them into contact with Native American women. Above all, the descriptions of relationships reveal the exploitation of women who were often forced into prostitution or victimized by mass rape.

Staples, Robert. *The Black Woman in America: Sex, Marriage and the Family.* Chicago: Nelson-Hall, 1973. 269p.

Staples is a black sociologist who has specialized in studying the black family. In this book he presents a sympathetic portrayal of black women in chapters devoted to sexuality, prostitution, marriage, motherhood, and the relationship of black women to the women's liberation movement. He points out that the lives of black women are more ambiguous and difficult than those of any other group in our society.

Terrell, John Upton and Donna M. Terrell. *Indian Women of the Western Morning: Their Life in Early America.* New York: Dial, 1974. 214p.

Gleaning their information from other books on Native American life, the authors present here a popular book which describes the cultural role of women. The book is divided topically and covers roles, food, crafts, sex and patterns of child rearing.

Udall, Louise. *The Life Story of Helen Sekaquaptewa* as told to Louise Udall. Tucson: The University of Arizona Press, 1969. 262p.

This document of Hopi life is narrated by a woman who describes the details of tribal living and relates how she moved away from Hopi traditions. Unlike others of her people who resisted the white man's schools, Helen Sekaquaptewa, her husband and eight children, absorbed some of the outside culture without completely giving up their own traditions. The everyday details of their adaptation is the focus of this autobiography.

Watkins, Mel, ed. *To Be a Black Woman: Portraits in Fact and Fiction.* New York: William Morrow, 1970. 285p.

This anthology is packed with almost forty selections containing poetry, fiction, excerpts from autobiography and scholarly studies written by or about black women. It is a useful starting place for readers wanting to acquaint themselves with available material in the field.

Yetman, Norman R. *Voices from Slavery.* New York: Holt, Rinehart and Winston, 1970. 368p.

In 1937-38, the Federal Writers Project under the Works Progress Administration interviewed former slaves who were living in seventeen of the states. Yetman has taken excerpts from 100 of the existing 2,000 interviews for his book. The subjects, a third of whom are women well into their eighties and older, recount childhood memories of life in the ante-bellum South.

Crime and Imprisonment

Recently the woman criminal has been a subject of interest to both scholars and to feminist activists. Feminist periodical literature frequently features articles about women prisoners and, occasionally, their poetry and fiction. Feminists tend to see imprisoned women as a subculture ignored by the larger society and as an oppressed group whose problems are exaggerations of the problems of all women. Scholars generally point out that the woman criminal is excluded from the general literature of criminology produced by social scientists. As if to compensate for past omissions, some recent scholars make much of the fact that women criminals are women, and give little consideration to their similarities to male criminals. This kind of thinking has, perhaps, led Freda Adler to the hasty generalization that the rising crime rate for women is a direct effect of the women's liberation movement. She feels, for instance, that the movement has led to greater opportunities for women to attain white collar jobs, and that they are in positions which enable them to commit embezzlement and fraud.

Since the greater participation of American women in the work force is a phenomenon that has increased since World War II, it is simplistic to connect women's rising crime rate with the women's movement. Furthermore, the evidence on women's employment does not indicate that women are getting top jobs; on the contrary, they are filling the same job categories they have always filled.

One can understand why women in prison, a group long ignored, have taken on symbolic meaning for feminists. But Kathryn Burkhart powerfully evokes the truth about these women who come from the same disadvantaged sections of society as their male counterparts and commit crimes for the same reasons.

Clearly more evidence is needed to understand the nature of and motivation for the crimes committed by women and Rita Simon's study, which provides statistical data, begins to fulfill this need.

Adler, Freda. *Sisters in Crime: The Rise of the New Female Criminal.* New York: McGraw-Hill, 1975. 287p.

Freda Adler's thesis is that the women's movement, with its emphasis on female assertiveness and extended opportunities for women, has a dark side. Women are now committing more crimes than ever before, and the crimes are more serious in nature. She states that ''although males continue to commit the greater absolute number of offenses, it is the women who are committing those same crimes at yearly rates of increase now running as high as six and seven times faster than males.'' Furthermore, the nature of these crimes is changing. Formerly, typical female crimes were passive and victimless, e.g., prostitution and shoplifting, the more violent crimes being the prerogative of men. Today, however, the female criminal is arrested for armed robbery, grand larceny, and embezzlement, the latter the result of rising opportunities for women in the white collar world.

Changes have occurred not only in the overall pattern of criminal behavior, but also within the traditional categories as well. In her chapter on prostitution, Adler brings together evidence which points to the changing profile of the prostitute. No longer as dependent on pimps as in the past, and even less so on the syndicate criminal, the prostitute is more likely to be a drug addict and is more inclined to rob customers, often violently. New sexual mores have also created change, for the streetwalker is no longer the only kind of prostitute operating today. A new breed of semi-professional has appeared, often housewives who use their earnings to contribute to family goals, an aim, Adler says, which tends to neutralize their sense of guilt.

Other chapters in the book deal with juvenile delinquency, the world of drugs, class and race differences in crimes, the prison system, and the historical attitudes of the legal profession toward women. Adler relates particular phenomena of female crime to the larger culture to emphasize the dramatic change. Although sometimes effective, this method can cause her to pay short shrift to historic fact. For instance, when she compares the black experience to that of white women, Adler says that white women did not emerge as individuals until a hundred years after black women, that the white woman ''had been securely established in the role of homemaker, protected for the most part from financial responsibilities, and ... educated sufficiently to qualify for white male positions.'' By looking at white women monolithically, Adler ignores the lives of important groups like immigrant women and other poor urban dwellers as well as poor rural whites whose experiences in America have not been so comfortable.

However, Adler's observations and data concerning the criminal behavior of American women are impressive. Her conclusions may be disheartening to those who have pictured only the positive results of the women's movement.

Burkhart, Kathryn Watterson. *Women in Prison.* **Garden City, New York: Doubleday, 1973. 465p.**

Most popular impressions of women in prison come from dramatic film portrayals — Susan Hayward awaiting execution for a crime she did not commit, or

Ida Lupino imprisoned because of a confusion over her identity. The public is momentarily interested in sensational crimes as they are fictionalized or as they occur in real life. But Kathryn Burkhart is interested in typical women who are imprisoned. She says, ''The majority of women in this book are not women you've read about in newspapers. They're the women who are listed as police and court statistics. Occasionally they have been mentioned by name in a paper — 'Mary Smith Charged with Homicide' or 'Police Make Morals Raid on Locust Street' or 'Three Suspects Rounded Up in Drug Bust.' That is the last you usually hear of them, if you hear of them at all.''

By letting the inmates speak for themselves through excerpts from the 400 interviews she conducted, Burkhart reveals the nature of prison life. Gradually, a portrait of places with rigid structures, meaningless activities, and no promise for the future emerges. Burkhart describes the prison environment as a ''concrete womb'' where poor women pay for crimes from which the rich are generally absolved, and where a sense of docile acceptance creeps over trapped women who become accustomed to their dehumanizing environment.

Inmates repeatedly told her, ''They treat us just like children,'' and, ''They think we're four years old. They think we can't think for ourselves ... they call us girls, but we're *women.*''

The confinement and routine of prison life give women a sense of security even though they despise the institution that is taking care of them. They are never prepared to deal with the outside world. In anticipating her release one prisoner said, ''I'm just so scared of going out there. I don't know. I'll have to wake myself up in the morning and get up and carry myself to work and make all my own decisions. I'll have an apartment of my own. I just don't know if I can make it.''

In this powerful book, Burkhart draws a portrait of the realities of prison life and reveals its stultifying effect on its inmates. She brings attention to a society of women whose existence has been generally forgotten.

Simon, Rita James. *Women and Crime.* Lexington, Mass.: D.C. Heath, 1975. 126p.

Simon, an academic trained in law and sociology, provides an overview of the participation of women in crime in the United States. The first important point she makes is that the female criminal has been ignored by social scientists, lawyers and penologists, although information about the male criminal is abundant. The purposes of her book are to gather and interpret existing data to see how many women are engaged in various types of crimes, to determine how they are treated by authorities, and to offer a prognosis about future participation of women in crime.

The statistics Simon presents lead her to conclude that ''there are more women involved today than there has been at any time since the end of World War II, and probably before that. But the increase has been in certain types of offenses; theft, forgery, fraud, and embezzlement, not in crimes of violence or in the traditional female crimes, such as prostitution and child abuse.'' She also proves that the court system is lenient toward women, showing that although one in 6.5 arrests are women, only one in 30 of those sentenced to prison are women.

Simon points out that feminists view as paternalistic the preferential treatment of women criminals. Just as feminists would insist on equal rights and opportunities for women, so would they expect no special privileges for women under the law.

In acquiring some of her data Simon interviewed thirty criminal trial court justices and state attorneys. These experts were asked if they anticipated future changes in the profile of the woman offender. Only twenty-five percent thought ''that more women would be involved in financial or white-collar crimes than in the past, because more women would be in the labor force and, therefore, would have more opportunities to embezzle and defraud. Only three of the respondents mentioned the women's movement as a possible source of influence. Those who did felt that the women's liberation movement gave women a greater sense of independence and a belief that they could do anything that a man could do. If men can commit all types of crimes, so can women.''

*   *   *

Brodsky, Annette, ed. *The Female Offender*. Beverly Hills: Sage, 1975. 108p.

Some of these readings originally appeared as a special issue of *Criminal Justice and Behavior* and others came out of a symposium called ''Planning for the Female Offender.'' Most contributors agree that women offenders tend to be forgotten, that they need a better quality of attention from law enforcement personnel and more attention from researchers.

Colebrook, Joan. *The Cross of Latitude: Portraits of Five Delinquents*. New York: Knopf, 1967. 340p.

This is an account of the lives of five young girls who spend their time moving between prisons and the streets of their slum. Colebrook observed them over several years and writes with sympathy about their lives which include drug-use, promiscuity and crime.

deRham, Edith. *How Could She Do That?: A Study of the Female Criminal*. New York: Clarkson N. Potter, 1969. 340p.

deRham studies the female criminal not in the sociological sense, but out of a personal interest in her as woman. She presents a series of case histories on women who have been convicted of serious crimes, and concludes that women commit all the crimes that men commit with the exception of rape. Their participation in crime tends to be concealed because they induce men to do the things which require physical strength, thus appearing innocent when in fact they are only secretive.

Giallombardo, Rose. *Society of Women: A Study of Women's Prison.* **New York: Wiley, 1966. 248p.**

The author spent 1962-1963 at the Federal Reformatory for Women in Alderson, West Virginia in order to examine prison life from a sociological perspective. She compared what she saw with the literature on male prisons and found differences which indicated that women bring to the prison setting the sex roles ascribed to them in the larger society. Giallombardo found that at least 75 percent of the inmates simulated family life by involving themselves in homosexual relationships, with the "females" doing all of the housework and in general being subservient to those women who acted out roles as husbands.

Hanson, Kitty. *Rebels in the Street: The Story of New York's Girl Gangs.* **Englewood Cliffs, New Jersey: Prentice-Hall, 1964, 183p.**

This is a narrative about a New York street gang from Spanish Harlem called the Dagger Debs. The book is written from the point of view of a social worker who was placed by the New York City Youth Board as a street worker. She observes the gang's affiliation with a male gang, and the violence and promiscuity that take the place of positive direction in the lives of these girls.

Harris, Sara. *Hellhole.* **New York: Dutton, 1967. 288p.**

The title refers to the New York City House of Detention for Women located in Greenwich Village. Harris writes an exposé of the overcrowded, generally disreputable facility which was geared more to retribution than to rehabilitation. She describes the poor treatment of addicts and the mentally ill, and the poor quality of all attention, including medical care.

Lampman, Henry P. *The Wire Womb: Life in a Girls' Penal Institution.* **Chicago: Nelson-Hall, 1973. 181p.**

Lampman worked as a psychologist in a girls' rehabilitation home in New Mexico, and presents here the conclusions he drew out of that experience. He sees as the most profound drive in every delinquent the search for family and a real home, a drive which institutions fail to realize.

Education

From the onset of the women's movement, education has been the focus of wide-spread feminist attack. It has been seen as an institution which teaches females to be subordinate to males to whom it provides better opportunities and positions of leadership.

A whole category of educational material which attempts to redress the sexism rampant in children's textbooks and literature has appeared, such as Barbara Sprung's *Non-sexist Education for Young Children.* It takes issue with such objectionable biases as the portrayal of girls as passive and of less consequence than boys. To some extent textbook publishers have taken heed of the objections raised by teachers who want books that provide a positive image of girls and women. More women's history and creative literature written by women are appearing in recent books.

Discrimination against women is perpetuated not only by what is taught but by who gets taught, especially in graduate and professional schools. Such schools have systematically excluded women from entering fields traditionally dominated by men: medicine, law and business, most obviously. Moreover, sexist counselling practices have discouraged young women from setting career goals which lead to professional lives in these areas.

Women who do receive graduate training often have special problems which are ignored, like the need for part-time study and child-care facilities. Academic women like Alice Rossi, Florence Howe and Patricia Graham discuss such issues as these and the career problems that generally face academic women: the difficulty of getting teaching jobs and tenure. They offer strategies which would enable women to gain stronger leadership positions within fields like nursing, social work and education, areas in which women are already strong.

Harrison, Barbara Grizzutti. *Unlearning the Lie: Sexism in School.* **New York: Liveright, 1973. 176p.**

At first Harrison's book appears to be a straight-forward account of how a group of mothers of children in a Brooklyn private school joined together to combat sexism in their children's classrooms. But the issues in the book become complex, for Harrison notes that when women of dissimilar backgrounds met to discuss sexism, other issues inevitably grew out of their meetings. Differences of opinion became intense. The group accomplished the desired changes in the school, but not before they learned to work within a political group, and not before they learned to recognize some personal attitudes and goals in themselves which had never before been clearly defined.

The ''Sex-role Committee'' was made up of middle-class New York women who responded to the women's movement early in 1970 by seeking an improved educational experience for their children. They met to find ways of ridding the classrooms of sexist attitudes. (Boys in the block corner and girls in the doll corner). During the course of their meetings they met the problems women's groups have been facing since the advent of the new feminism: Should they be more concerned with consciousness-raising or with political activity? How could they get things accomplished within the confines of a leaderless group where absolute democracy seemed to bog down progress? How were they to deal with people who were at different stages of feminism? Recent joiners raised questions that had already been thrashed out and were boring to more seasoned members who, in turn, made newcomers uncomfortable by failing to respond to them. One woman expressed the problem well when she said, ''When women experience a leap into feminist belief, they tend to have contempt for people who are not where they're at. We hold others responsible for what we did before our conversion.''

Perhaps the most difficult confrontation, and the one that has the most impact in Harrison's recounting, was the conflict between blacks and whites. Black women, embittered because the women's movement was taking away the energy of liberals who had been involved in civil rights, were at serious odds with white women. They could not accept the feminist definition of ''oppression.'' Blacks saw a difference between being oppressed and loved (the position of white women) and being oppressed and hated (the position of black men and women). Some misunderstandings were cleared away, but Harrison makes clear that mistakes were made on both sides during the painful process of trying to reach agreements in order to create a better place for their children.

Men were eventually brought into the group, and Harrison provides an insight that is startlingly true. Others have noted that when men are included in meetings they tend to direct the talk, silencing otherwise articulate women. But Harrison points out that ''a woman whose husband has publicly played the fool feels literally devastated as if she has been robbed of her own worth.'' That is a keen observation by a writer who has succeeded in describing a difficult and complicated set of circumstances with liveliness, intelligence and truth.

*   *   *

Abramson, Joan. *The Invisible Woman: Discrimination in the Academic Profession.* San Francisco: Jossey-Bass, 1975. 248p.

Joan Abramson taught in the English Department of the University of Hawaii where she experienced such repeated discrimination that she felt like an invisible woman. She describes the frustration of her expectations in trying to deal honestly with colleagues, university committees and government agencies in her quest for tenure. She has written this book in the hope that it will serve as a warning to other academic women, and that it will educate faculty men who perpetuate discrimination against women.

Bernard, Jessie. *Academic Women.* University Park: Penn State University Press, 1964. 331p.

Bernard, whose recent work is explicitly feminist, wrote this book in the years before the women's movement. Using biographical data to support her observations, she describes discrimination against academic women, indicating how they functioned in spite of it. She remains a detached observer, never commenting on the injustice of the system that created such problems for women.

Carnegie Commission on Higher Education. *Opportunities for Women in Higher Education.* New York: McGraw-Hill, 1973. 282p.

This is an overview of the status of women in higher education. Problems facing female students, faculty, and administrators are analyzed, and suggestions for change are offered. The Carnegie Commission recognized that only equal access to higher education and the jobs to which it leads can ensure women the opportunity to develop and utilize their abilities.

Centra, John A. *Women, Men and the Doctorate.* Princeton, New Jersey: Educational Testing Service, 1974. 214p.

The purpose of Centra's study is to describe the current status and professional development of a sample of women Ph.D's and to compare them to a sample of men who have attained the same educational status. With this approach he is able to document what female academics already know — that discriminatory practices exist, and that women receive far fewer academic awards than do their male colleagues.

Cross, Barbara M., ed. *The Educated Woman in America: Selected Writings of Catharine Beecher, Margaret Fuller, and M. Carey Thomas.* New York: Columbia University, Teachers College Press, 1965. 175p.

In a brilliant introduction to these selected writings, Barbara Cross analyzes the contributions which each of these women made to American thought about the purpose of female education. She concludes that none of them offered a comprehensive plan for specific goals, but rather "bequeathed to their successors the nervousness, the risk, and the liberty of having many choices."

Feldman, Saul D. *Escape from the Doll's House: Women in Graduate and Professional School Education.* New York: McGraw-Hill, 1974. 208p.

In preparing this report for The Carnegie Commission on Higher Education, sociologist Saul Feldman observed the inferior position of women in graduate and professional schools. By analyzing questionnaire data, Feldman found that there are fewer women than men in every field outside the humanities, and that women have low self-esteem which is intensified by the discrimination they find within the schools. Increasing the number of graduate women will not solve the problem, Feldman concludes. The solution must come from changes in earlier levels of education and from changes in the general society.

Frazier, Nancy and Myra Sadker. *Sexism in School and Society.* New York: Harper and Row, 1973. 215p.

This book is meant for professional educators, teachers and administrators who, as a group, have been slow to respond to feminist issues as they apply to classroom situations. The authors define sexism as it usually occurs in classes, and then, by using anecdotes and referring to other readings, suggest ways to combat the biases of our culture which are reflected in the schools.

Furniss, W. Todd and Patricia Albjerg Graham, eds. *Women in Higher Education.* Washington, D.C.: American Council on Education, 1974. 336p.

The papers in this book were presented at the 55th Annual Meeting of the American Council on Education. The participants deal with a variety of issues that relate to the higher education of women: aspects of discrimination; the role of women's colleges; and the place of women's studies, feminism and black feminism in the curriculum.

Gersoni-Stavn, Diane, ed. *Sexism and Youth.* New York: Bowker, 1974. 468p.

This is a collection of articles which criticize the perpetuation of sex-role stereotyping by the use of such educational materials as books, films, television programs and toys for children.

Gray, Eileen. *Everywoman's Guide to College.* Millbrae, Calif.: Les Femmes, 1975. 168p.

In this practical guide for mature women who are returning to college, Gray offers sound advice in such areas as the development of study skills and preparation for employment after graduation.

Howe, Florence, ed. *Women and the Power to Change.* New York: McGraw-Hill, 1975. 182p.

This volume, sponsored by The Carnegie Commission on Higher Education, contains four essays written by feminist academics. Each one envisions important ways in which universities will have to change before women can enjoy their rightful places within institutions. Adrienne Rich writes about the need for university-supported child care and opportunities for part-time study and work. Arlie Hochschild perceives universities as male bastions organized around the employment of males with supportive families, thus putting women at a disadvantage. Aleta Wallach looks at law schools' responsibility for maintaining the inferior status of women and considers the possibility of establishing separate feminist institutions. In the closing essay, Florence Howe examines ways in which women can increase their power within institutions, concluding that they should work within those areas in which they are already strong — education, nursing and social work, for example.

Lever, Janet and Pepper Schwartz. *Women at Yale: Liberating a College Campus.* Indianapolis: Bobbs-Merrill, 1971. 274 p.

The authors are sociologists who arrived at Yale to do graduate work the year before that institution became coeducational, when 500 undergraduate women were admitted. They viewed Yale as a microcosm of the larger male-dominated society, and comment on the male/female role in education, careers and family.

Maccia, Elizabeth Steiner, ed. *Women and Education.* Springfield, Illinois: Charles C. Thomas, 1975. 381p.

The twenty-five essays in this collection study the effect of the educational system on American women. Contributors conclude that the system operates in tandem with socialization, in that women are taught to be subordinate to men. They suggest ways to correct this situation. The book includes essays by such well known feminist educators as Florence Howe, Alice Rossi, Sheila Tobias and Wilma Scott Heide.

Richardson, Betty. *Sexism in Higher Education.* New York: Seabury, 1974. 221p.

In writing about sexism in higher education, Richardson blames not only institutions and the men who dominate them, but also women who have allowed themselves to be exploited. One example is the faculty wife who agrees to teach part-time at low pay.

Rossi, Alice S. and Ann Calderwood, eds. *Academic Women on the Move.* New York: Russell Sage, 1973. 560p.

The purpose of this sizable collection of essays was to bring together the findings of numerous studies about the status of women in American higher education. The point of view of contributors to this anthology is political — the shared desire to see the status of academic women improved. Writings are about such diverse subjects as: ''Institutional Barriers to Women Students in Higher Education,'' ''The Dilemma of the Black Woman in Higher Education,'' ''Sex Discrimination in Academe'' and ''Political Action by Academic Women.''

Schmuck, Patricia Ann. *Sex Differentiation in Public School Administration.* Arlington, Va.: National Council of Administrative Women in Education, 1975. 119p.

The author deplores the low status of women in educational administration, a field called a ''woman's profession'' which in fact blocks women from rising to their professional peak. It is the socialization process which has lowered the self-esteem of women, Schmuck contends, and discrimination has kept women out of management jobs throughout society.

Sprung, Barbara. *Non-sexist Education for Young Children: A Practical Guide.* New York: Citation, 1975. 115p.

There is much theoretical discussion of the harm caused by the rigid sex-role indoctrination of children. Here the author provides a practical guide for teachers and parents, showing how to overcome the stereotypes seen by children on TV programs and commercials and in the society at large. Sprung describes how inexpensive non-sexist environments can be created for children's play, and how to make or where to buy appropriate toys and games.

Stacey, Judith, Susan Béreaud, and Joan Daniels, eds. *And Jill Came Tumbling After: Sexism in American Education.* New York: Dell, 1974. 461p.

The editors of this anthology are concerned with the role of education in establishing and maintaining wasteful and unfair sex-role limitations for women. The collection "brings together writings that document the extent to which sexism pervades our educational system from romper rooms to post-doctoral 'fellow'ships. It shows that women in our culture are educated less seriously, less expensively, and even less often than men. The barriers to their education come in three basic styles — institutional, cultural, and psychological."

Contributors include Florence Howe, Elaine Showalter, Alice Rossi and Barbara Harrison. The book serves as an excellent introduction to the kinds of discrimination facing women at all stages of the educational process.

Feminism

The contemporary feminist movement in America has been, for the most part, a middle-class movement. Its beginnings are usually traced to *The Feminine Mystique* by Betty Friedan who deplored the waste of the talents of more than half the people in this country. She perceived the enemy of women to be all of the institutions which give preferential treatment to males, and saw as ideal a society in which women would be free to rise to the same level of achievement as men. Such a solution for sexism failed to realize that for the working class paid work does not offer choices and is not liberating, but instead is often mindless and physically grueling.

Subsequent feminist writers have also tended to analyze sexism within a framework of feminist consciousness not related to a broader political analysis. Shulamith Firestone, for instance, dismisses economic factors as primarily responsible for sexism. Instead she believes that the origins of the sex/class system lie in the biologically determined reproductive roles of men and women. She postulates that only a biological revolution will lead to the elimination of male privilege and ultimately to the elimination of sex distinction. She relies on technology — the future possibility of test tube babies — and on the conviction that apart from the reproductive process no biological differences exist between men and women. The possibility of such a biological revolution is not only repugnant to many women but may also be unrealizable. At the present time no scientist can be sure that significant differences between the sexes apart from reproduction do not exist. Nor can scientific verification of Firestone's thesis occur until gender differences imposed by the process of socialization cease to exist.

Writers like Elizabeth Janeway and Carolyn Heilbrun offer still another approach. With wisdom and rationality they point out the myths and willful ignorance of a society that permits polarization between the sexes. They conceive of a solution in terms of an androgynous ideal in which prescriptive sex-roles will no longer exist. Their basically apolitical approach is different from Friedan's in that they do not see the male model as an ideal. It is doubtful, however, that the androgynous ideal they recommend will solve the problems of a working class which is more concerned with survival than with sensibility.

A number of other feminist theorists are finding answers in a Marxist feminist approach. They see capitalism as a system which uses the free services of women in the family to raise a new supply of cheap labor. Juliet Mitchell, who presented her analysis as early as 1966, expressed concern over the necessity of developing both a radical feminist consciousness and a socialist analysis of the oppression of women. Even though traditional radical ideology failed to support women, Mitchell feels that for women to ignore socialist theories will be self-defeating. Without a cohesive political theory, feminist thought has led to devisiveness not only with men but within the women's movement.

Carden, Maren Lockwood. *The New Feminist Movement.* **New York: Russell Sage, 1974. 234p.**

Although this book covers many of the issues and some of the history of the modern women's movement, the author, a sociologist, is particularly concerned with questions about motivation and group behavior — why do women participate in feminist organizations and how do the groups operate?

She examined more than a hundred periodicals and newsletters written by people affiliated with reformist groups like NOW and WEAL, and with the more revolutionary radical groups which were located in the larger cities or on college campuses, but these sources proved less informative than the extensive interviews she conducted nation-wide. From the interviews she was able to draw some conclusions about individual motivation or the dynamics of particular groups, which she categorizes as "women's rights" advocates (moderate groups); "women's liberation" members (more extreme groups), after Ellen Levine and Judith Hole in *The Rebirth of Feminism.*

We learn that, in both groups, the members were 90 percent middle- and upper middle-class white women. To explain this, Carden tells us, "All American women grow up learning, on the one hand, such societal values as achievement and individualism and, on the other hand, the frequently contradictory demands of the traditional feminine role. Middle- and upper middle-class college graduates are likely to feel the ensuing conflicts most acutely; their expectations are highest and their relative deprivation is the greatest. It is from these women that, so far, the new feminist movement has drawn the majority of its members."

The major difference, Carden notes, is that people who joined organizations like NOW were working within a broad-based group which was seeking changes within the established order, while the more fragmented radical groups were proposing extreme change if not a total destruction of the status quo. Members who joined the women's liberation movement after having worked within radical politics often grafted feminism onto earlier ideas which were taken from their New Left Marxist orientation.

Carden offers objective, reliable information about the emergence and growth of the women's liberation groups throughout the country. She discusses their individual structures and the coalitions they formed, and presents insights into the conflicts that existed both within and among groups. Her writing is precise while at the same time jargon-free, and offers a particular point of view which other studies do not. One should, perhaps, go to *The Rebirth of Feminism* for the best early history of the movement, and to Barbara Deckard's *The Women's Movement* for the most complete discussion of feminist issues, but to Maren Carden's book for sociological insights into the nature of groups and their members.

Deckard, Barbara Sinclair. *The Women's Movement: Political, Socioeconomic, and Psychological Issues.* New York: Harper and Row, 1975. 450p.

Barbara Deckard has assimilated an enormous amount of material from the best of the available secondary sources, and has compiled a veritable handbook of the history and the issues of the women's movement. An impressive and singular effort, this is the book for people who do not have the time to go to all the original sources or for those who need to clarify the reading they have already done.

The book is divided into two parts. The first, "American Women Today: Patterns of Discrimination," has six chapters which deal with feminist issues: psychological theories about women; sex-role socialization; the family; working women; professional women; and women and the law. Deckard includes with this part of the book summaries of such important issues as the abortion controversy and the Equal Rights Amendment. Part two of the book is a survey of women's history which includes: women in primitive, slave, and feudal societies; women in capitalist and socialist societies; the history of American women 1820-1920, 1920-1960, 1960-1975; current issues of the women's movement; and theories of women's liberation.

Figes, Eva. *Patriarchal Attitudes.* New York: Stein and Day, 1970. 191p.

Patriarchal Attitudes appeared at almost precisely the same time as Kate Millett's *Sexual Politics.* Eva Figes, a British writer, indicts what she sees as a patriarchal society where women have been manipulated and used not only because of pervasive male chauvinism but also because females have always colluded by making the pleasing of men their primary function. Her point of view, and many of the ideas she expresses are similar to Millett's, but unlike *Sexual Politics,* Figes' book is not a polemic. It is, rather, a thoughtful study of how men have viewed women through the ages, and why patriarchy is inappropriate for modern society.

She is critical of Freud's psychological profile of women and their sexual response, and of the strictures that he and the neo-Freudians have imposed on women's options. Figes also examines myth to show that the image of woman has always been denigrated — Pandora was made responsible for the evils of the world, and Eve caused man's mortality and fall from Grace. Within the culture itself, Figes believes, men have always set the standards for womanhood, and they have set them too high. "She is either an absolute woman or nothing at all, totally rejected." This has led to a male image of woman which either puts her on a pedestal (The Virgin Mary) or tramples her underfoot (Hester in *The Scarlet Letter*). Marriage, says Figes, is an institution established out of economic necessity. Wives do a certain amount of domestic work. In return they and their children receive financial support from husbands. Figes considers this customary arrangement archaic and destructive, a sinister product of capitalism.

The relationship between capitalism and patriarchy interests Figes, and she makes what has become a commonplace feminist analysis tracing the beginnings of female oppression to the industrial revolution. Before then, women worked at home and received wages. Later they were obliged to work long hours in factories if they needed jobs, or kept idle at home as symbols of their husbands' success. In Western culture their role as consumers has made women major perpetuators of the capitalist system.

Perhaps the most interesting question Figes deals with is why, if women are not inferior to or weaker than or different from men, has a patriarchal system been able to continue throughout history? Or, stated another way, why have so few women achieved genius? Where are the female Michelangelos? Figes suggests that women themselves are largely responsible for their subordinate position, for in most ages they have accepted the position assigned to them by society. It also stands to reason, she says, that men are reluctant to concede power, that "human beings have always been particularly slow to accept ideas that diminished their own absolute supremacy and importance." As for the lack of female Michelangelos, she offers the obvious answer: there are remarkably few male Michelangelos. More to the point, women have historically lacked opportunity for achievement, and they have lacked motivation. Women have been educated to respond to the needs of men. Taught to suppress their strength and independence for the more acceptable role as helpmate, women have become narcissistic and dependent in their pursuit of social approval.

Although each of the arguments Figes pursues is not necessarily unique to feminist thought, her book offers a rational and literate discussion of some of the essential ideas of contemporary writing on the subject.

Firestone, Shulamith. *The Dialectic of Sex: The Case for Feminist Revolution.* **New York: William Morrow, 1970. 274p.**

As radical feminism grew into a movement, some members whose earlier political experience had been with New Left politics felt the need to examine the politics of feminism within an ideological framework. The predominant group felt that women's oppression had its origins in the class structure: capitalism was the major cause of the gross inequities between men and women. Women in the labor force are paid low wages which result in higher corporate profits. The unpaid work performed by women in the home results in a cheap supply of a new generation of workers for the labor force. Such major feminist writers as Juliet Mitchell and Evelyn Reed believe that a radical socialist revolution would counteract this system which has created inequality between the sexes.

Shulamith Firestone, on the other hand, sees the primary cause of sexism as biological rather than economic. The origins of the sex/class system, she says, lie in the biologically determined reproductive roles of men and women. Men remain relatively free while women bear and nurse children. The biological family creates a system of dependency in which women are vulnerable and are made to feel that they need protection. Firestone says, ''Current leftist analysis is outdated and superficial because this analysis does not relate the structure of the economic class system to its origins in the sexual class system, the model for all other exploitive systems and thus the tapeworm that must be eliminated first by any true revolution.'' In constructing her vision for a feminist revolution, Firestone relies on technology. She believes that artificial reproduction (test-tube babies) will be technologically possible in the future and that such advances can lead to a total restructuring of society. ''The end goal of feminist revolution,'' she says, ''must be ... not just the elimination of male privilege but of sex distinction itself: genital difference between human beings would no longer matter culturally.''

Firestone sets out four conditions under which the society she envisions should function: 1) Women must be freed from childbearing as well as childrearing. Technological advances will eventually make artificial reproduction possible. 2) Women and children must be economically independent and free from dull repetitive jobs that will be completely automated in the future. 3) Women and children must be totally integrated into all aspects of the larger society. 4) Women and children must be guaranteed full sexual freedom.

Firestone believes that the accomplishment of the first two conditions would eliminate the entrapment of family life, and the fulfillment of the latter points would ensure the end to all forms of social oppression. She describes varieties of nonreproductive lifestyles in which people could live singly or within groups depending on their own particular needs and desires. Children would be raised not as possessions, but freely within households of adults who would share responsibility for their rearing.

Firestone thus provides not a step-by-step plan for radical revolution, but rather a theoretical solution to the inequities inherent in a society based on a sexual division of labor. The stumbling point which inevitably arises within any serious discussion of the problems of women has to do with the rearing of children. Instead of offering suggestions which would basically accommodate the existing structure — sharing household tasks, day-care centers — Firestone abolishes the structure itself. She is convinced that sex-role assignments based on biological facts will be changed only when those very facts themselves no longer exist.

Freeman, Jo. *The Politics of Women's Liberation*. New York: David McKay, 1975. 253p.

Jo Freeman is a political scientist who was a student at the University of Chicago in the 60's when the women's movement was starting. She has written articulately about the movement from a politically active position.

This book, based on her doctoral dissertation, is largely concerned with the relationship between the women's movement and the establishment of public policy. Both her active participation and her position as a trained observer allow her to bring forth an accurate account of how the movement developed, and very often, an explanation of why things happened as they did. She traces, for example, the establishment of early women's groups and analyzes differences between campus radicals and the moderate groups such as the National Organization for Women and the Women's Equity Action League. Not only does she analyze the origin and development of groups but she also describes how small groups functioned, emphasizing their decision-making processes and the practice of consciousness-raising.

Freeman concludes that the movement had a mushroom effect, that, for instance, the higher education campaigns of WEAL and the continuing fight for the Equal Rights Amendment brought people together in effective ways. Sympathetic women within government were brought into the fight alongside of people who had been long identified with the movement. She also views the movement within the context of broader social movements and concludes that the civil rights activities had broken the ground for feminists in that existing legislation was made to accommodate women's rights issues.

Friedan, Betty. *The Feminine Mystique.* **New York: Norton, 1963. 410p.**

Betty Friedan came to maturity in the 1940's, married and had children in the 50's and soon found herself tucked away in a large house in a stylish suburb of New York, asking of life, "Is this all?" "This," to be sure, would have been enough for women living in poverty with little hope of improving their lot, but middle and upper-middle class women like Friedan were experiencing problems, less drastic, more subtle to be sure than the lack of material things, but problems that were nevertheless serious and debilitating. What was it that was dissatisfying large numbers of educated American women who had lived through the Depression and World War II and finally arrived at domestic and financial security? Were they not acting out at last the American dream with men and children to care for in comfortable and affluent surroundings? Popular writers and psychologists began to talk about "the trapped housewife" or women who suffered from "housewife's fatigue." They spoke of "the problem that has no name." But Friedan had a name for it. For her the unhappiness of women was not a matter of the failure of individuals to adjust but rather the result of the expectations of a society that insisted that women take on subordinate and unfulfilling roles, what she called "the feminine mystique."

Convinced of the conspiratorial nature of this "mystique," Friedan took off in a fury of indignation spending five years compiling evidence to prove that for fifteen years at least women had been systematically brainwashed. She found that during the War women had been encouraged to enter the work force and had proved that they could achieve economic independence, but they were just as forcefully encouraged after the War to retire, to serve the men coming home and make way for them in the labor market. Even though women continued to work in increasing numbers in the years following the War, the myth had been created that women belonged in the home.

Many influential groups were helping to perpetuate that myth. Publications like *The Ladies' Home Journal, McCall's* and *Redbook* printed articles and fiction that failed to present an identity for women other than happy homemakers whose only valid destiny was in serving others. Friedan analyzed these writings and observed that the themes were in marked contrast to the pre-war publications which contained stories with independent heroines and articles about working women. She found that Freudian psychology had become so popularized that women feared being accused of penis envy or the desire to castrate males. She observed that in sociology the functionalist school prescribed roles for women within a rigid framework. While husbands were expected to work outside the home, wives were assigned most of the tasks of household maintenance. At the same time, professional educators contributed to the "mystique" by persuading women to stay out of male-dominated professions "for their own good."

Within this climate, Friedan predicted dire results not only for women already affected but also for their children. It seemed to her that excessive mothering could only lead to passivity and dependency in children. She warned: "If we continue to produce millions of young mothers who stop their growth and education short of identity, without a strong core of human values to pass on to their children, we are committing, quite simply, genocide, starting with the mass burial of American women and ending with the progressive dehumanization of their sons and daughters."

The Feminine Mystique became not only a publishing phenomenon but also a social catalyst because it told its readers that they were not alone in thinking their dark and unhappy thoughts, that other women were rejecting the loud insistence on "togetherness" and listening to the quieter voices within themselves that were saying, "Yes, there must be more."

Hole, Judith and Ellen Levine. *Rebirth of Feminism*. New York: Quadrangle, 1971. 488p.

The authors of *Rebirth of Feminism* present an encyclopedic account of the origins and organizational development of the new feminist movement, an analysis of the ideas and issues it contains, and a description of the social institutions it has sought to change. Through research and interviews with feminists, Judith Hole and Ellen Levine have brought together a comprehensive account of this period of women's history.

In explaining the origins of the women's movement, Hole and Levine provide thorough information. Most writers who describe this period relate the movement to other social reforms of the 1960's — civil rights, the peace movement and new left politics. Everyone points out that radical women left these groups when they realized that they were the victims of anti-woman bigotry. But Hole and Levine argue that the new feminism actually began in 1960 when President Kennedy established the Commission on the Status of Women, the first official recognition of women's issues since ratification of the suffrage amendment in 1920. No one is quite sure what moved Kennedy to become involved with women's problems, but the authors believe that a combination of politics and altruism motivated him. The establishment of the Commission allowed the new president to discharge his responsibilities to women who had worked for his election but had not received appointments.

In addition Hole and Levine state that women who had been involved in the civil rights movement tended to become feminists more frequently and more quickly than women in the peace movement or in new left organizations. One explanation offered is that by witnessing other people's subjugation, women became more conscious of their own powerlessness. More politically oriented women tended to see women's liberation as connected to, but not at the center of other social concerns.

The authors present discussions about the whole canon of important women's movement issues such as the abortion conflict, Equal Rights Amendment arguments, the conflict between women's rights and organized religion, and more, making their book the most comprehensive analysis of the origins, development and issues of the women's movement that has yet appeared.

But since their book came out in 1971, a year of peak activity in the movement, there is now a need for a similar study which would trace the activities of the movement through subsequent years.

Janeway, Elizabeth. *Man's World. Woman's Place: A Study in Social Mythology*. New York: William Morrow, 1971. 319p.

Elizabeth Janeway's book appeared shortly after the publication of Kate Millett's *Sexual Politics,* a radical explanation of the war between the sexes and viewed as a polemic by many. Janeway, though she challenged many of the same social biases Millett had, found critical enthusiasm for her work, partly no doubt because her approach was gentle.

Janeway finds that the long and firmly held precepts, ''it's a man's world'' and ''woman's place is in the home,'' are based on myths.

In examining these myths, Janeway contends, with the support of Philippe Ariès's *Centuries of Childhood,* that the family is, historically speaking, a relatively new institution. Then why, she asks, do men prefer to have their women at home? And why has a social mythology been built to rationalize this desire? Janeway explains it as ''a demand for the renewal of past happiness which might be stated ... 'I want a woman of my own whom I can command, and who will respond willingly, to comfort me in my lack and loneliness and frustration as my mother did long ago.' With such a plea we can surely sympathize. This is the internal, remembered reality which corresponds with the external social reality, the emotion imprinted by the fact that children need mothering and get it most often and most easily from their mothers.'' Out of this need, Janeway believes, has grown the demanding mythic imperative that men have natural rights to women.

She also believes that men are afraid that if women leave the home they will seize power, that unless they are kept dependent they will become tyrants. It is Janeway's conviction that, far from wishing to become tyrants, what women want is autonomy — "control over their own lives and authority or influence commensurate with their abilities in the external world."

Millett, Kate. *Sexual Politics.* **Garden City, New York: Doubleday, 1970. 393p.**

Sexual Politics caused a tremendous stir when it was published; its author appeared on numerous television talk shows and ultimately on the cover of *Time Magazine.* Its critical reception was mixed. For those who disliked the book, it represented the most unpleasant aspects of the new feminist movement — an angry, humorless, brooding disposition. It has since become the standard for reviewers who compare other feminist books with it to see if they are more or less hostile, humorous or graceful in style than *Sexual Politics,* which has come to epitomize that worn-out phrase, "a strident, feminist polemic."

It is a difficult book, a reworked doctoral dissertation which analyzes certain intellectual traditions that perpetuate the patriarchal system in America. Kate Millett was the first contemporary American intellectual who, like Simone de Beauvoir in France, made a fundamental and systematic feminist attack on society. Although Betty Friedan's *The Feminine Mystique* had also made a broad attack on American thought, her evidence came largely from popular culture and not from an analysis of intellectual ideas, the substance of Millett's indictments.

The theme of the book is that sexual politics is a "power-structured relationship" based on sexual differentiation "whereby one group of persons is controlled by another." In developing her theme, Millett is most effective when she discusses literature.

She traces misogyny in the writings of D.H. Lawrence, Henry Miller, Norman Mailer and Jean Genet. Except for Genet, the writers are described as perpetrators of male-chauvinist attitudes who portray women as inferior beings with such depersonalized sexuality that the rest of their beings are "divorced from their genitals." Genet, on the other hand, understands that the "sexual role is not a matter of biological identity but of class or caste in the hierocratic homosexual society" of the world created in his novels and plays. Millett ingeniously considers that world of pimps and queens to be the mirror-image of heterosexual society where the contempt with which homosexual female characters are treated by male characters is a reflection of the sexual caste system operating in the heterosexual world.

Millett's literary criticism has already influenced other critics and is an important contribution to feminist thought.

Mitchell, Juliet. *Woman's Estate.* **New York: Pantheon, 1971. 182p.**

Juliet Mitchell wrote the widely-circulated article "Women: The Longest Revolution'' for the *New Left Review* in 1966. In that article, she criticized traditional socialist analysis for its inability to incorporate the issues of women's liberation in its more general criticism of society. That piece is included in this book which assesses the political background of women's liberation, its origins, and the ideas it shares with other radical movements of the sixties.

One of her major concerns is the failure of communication between socialists and feminists, groups which need one another in order to accomplish common goals. The conflict that sprang up between them was premature because neither group had developed a theory. She argues for the necessity of developing both a radical feminist consciousness and a socialist analysis of the oppression of women. ''The two are coextensive and must be worked on together. If we simply develop feminist consciousness (as radical feminists suggest) we will get, not political consciousness, but the equivalent of national chauvinism among Third World nations... On the other hand, if our socialist 'theories' ignore our feminist consciousness they cannot understand the specific nature of our oppression as women.''

In the second part of the book, Mitchell analyzes women's failure to respond to the oppression which has traditionally beset their lives. The answer, she believes, lies in the nature of the family. Women are usually at home raising small children at a time when they might be developing class consciousness within the labor force. Thus they provide a permanent source of the cheapest labor found within capitalist countries. Trapped within the family, they fail to recognize the contradiction between the ideology of their freedom assumed in a democratic society and the reality of their economic deprivation in a capitalist society that makes the ideology a farce.

Mitchell believes that psychoanalysis is crucial to the understanding of women and the family. ''In studying women we cannot neglect the methods of a science of the mind, a theory that attempts to explain how women become women and men, men. The borderline between the biological and the social which finds expression in the family is the land that psychoanalysis sets out to chart; it is the land where sexual distinction originates.'' That so many feminists have excoriated Freud and his science is an attitude Mitchell finds simplistic, and one she sets out to correct in her second book, *Psychoanalysis and Feminism.*

West, Uta, ed. ***Women in a Changing World.*** **New York: McGraw-Hill, 1975. 170p.**

The women's movement has changed the lives of many people, and the contributors to this volume are concerned with problems that are the result of these changes. In her essay, ''The New Anxiety of Motherhood,'' Caryl Rivers discusses the pressures placed on young women who no longer assume they will have children, but instead agonize over the difficult decisions involved. In ''If Love is the Answer, What is the Question?,'' Uta West deals with the problems of love and loneliness for women who have already achieved feminist goals — autonomous lives with high-paying jobs and positions of power. West points out that these women still long for intimate relationships with men, and often pay a heavy price for even temporary satisfactions. They sometimes financially support men who offer no personal commitment to them, or involve themselves with men whose severe problems have led them to alcoholism or drug addiction. A selection by Jane Lazarre, "What Feminists and Freudians Can Learn from Each Other" defends traditional psychoanalysis as a tool for helping people to understand themselves in order to deal more successfully with life and with changing ideals. This anthology also includes articles by Mary Daly and Elizabeth Janeway and fiction by Doris Lessing, Grace Paley and Donald Barthelme.

In general, the problems dealt with by these writers are advanced — many steps beyond the basic arguments of the battle between the sexes which characterized earlier feminist writing. The book is addressed to educated people of the '70's who are beyond coping with social inequities and must now handle the new social styles they have chosen.

Yates, Gayle Graham. *What Women Want: The Ideas of the Movement.* Cambridge, Mass.: Harvard University Press, 1975. 230p.

Yates studied some of the essential writings of contemporary feminists and perceived their philosophies to fall into three major categories: the male as superior to female model; the female as superior to male model; and the androgynous ideal. The first and largest of these categories contains the views of such organizations as the National Organization for Women, the Women's Equity Action League and the National Women's Political Caucus. Members of these groups view men as having been in a superior position historically, and define as their goal the desire to achieve equality with men. The second group has a more radical position, its views expressed by such writers as Kate Millett and Shulamith Firestone. Their position is "antimasculinist, against things male-derived and sometimes against males themselves. Its primary focus for change is social. Its strategy is conflict. The source of its standard for a new social order is in women themselves." As her third category, Yates describes the androgynous perspective which uses as its model the ideology that women and men are equal to each other. She includes in this group the writings of Carolyn Heilbrun, Elizabeth Janeway and Germaine Greer, and believes that this model is the desirable approach for future feminist goals.

*   *   *

Anticaglia, Elizabeth. *A Housewife's Guide to Women's Liberation.* Chicago: Nelson-Hall, 1972. 231p.

This is an example of a book totally derived from *The Feminine Mystique,* claiming to be special in that the feminist message is delivered in terms a housewife can understand.

Atkinson, Ti-Grace. *Amazon Odyssey.* New York: Links, 1974. 226p.

The essays and speeches in this book cover the years between 1967 and 1972 when Atkinson evolved as a radical feminist. She includes her 1968 resignation speech from NOW which occurred after she lost a battle to rid the organization of positions of power; and the speech she gave at Catholic University in 1971 when she was attacked by Mrs. Bozell, William Buckley's sister, for insulting the Virgin Mary.

Billings, Victoria. *The Womansbook.* **Los Angeles: Wollstonecraft, 1974. 266p.**

Billings has written a feminist pep-talk, encouraging women to shake off all of the old stereotypes which have prevented them from developing their potential and independence. She offers suggestions for doing so, and includes biographical snippets from the lives of such women as Gloria Steinem and Golda Meir for inspiration.

Burton, Gabrielle. *I'm Running Away from Home But I'm Not Allowed to Cross the Street.* **Pittsburgh: Know, 1972. 206p.**

Written as an alternative to the weighty classics of the women's movement, the book is a primer of women's liberation, a pocket-sized guidebook for those who want to understand feminist issues in a hurry. It is intelligent and witty and therefore ideal for young readers and for those who cannot make it through *Sexual Politics.* Burton at all times acknowledges her intellectual debts to her ambitious predecessors.

Decter, Midge. *The New Chastity and Other Arguments Against Women's Liberation.* **New York: Coward, McCann and Geoghegan, 1972. 188p.**

Decter, a bright woman with an impressive prose style, uses her gifts to diminish the credibility of what she interprets to be some fundamental principles of the women's movement. In her chapter entitled "Shitwork" she trivializes the origins of the movement by pointing out that an inherent absurdity exists when a social movement springs up over fights about housework. On the other hand, when it suits her, she exaggerates aspects of the movement to make her point. For example, she relates negative reactions to motherhood to evidence of self-hatred, much as kinky religions and suicidal cults express self-hatred in the name of social justice.

deRham, Edith. *The Love Fraud.* **New York: Pegasus, 1965. 319p.**

The author subtitles her book, "A direct attack on the staggering waste of education and talent among American women." Like Betty Friedan, deRham writes about the middle-class woman who has been persuaded that her entire future rests with the care of husband and children. She sees no future in motherhood, and among other things, calls for the social acceptance of day-care centers, institutions which met with success in Russia, Israel and Sweden.

Dreifus, Claudia. *Woman's Fate: Raps from a Feminist Consciousness-Raising Group.* **New York: Bantam, 1973. 277p.**

Consciousness-raising, a concept inherited from the Speak Bitterness meetings held by Chinese women in the 1940's, has been one of the most political activities of the women's movement. Like Chinese women, Americans converted their private laments into political acts, recognizing that what had seemed to be individual problems were affecting many other women, and were the result of social inequities, not individual failures. In this book, Dreifus describes the rap sessions of her group of eight women. She illustrates the dynamics of the functioning consciousness-raising group as a guide for other women to follow.

Dworkin, Andrea. *Woman Hating.* **New York: Dutton, 1974. 217p.**

Dworkin sees herself as part of the anti-male feminist tradition inspired by Kate Millett and Robin Morgan. She is enraged by the historic oppression of women, and points to classic examples which support her claims — the burning of witches, foot-binding in China, pornography.

Freeman, Jo, ed. *Women: A Feminist Perspective.* **Palo Alto, Cal.: Mayfield, 1975. 487p.**

Unlike numerous other anthologies of feminist writings, this one contains all new material. Manuscripts were solicited by Freeman from any woman who could offer intellectually provocative material from a feminist perspective. The collection focuses on the socialization process and its damaging effects on women. Sections deal with family life, the work world, and institutions of social control such as law, politics and psychology. Most of the contributors are academic women, and many are familiar because of their previous contributions to feminist thought, e.g., Phyllis Chesler, Pauline Bart and Rosalyn Baxandall.

Fritz, Leah. *Thinking like a Woman.* **New York: WIN Books, 1975. 160p.**

Leah Fritz has collected her essays which were published between 1967 and 1975. Together they form a documentary of her developing feminist awareness, tracing her emergence from radical politics through the peace and civil rights movements. Though her response to the women's movement is personal, many of her perceptions will be familiar to other women.

Gornick, Vivian and Barbara K. Moran, eds. *Woman in Sexist Society: Studies in Power and Powerlessness.* **New York: Basic Books, 1971. 515p.**

These essays deal at length with contemporary issues that have concerned feminists. Writers have moved beyond manifestoes and personal reminiscences to offer scholarly and critical analyses of the position of women in America. Some important articles appear here for the first time — Kate Millett's ''Prostitution: A Quartet for Female Voices'' and Ethel Strainchamps's ''Our Sexist Language.''

Greer, Germaine. *The Female Eunuch.* **New York: Bantam, 1972. 373p.**

Germaine Greer is from Australia, received her Ph.D. at Cambridge, and now lives in England where she teaches and works as a television journalist. Her book is an appraisal of the battle between the sexes which Greer believes can be avoided if women will only understand the power of their own sexuality. As things have stood, she says, women have become castrated — female eunuchs unaware of their potentialities for freedom. She writes with style and wit, exploding myths about the content of women's lives. One by one she dismisses romance, marriage, family and childrearing as institutions which have been highly overrated. Her purpose is to raise important questions, not to provide answers to them. She is not interested in suggesting collective action as a way for women to improve their lives. When she does suggest solutions, they seem to apply only to herself, a talented and successful woman who managed to find her own way in the world.

Harris, Janet. *The Prime of Ms. America: The American Woman at Forty.* **New York: Putnam, 1975. 250p.**

Harris has written still another version of *The Feminine Mystique,* this time directed at middle-aged women, an audience she presumably feels could not be reached by Betty Friedan's book.

Janeway, Elizabeth. *Between Myth and Morning: Women Awakening.* **New York: William Morrow, 1974. 279p.**

Elizabeth Janeway's earlier book, *Man's World, Woman's Place* brought to her a deserved reputation as a wise and graceful writer on contemporary issues about women. In this book she has collected her essays, speeches and book reviews written on the subject of women, and presents them in support of an overall theme — that women have attained a new status in the years between 1965 and 1975, a view she supports by referring to the appearance of new views on women's careers, childrearing methods and sexuality.

Jenness, Linda, ed. *Feminism and Socialism.* **New York: Pathfinder, 1972. 160p.**

This is an anthology of articles, interviews and resolutions representing the socialist position on the oppression of women and on strategies for winning full liberation. The writers condemn capitalism and call for a socialist revolution. Fundamental issues taken up include the rights of black women and Chicanas, comments on abortion rights and the ERA, and the structure of the family. The collection includes a Marxist analysis of *Sexual Politics* and a socialist response to Norman Mailer's *The Prisoner of Sex.*

Koedt, Anne, Ellen Levine and Anita Rapone, eds. *Radical Feminism.* **New York: Quadrangle, 1973. 424p.**

This anthology of contemporary feminist writing is unusually good, for it contains essays that are now classics: "Why I Want a Wife," by Judy Syfers; "The Building of the Gilded Cage," by Jo Freeman; "Psychology Constructs the Female," by Naomi Weisstein; and "The Myth of the Vaginal Orgasm," by Anne Koedt. Many of the entries are reprints from *Notes,* a radical feminist journal.

Lifton, Robert Jay, ed. *The Woman in America.* **Boston: Beacon Press, 1967. 293p.**

These essays first appeared in a 1964 issue of *Daedalus,* and came out of a conference on women sponsored by that journal. Contributors include such well-known scholars as Erik Erikson, David Riesman, Carl Degler and Jill Conway. But the best-known essay among several fine ones is by Alice Rossi, "Equality Between the Sexes: An Immodest Proposal." Writing at a time when feminism was a dead issue in America, Rossi spoke of the "need to reassert the claim to sex equality and to search for the means by which it can be achieved." The essay has become a classic. Rossi anticipated many of the issues which began to engage feminists five or six years later when the women's liberation movement took hold. She speaks, for instance, of an androgynous ideal as the solution to the injustices perpetuated by sex-role stereotyping. She has become a major contributor to feminist thought.

Martin, Wendy, ed. *The American Sisterhood: Writings of the Feminist Movement from Colonial Times to the Present.* New York: Harper and Row, 1972. 373p.

Almost half of the forty-six selections included here were written after 1969. The focus of the book is on the relationship of the issues of the new feminist movement to earlier feminist thought. The range of topics is broad, and the editor has grouped them around two general themes: "Political, Legal and Economic Questions;" and "Social, Sexual, and Psychological Questions." Writings range from excerpts from "The First Trial of Anne Hutchinson" to Robin Morgan's "Goodbye to All That."

Merriam, Eve. *After Nora Slammed the Door.* Cleveland: World, 1964. 236p.

Eve Merriam examined the "woman question" in the 1950's and early 60's, and like Betty Friedan, saw that all was not well with the lives of middle-class women in America. She explores the inadequacies of suburban life and offers solutions to the myths that have led to the narrow restrictions caused by sex-role stereotyping.

Millett, Kate. *Flying.* New York: Knopf, 1974. 546p.

Flying is a free flowing verbal monologue in which the author takes the reader everywhere but particularly into the troubled corners of her mind. The years following the publication of *Sexual Politics* were difficult for Millett and filled with pain. The sensation caused by the book and by her press conference in which she discussed her bisexuality, brought her fame, but made her vulnerable to attack from all sides. She was anguished by people in the women's movement who, according to the ethic of a leaderless movement, felt she was looking for personal power at the expense of others. The book, then, becomes a way for Millett to exorcise herself from the blame and guilt which had been heaped upon her by others.

Morgan, Robin, ed. *Sisterhood is Powerful: An Anthology of Writings from the Women's Liberation Movement.* New York: Vintage, 1970. 602p.

This is the most comprehensive anthology of early writings on the contemporary women's movement. The collection contains the whole range of themes that have long been identified with the new feminism — abortion and birth control, psychological and sexual oppression, the persecution of lesbians, prostitution, discrimination against black women, and the low status of housewives. The articles were written by fifty contributors showing the energy and anger that are as much a part of the early years of the movement as the issues that the writers discuss.

Reed, Evelyn. *Problems of Women's Liberation.* New York: Pathfinder, 1971. 96p.

Reed's essays discuss women's problems from a Marxist point of view. She sees women as duped consumers, victims of capitalists who "profiteer in female flesh." Reed explores the origins of patriarchy, and is convinced that it was preceded by a matriarchy in primitive society.

Roszak, Betty and Theodore Roszak, eds. *Masculine/Feminine: Readings in Sexual Mythology and the Liberation of Women.* New York: Harper and Row, 1969. 316p.

This fine anthology contains essays which provide a brief history of modern anti-feminist thought, and essays which offer contemporary feminist responses. The readings are divided into four sections: 1) misogynist writings by Strindberg, Freud and Lionel Tiger; 2) more enlightened views of women held by George Bernard Shaw, Havelock Ellis and Gunnar Myrdal; 3) feminist writings from the 1950's and 1960's by Ruth Herschberger, Simone de Beauvoir, Alice Rossi, Marlene Dixon and others; 4) radical feminist contemporary pieces such as Valerie Solanas' "SCUM Manifesto" and the "Redstockings Manifesto."

Rowbotham, Sheila. *Woman's Consciousness, Man's World.* Baltimore: Penguin, 1973. 125p.

The author, a socialist, is interested in identifying the origins of the feminist movement within capitalist societies and in analyzing the condition of women to show the need for a feminist revolution. For the task ahead, she sees the need for a movement largely made up of working-class women who have been exploited because of their class origins as well as because they are women.

Stambler, Sookie, ed. *Women's Liberation: Blueprint for the Future.* New York: Ace, 1970. 283p.

This early collection includes essays by Susan Brownmiller, Kate Millett, Rita Mae Brown and many other contemporary feminists.

Tanner, Leslie B., ed. *Voices from Women's Liberation.* New York: New American Library, 1970. 443p.

Tanner has compiled brief excerpts from feminist writings beginning with Abigail Adams and ending with an essay by Shulamith Firestone. The point made is that women have objected to their subordinate role for centuries, and that complaints made hundreds of years ago are the same as those made today.

Thompson, Mary Lou, ed. *Voices of the New Feminism.* Boston: Beacon Press, 1970. 246p.

An excellent anthology which presents the new feminist movement within a historic context, the book includes some reprinted articles and some new statements by well-known feminists. Included are: ''Pioneers of Women's Liberation,'' by Joyce Cowley; ''Sex Equality: The Beginnings of Ideology,'' by Alice Rossi; and ''Toward Partnership in the Church,'' by Mary Daly. The book also contains an abridged version of Lucinda Cisler's bibliography on women.

Ware, Cellestine. *Woman Power: The Movement for Women's Liberation.* New York: Tower, 1970. 176p.

This is an analysis of the new feminist movement and contains some interesting material on the relationship between the movement and black women.

Wortis, Helen and Clara Rabinowitz, eds. *The Woman Movement: Social and Psychological Perspectives.* New York: Halsted, 1972. 151p.

Most of the essays in this book originally appeared in a special section of the *American Journal of Orthopsychiatry.* Contributors are professionals who share general concerns about the changing role of women in America and what the impact will be on women and on the family.

Health

The medical profession has been criticized in recent years by feminists who feel that male physicians have not been properly responsive to the needs of female patients. These feelings have led to the self-help movement in health in which women are learning routine medical procedures and are gaining knowledge about the functioning of their own bodies. The popularity of *Our Bodies Ourselves* is further proof that women have not previously received the information they need through the regular channels of the medical establishment.

Other books in this section explore medical subjects that are of concern to women such as: relating the history of attitudes toward childbirth in America; documenting the suppression of women as healers; and exposing the dangers of birth control pills.

The Boston Women's Health Collective. *Our Bodies Ourselves: A Book by and for Women.* **Second Edition. Completely Revised and Expanded. New York: Simon and Schuster, 1977 (c1971, 1973) 383p.**

The groundwork for this book began when a small discussion group on "women and their bodies" began meeting to gather information on the health of women. Feeling that many doctors were "condescending, paternalistic, judgmental and non-informative," the women decided to share information. This led to their offering a course to other women and finally to their distributing their information in a mimeographed form. They received an enthusiastic response from other women and this led ultimately to the decision to publish their work commercially. Enormously successful, it has since been reprinted. Royalties from the book are used to support health education work within their own and within other women's groups.

The innovative aspect of the book is that it offers information about women's feelings as well as factual information about the parts and functions of the body. Although emphasis is on sexuality and the reproductive cycle, the book also contains information about good nutrition and other recommended health habits. It also includes a chapter on lesbians and a discussion of lesbian mothers.

*   *   *

Arms, Suzanne. *Immaculate Deception: A New Look at Women and Childbirth in America.* Boston: Houghton Mifflin, 1975. 318p.

Arms's thesis is that modern society has mystified childbirth and removed it from its natural process, giving rise to the modern deception that normal childbirth is inherently dangerous, risky, painful and terrifying. She blames Christianity as the source of misguided attitudes about childbirth that have gradually taken all determination away from women, and put it into the hands of men.

Ehrenreich, Barbara and Deirdre English. *Complains and Disorders: The Sexual Politics of Sickness.* Old Westbury: Feminist Press, 1973. 94p.

The authors perceive sexism in medicine "as a social force helping to shape the options and social roles of all women." By looking at the historic relationship between women and medicine they argue that women have continually been denigrated by male doctors. They conclude that women must demand control over their own bodies, away from the medical profession which holds power over women.

————. *Witches, Midwives and Nurses: A History of Women Healers.* Old Westbury: Feminist Press, 1973. 45p.

Here the authors provide a brief history of the suppression of women as healers. Beginning with a discussion of witches who were lay healers serving the peasant population, they trace the disappearance of women from the decision-making areas of medicine. The book provides historic background relevant to the current women's health movement.

Frankfort, Ellen. *Vaginal Politics.* New York: Quadrangle, 1972. 250p.

Frankfort has collected for this volume many of her articles which originally appeared in *The Village Voice.* Included are her views on the drug industry, abortion clinics, the treatment of cancer, and male dominance in the medical profession. She points out, for instance, that males overwhelmingly control the field of gynecology because it involves surgery, the male territory.

Horos, Carol V. *Vaginal Health.* New Canaan: Tobey, 1975. 174p.

Horos provides a handbook on what every woman should know about daily vaginal care and about the gynecological exam. Included are discussions of problems ranging from minor infections to venereal disease.

Lanson, Lucienne. *From Woman to Woman: A Gynecologist Answers Questions About You and Your Body.* New York: Knopf, 1975. 358p.

Dr. Lanson responds to the upsurge of interest of women in their bodily functions, and presents straight-forward answers to frequently raised questions. She discusses the normal functions of women's bodies as well as the prevention and treatment of disease.

Maddux, Hilary. *Menstruation.* **New Canaan: Tobey, 1975. 191p.**

This book provides an uncomplicated discussion of menstruation. It describes the function of genital organs, the role of hormones and problems of menstruation in an attempt to demystify basic information about women's bodies. Maddux has included a directory of women's centers, health care clinics and referral services, which was compiled by the Women's Action Alliance.

Seaman, Barbara. *The Doctors' Case Against the Pill.* **New York: Wyden, 1969. 279p.**

As more and more women have been finding out, the birth control pill has not been the panacea physicians and patients thought it to be. Barbara seaman has gathered startling evidence pointing to the medical dangers inherent in the use of the pill. She attacks those physicians who continue to prescribe this potent drug without properly evaluating its effects on individual women, or at least informing them of the potential risks.

Tucker, Tarvez. *Prepared Childbirth.* **New Canaan: Tobey, 1975. 143p.**

Tucker discusses alternatives to traditional methods of childbirth in clear, straight-forward language. Some of the topics included are pain, use of drugs, and courses which prepare women for childbirth.

History

At the present time, historians of women are attempting to work out a way to evaluate women's involvement in history. Gerda Lerner, in particular, has analyzed various theoretical approaches. She sees traditional history as patriarchal, a fact most obviously reflected in the terminology of most historians — ''man, men, mankind'' — women being subsumed or ignored under those rubrics. To counteract this male-centered view of the past, historians of women are attempting a variety of approaches. Some are investigating the movement in history for woman's rights and opportunities, an approach Lerner calls ''compensatory,'' and one which has led to numerous studies of the suffrage movement. Other historians are focusing on other movements not directly involving women's rights in which women have participated. This ''contribution'' theory of women's history, according to Lerner, is limited by a failure to evaluate what that participation meant for women. (William O'Neill neglected this question when he concluded that the 19th-century suffrage and reform movements were failures.) Now social historians and Marxist theorists have a broader perspective than that of traditional historians but, though they avoid an elitist interpretation of the past, they still treat women as marginal. Marxist theory, Lerner points out, still regards women as a subclass. Finally there is Mary Beard's theory — that women have been powerful and creative forces in history, and not merely abject, passive victims.

Most of the books in this chapter are studies and biographies of women who were suffragists or who sought other social reforms. They reflect those categories Lerner calls ''compensatory'' and ''contribution.'' Still other books are social histories which provide historical analyses of broader segments of American women. William Chafe studies the changing status of women in the fifty years following the passage of suffrage; Anne Scott interprets the Southern lady over a hundred years beginning with 1830; Mary Ryan provides an analysis of the social roles prescribed for women throughout American history; Kathryn Sklar, in her biography of Catharine Beecher, uses her subject's life to reveal aspects of 19th century social thought.

Recent scholarship concerned with historiography and social history occurs more frequently in journal articles than in books. For this reason, anthologies presenting primary sources or new historical scholarship are featured in this chapter.

GENERAL STUDIES

Chafe, William Henry. *The American Woman: Her Changing Social, Economic, and Political Roles, 1920-1970.* New York: Oxford University Press, 1972. 351p.

Chafe's history of American women begins with the granting of suffrage in 1920. By examining women's political and economic positions in the decades following the passage of the 19th amendment, Chafe found that gains in these areas were prevented by the widespread attitude that woman's place was in the home. The author perceived that this attitude persisted through the Depression right up to World War II when women were actively solicited for the job market.

Chafe sees war-time work experiences as a turning point for women and their place in society. Refuting the commonly held assumption that women returned to their homes at the war's end, Chafe demonstrates that more women than ever, particularly those in the middle class, entered the job market, thereby creating a setting for the new drive for equality that appeared in the 1960's.

Chafe discusses the changes that have been occurring within the domestic setting. Women's responsibilities as wage earners have led to an overlapping of domestic roles, with husbands often sharing the running of the home. He concludes that this restructuring of roles will have to continue if the modern feminist movement is to succeed, and that its success will affect not only how society perceives women but how they perceive themselves.

Davis, Allen F. *Spearheads for Reform: The Social Settlements and the Progressive Movements 1890-1914.* New York: Oxford University Press, 1967. 322p.

This book is similar in scope to Daniel Levine's study of Jane Addams, for its concern is also with the influence of the settlement movement on the progressive movement. However, it differs from the Levine book in that it looks at the history and development of the settlement movement as a whole rather than only the influence of Jane Addams and Hull House. Davis points out that settlement workers took part in the labor movement, the establishment of the NAACP, and provided the first director for the Children's Bureau, Julia Lathrop. He documents the enormous difficulty these dedicated people encountered, for promoting social legislation often meant fighting the same battle over and over again.

Finally, Davis makes clear that these early social workers — most of them women — widened their spheres from the alleviation of neighborhood problems to the fight for change on a national level. In his concluding chapter, Davis points out that the emphasis in social work has changed from the crusading zeal for social reform during the Progressive Era to the modern tendency to treat problems as individual by promoting psychiatric adjustment.

Kraditor, Aileen S. *The Ideas of the Woman Suffrage Movement,* **1890-1920. New York: Columbia University Press, 1965. 313p.**

Kraditor's study is concerned with the ideas that were both implicit and explicit in the woman suffrage movement in America during the thirty years preceding the passage of the 19th Amendment. Using the last three volumes of *The History of Woman Suffrage, The Woman's Journal,* and other sources, the author presents and examines arguments used both by the suffragists and the antisuffragists to defend their opposing points of view.

Kraditor disentangles the inconsistencies which characterize the arguments on both sides of the suffrage issue. She traces the change in the premises of the suffrage leaders from arguments derived from the inalienable right of women to vote (the principle of the ''consent of the governed'') to the later question of expedience — that women needed the vote to institute important reforms. This shift in rationale from justice to expediency reflects the suffragists' reaction to the enfranchisement of black males and immigrants: To be denied long-sought rights which were freely handed over to people who in their eyes were less worthy citizens caused the suffragist leaders to change the premises of their arguments. They were no longer certain about universal, individual rights, and began to support literacy tests, for example, and property requirements.

Antisuffrage proponents used biological rather than ideological arguments and used them with an interesting inconsistency. On the one hand, they felt that women were weak and therefore incapable of assuming the responsibilities demanded by full participation in government; on the other hand, some antis believed that women, like men, had evolved specialized roles, an argument based on Social Darwinism, which was in vogue, and that the confusion of roles would be a dissolution of their particular strengths.

Kraditor's book is a rich intellectual analysis of the political activity of American women during these crucial years. The book deals with questions of religion, attitudes toward immigrants and labor, the Southern woman, the structure and policies of the Woman's Party, and the role of women and the home. Contemporary debates over the sex-role stereotyping of women are echos of arguments that occurred a hundred years ago. Anyone interested in the intellectual history of women must be indebted to Aileen Kraditor for identifying and documenting the ideas presented in this book.

Lutz, Alma. *Crusade for Freedom: Women of the Antislavery Movement.* **Boston: Beacon Press, 1968. 338p.**

Long before women's history became a subject of interest to more than just a handful of people, much less a course of study, Alma Lutz was writing books about women leaders of the 19th century. In *Crusade for Freedom,* she has written a history of the Abolition Movement, with particular focus on the women who contributed to its eventual success. Not heavily documented, this is a chronicle of the thirty years of the Movement, with anecdotes about the large and fascinating group of people who were making history during the period.

As Alma Lutz makes clear, the Abolitionist Movement was the first reform movement around which women organized. Female antislavery groups sprang up in Philadelphia, Boston, Lynn and other places, and women contributed to the cause in a number of ways. Maria Weston Chapman organized Abolition fairs which raised large amounts of money for the American Antislavery Society. Others, like Lydia Maria Child and Harriet Beecher Stowe, presented their views through their books. But it was women like the Grimké sisters and Abby Kelley, who chose to travel around the country delivering antislavery lectures, who are perhaps the most admirable. Not only did they meet with audiences who were hostile on ideological grounds, but within the movement they had to contend with a clergy that patronized women, and worse, male antislavery workers who felt that it was immoral for women to come out from behind the scenes to appear on the lecture platform. In spite of such resistance and the added discomforts of the grueling lecture circuit, these women persisted in the task they saw before them.

Like so many other organizations, the Abolitionists were beset with internal strife and divisions. Garrison and his followers were staunchly in favor of immediate emancipation and eventually favored disunion, believing that the Constitution was a pro-slavery document. Others felt that political activity within the existing system was the wiser course. The women, who generally remained in Garrison's camp, saw another kind of division arising from their work, the question of woman's rights. Lucretia Mott, Elizabeth Cady Stanton, Susan B. Anthony, and Lucy Stone all launched into woman's rights work after having experienced injustice as Abolitionists.

Alma Lutz captures the sense of the times, and takes particular delight in giving credit where it is due. Writing in the '60's, Lutz again could see the significance of the involvement of women in Civil Rights activities, and predicted a resurgence of feminist activity which would lead, she hoped, to the passage of the Equal Rights Amendment.

Morgan, David. *Suffragists and Democrats.* **East Lansing, Mich.: Michigan State University Press, 1972. 225p.**

David Morgan's study focuses on that important period in the history of suffrage, the years between 1916 and 1920 when the 19th amendment was ratified. He is concerned with the political battle over suffrage, and deals specifically with President Wilson's position and style of leadership during this period when the suffrage movement had become enmeshed in party politics.

The proponents of the 19th-century suffrage movement had gradually changed from a group of elite women struggling for personal rights to a broader based group interested in social reform during the Progressive Era. As the relationship between suffrage and other reform issues became more closely identified, combative political factions came into the fight against woman suffrage. Morgan has analyzed why regional interest groups took this negative position. Southern racists resisted federal meddling in local elections; the liquor industry feared women's newly exhibited power as temperance workers; and the textile industry resisted political power for women because they feared their support for child labor laws. Morgan provides a tightly organized, readable account of these vital years in the history of reform in America.

O'Neill, William. *Everyone Was Brave: A History of Feminism in America.* Chicago: Quadrangle, 1971. 379p.

In his examination of the suffrage movement, O'Neill concludes that the seventy-year battle for woman's rights was finally a failure; that after 1920 feminism in America was virtually dead. His thesis is that by narrowing their aims to suffrage, feminists failed to take into account that women's fundamental problems were social rather than political. Societal expectations for women as wives and mothers, although examined and criticized by an important feminist like Charlotte Perkins Gilman, were never seriously condemned by the women who made up the mainstream of woman's rights activities. Instead of discarding the Victorian principle that motherhood was the natural state for women, feminists argued that as mothers of the race women were responsible for the moral standards of all society and must therefore have the vote. To O'Neill, only a truly socialist movement which included a restructuring of the family would lead to the emancipation of women. Other strategies, though temporarily beneficial to individuals and to society, were not long lasting.

With the new feminist movement O'Neill sees greater possibilities for a more lasting success because women are questioning such fundamentals as the definition of the female role in our society.

O'Neill's conclusions about the failure of the suffrage movement have been criticized by some historians. They point out that women gained valuable experience by working and taking leadership in the movement. After the passage of the 19th amendment, women formed new groups like The League of Women Voters and other organizations in which they continued to work for social reform.

Ryan, Mary. *Womanhood in America: From Colonial Times to the Present.* New York: New Viewpoints, 1975. 496p.

Mary Ryan has provided an historic survey of the roles women have occupied in American society from Colonial times to the present. To develop her thesis that the social and economic systems have maneuvered women into roles they neither chose for themselves nor could escape from, Ryan makes important generalizations about the three centuries of women's history: the Colonial period when women did have autonomy; the nineteenth century with its restrictive "Cult of True Womanhood;" and the twentieth century in which women are simultaneously trying to be domestic, maintain femininity and hold down outside jobs. Ryan concludes that the long-awaited equitable society will come about only when women form a strong socialist feminist movement.

By looking at women's history with the intention of separating cultural attitudes from actual behavior, Ryan is the first historian to attempt a comprehensive survey revealing women's actual experiences.

Scott, Anne Firor. *The Southern Lady: From Pedestal to Politics, 1830-1930.* Chicago: The University of Chicago Press, 1970. 247p.

Anne Scott has provided a new interpretation within which she has traced the changing role of the Southern woman over a crucial period of American history. Calling upon diaries, family papers and the records of organizations, she has examined "women's sphere" (that catch-phrase for the stereotyped role of women which appeared again and again in the 19th century). She convincingly demonstrates that the lives of women in the South were changed in dramatic ways in the course of the hundred years with which her study is concerned. Though the Southern woman was considered less progressive than women in other parts of the United States, she finally operated within a world that offered her significant choices. Her world was changed most abruptly by the Civil War, but also by the suffrage movement which improved her lot even though it did not completely fulfill the wildest hopes of its most ardent advocates.

It is Scott's feeling that a great many myths have surrounded the Southern woman, some of them perpetuated by the women themselves. Religion taught them they were inferior to men. Lack of education persuaded them that their proper place was within the domestic setting and their greatest expectation the satisfactions of motherhood. But the brute realities of life in the predominantly rural South cut sharply into these myths. Motherhood came to mean a baby a year. Notions about helplessness and servility had to be replaced by the obligations of managing a large and complicated household and the many slaves involved in that management. Apart from the physical demands of daily life, there were the emotional strains the Southern woman suffered. It was, for example, an inescapable fact (since mulatto children were everywhere) that their husbands commonly took sexual advantage of slave women.

Scott suggests that the threat of social disorganization posed by a change in the role of women, let alone by changes in the system of slavery, made men in power defend the patriarchal structure. It was, of course, the Civil War that brought change. Almost single-handedly women took over the running of plantations, the setting up and maintenance of hospitals, and the compounded responsibilities of war-time survival. In doing so they gained confidence, a sense of self-worth and a sense of the contributions they might make. By participating in voluntary associations, Southern women moved from missionary societies, to WCTU work and suffrage, and ultimately to club work and social reform.

Anne Scott does not claim her absorbing book to be an exhaustive study. She points out what related areas of concern remain to be investigated — the question of the racial attitudes of the "Southern lady" and the equally pressing question of poor white and black women who were never considered "ladies."

Sinclair, Andrew. *The Better Half: The Emancipation of the American Woman.* New York: Harper and Row, 1965. 401p.

Sinclair has written one of the few broad surveys of the social history of women in America. He explores such general themes as the relationships between various reform movements, and the effect of western expansion on the nineteenth-century woman's movement. He draws a comparison between the 1840's and the 1960's as decades when reformers were preoccupied with the position of black people, and predicted that a new movement for women's liberation was about to take place. He reasoned that just as nineteenth-century women had become sensitized to their own subordinate position after working as abolitionists, so would the modern civil rights worker be made aware of her unequal position.

He traces geographic as well as historic patterns that emerged from reform movements. Although antislavery and suffrage activity began in the cities of the eastern seaboard, vitality shifted to small towns in the West and eventually to the frontiers. Boston and Philadelphia became conservative, and the smaller towns produced the new leaders — Theodore Weld, Elizabeth Cady Stanton and Susan B. Anthony. When the towns eventually became conservative, the cities again were radicalized by younger people who were bringing forth newer ideals for reform.

Considering that few other historians had inquired into women's history at the time Sinclair wrote this study, he offers interesting information and commentary. He points out, for example, that nineteenth-century feminists had to be assured that they were ''ladies''; that progress was made within the movement only when middle-class suffragists joined with working-class women; and that little could be accomplished within reform groups until a zealous group of women sacrificed other social aims for those of their own.

Sochen, June. *The New Woman: Feminism in Greenwich Village, 1910-1920.* New York: Quadrangle, 1972. 175p.

June Sochen has chosen to write about five feminists whom she sees as representative of the Greenwich Village scene between 1910-1920: Crystal Eastman; Henrietta Rodman; Ida Rauh; Neith Boyce; and Susan Glaspell. Boyce and Glaspell were professional writers who were producing works with feminist themes. Rodman and Eastman were activists as well as writers — Rodman fought for progressive change within the New York School System, and Eastman worked within the Peace Movement. Ida Rauh was an actress with the Provincetown Players, a group which performed a number of feminist plays written by Susan Glaspell.

These women have not received much attention from historians. Sochen merely begins to fill this gap. Her thesis is that the five women championed radical causes but used much too moderate means to reach their goals. She feels that for this reason their feminism failed. One problem with this concept is that Sochen has lumped together a group of women who were involved in very different activities, all of whom achieved varying amounts of success within their fields. To indict them is to assume that they were a "movement" which, based on her own evidence, does not seem to be the case.

That these women are worthy of further investigation is clear. For example, Henrietta Rodman, who founded the Feminist Alliance, tried to implement some of Charlotte Perkins Gilman's ideas, most notably by trying to build a feminist apartment house in Washington Square. The building was to have had a centralized kitchen and a professional child-care facility. Rodman's dream was that the inhabitants would be made up of families with professionally committed wives. Sochen offers a few newspaper accounts in her discussion of the project, and we are told that it failed, but one is left with continuing curiosity about all that Henrietta Rodman put into the scheme and how she dealt with the opposition.

Sochen, June. *Movers and Shakers: American Women Thinkers and Activists 1900-1970.* New York: Quadrangle, 1973. 320p.

By expanding the parameters of her earlier study, *New Feminism in Greenwich Village, 1910-1920,* Sochen now looks at the principle feminist writers and activists who appeared throughout the 20th century, and provides an historic sequence of the recurring themes of American feminist thought. She defines the subjects of her study to be "the few American women, the movers and shakers, who found their purpose in life less than satisfactory and defined the problem as a woman problem, rather than a personal one." Sochen distinguishes between those feminists who were primarily writers and those who expressed themselves through political activity.

In the first twenty years of the century, Sochen notes, feminist writers and activists were all middle-class, educated women: Mary Heaton Vorse; Henrietta Rodman; Crystal Eastman; Neith Boyce and Susan Glaspell. The radical women, represented by people like Rose Pastor Stokes and Kate Richards O'Hare, had working class origins. Sochen uncovers some feminists from the period 1940-60, who have been overlooked in a period generally preoccupied with depression, war, and the dull stability of the 1950's. She discusses Pearl Buck's *Of Men and Women* (1941) and magazine articles by Dorothy Sayers and Dorothy Thompson as being in the tradition of feminist thought that had been strong before this period, and emerged again in the 1960's. The last portion of the book, which deals with the resurgence of feminism in the 60's, places Betty Friedan, Kate Millett, Robin Morgan and others into the perspective of all that came before.

Sochen's book succeeds in its attempt to put the modern feminist movement into perspective by bringing to light the thoughts and activities of feminists who have received little attention before now. Sochen's survey should serve the purpose of inspiring others to pursue studies of these women in greater depth, and to discover still more American women who have made contributions. Since Sochen based her study primarily on the published writings of these women, the work of examining their lives through collections of primary sources still needs to be done.

* * *

Adams, Mildred. *The Right to Be People.* Philadelphia: Lippincott, 1967. 248p.

This is an informally written history of the struggle for suffrage, using the *History of Woman Suffrage* as the primary source of information.

Altbach, Edith Hoshino. *Women in America.* Lexington, Mass.: D.C. Heath, 1974. 204p.

This book is intended as a general introduction to the history of American women; the author concentrates on what she calls "ordinary female lives" rather than the exceptional woman. The four parts of the book are divided into domestic history, women at work, the women's movement, and the new feminism. Altbach ends her work with a thirty-page chronology of the events of note in the history of American women.

Banner, Lois W. *Women in Modern America: A Brief History.* New York: Harcourt Brace Jovanovich, 1974. 276p.

Banner divides the modern history of women into three parts: 1) 1890-1920, a period of active feminism with women organized for action; 2) 1920-1960, a period with little active feminism because of the distractions of the Depression and World War II; and 3) 1960 to the present, the emergence of the most radical feminism in our history. Banner explores the social history of these periods and relates it to the activities of women. She provides excellent bibliographies throughout her book.

Fuller, Edmund. *Prudence Crandall: An Incident of Racism in Nineteenth-Century Connecticut.* Middletown, Conn.: Wesleyan University Press, 1971. 113p.

Fuller has recounted the incident of the arrest in 1833 of Prudence Crandall, a young, northern Quaker teacher, for accepting as students black girls from other states. The law she broke had been hastily passed and was aimed specifically at her. The abolitionists on one side and northern racists on the other fomented such violence that her school ultimately closed.

Gattey, Charles N. *The Bloomer Girls.* New York: Coward-McCann, 1968. 192p.

Writing a popular history of the nineteenth-century movement for dress reform, Gattey neglects to relate it adequately to other reform movements involving women, thereby trivializing its importance.

Gibbs, Margaret. *The Daughters of the American Revolution.* New York: Holt, Rinehart and Winston, 1969. 244p.

Gibbs, who qualifies as a member of the DAR, having descended from an early English forebear, has written a slightly irreverent book about that organization. She describes their patriotic and conservative activities in an amusing and anecdotal style.

Grimes, Alan P. *The Puritan Ethic and Woman Suffrage.* New York: Oxford University Press, 1967. 159p.

Grimes, a political scientist, studied the origins of the woman suffrage movement in Utah and Wyoming to determine why these frontier states were the first to pass suffrage. He concludes that although progressive elements did support it to some degree, the success for women in the West was largely due to male support of Prohibition and immigration restriction. He equates this conservative point of view with traditional, white Protestant values, and therefore sees a close relationship between suffrage for women and what he calls the Puritan ethic.

Gurko, Miriam. *The Ladies of Seneca Falls: The Birth of the Woman's Rights Movement.* New York: Macmillan, 1974. 328p.

This is a popular book which presents a lively account of the nineteenth-century movements for suffrage and other reforms in a readable form appropriate for general readers.

Haller, John S. and Robin M. Haller. *The Physician and Sexuality in Victorian America.* Urbana: University of Illinois Press, 1974. 324p.

By examining many books, pamphlets and journal articles on medical subjects that were written in the late 19th and early 20th centuries, the Hallers arrive at some interesting conclusions about Victorian attitudes about human sexuality. Physicians were encouraging moral standards which would accommodate the view that women were both physically and intellectually delicate and were better off in the home away from the difficult challenges of the world. Doctors also decided that neurasthenia was a socially acceptable disease and could be held accountable for women's lack of achievement.

The Hallers see the Victorian period as a time of tension between old and new roles for women, aggravated by the attitudes of physicians.

Jones, Katharine M. *When Sherman Came: Southern Women and the "Great March."* Indianapolis: Bobbs-Merrill, 1964. 353p.

Jones wrote this book because she had always wondered what women were thinking and doing during those five months — November 1864 to April 1865 — when General Sherman led his troops through Georgia. Much had already been published in praise of Confederate men, but Jones had to go to primary sources to learn about the women. Her book, then, is an anthology of first hand accounts of the occupation of Georgia as experienced by women, with descriptions of plundering, rape and the massive destruction of property.

Lemons, J. Stanley. *The Woman Citizen: Social Feminism in the 1920's.* Urbana, Illinois: University of Illinois Press, 1973. 266p.

Perhaps not for the casual reader, this book belongs on the reference shelf of the serious student of women's history. In it Lemons focuses on a brief but important period, the American 1920's. He argues that far from being moribund during this time, the feminist movement made progress in social reform. Lemons traces the activities of such groups as The League of Women Voters and the National Federation of Business and Professional Women's Clubs and clarifies what sides they took on such issues as the Equal Rights Amendment and why they held the positions they did.

Leonard, Eugenie A. *The Dear-Bought Heritage.* Philadelphia: University of Pennsylvania Press, 1965. 658p.

Leonard studied Colonial women to investigate the ways in which they helped civilize their new world. Her thesis is that next to conceiving and bearing children, women's main urge has always been to improve the conditions surrounding their families. How women in the New World fulfilled that aim is the focus of this book.

Lerner, Gerda. *The Woman in American History. Menlo Park, Calif.: Addision-Wesley, 1971. 207p.*

Since standard American history textbooks leave women out, Lerner has written a survey which is intended to be used as a supplement to other books. She provides an overview of American women from the Colonial period to the twentieth century.

Massey, Mary Elizabeth. *Bonnet Brigades.* New York: Knopf, 1966. 371p.

In spite of the title which trivializes the subject, this is a scholarly study of northern and southern women during the Civil War, describing the War's identical impact on both sides; women shared many of the same fears and doubts. It is Massey's thesis that the War compelled women to become more active, self-reliant, and resourceful, and that this ultimately contributed to their social, economic and intellectual advancement.

Noun, Louise R. *Strong-Minded Women: The Emergence of the Woman Suffrage Movement in Iowa.* Ames: Iowa State University Press, 1969. 322p.

Noun has written a study of the history of suffrage activity in Iowa exploring such themes as its relationship to the national scene. She notes that Iowa women vainly attempted to avoid the dissension which had divided the movement in the East, and describes the internecine warfare that occurred within its own ranks.

O'Neill, William. *Divorce in the Progressive Era.* New Haven: Yale University Press, 1967. 295p.

O'Neill sees the issue of divorce as an indication of other social changes which Americans underwent in the years between 1890 and 1920. He presents here not only a history of the debate over the divorce issue, but traces the development of social change in the early twentieth century.

Pivar, David. *Purity Crusade: Sexual Morality and Social Control,* 1868-1900. Westport, Conn.: Greenwood, 1973. 308p.

Pivar has written a social history of the purity reform movement. He defines it as having occurred before the Progressive Era, a period which has not received much scholarly attention. The purpose of this book is "to trace the major contours of the movement, including its accomplishments, the events in which purity reformers participated, the social functions of purity reform in the woman's movement and urban Progressivism, and its effects upon the development of the social hygiene movement." Although historians may argue whether such apparently differing activities constituted a movement, it is Pivar's contention that they did, and that they foreshadowed the more clearly defined reform impulses of the twentieth century.

Smith, Page. *Daughters of the Promised Land: Women in American History.* Boston: Little, Brown, 1970. 392p.

Smith's survey of the history of American women is generally considered to be an offensive book because of the condescending tone he uses throughout, and because of the derogatory comments about women he frequently injects. As part of his historical analysis, for instance, he writes that women are better than men at performing routine, unimaginative tasks.

Sochen, June. *Herstory: A Woman's View of American History.* New York: Alfred, 1974. 448p.

Sochen has packed into her book information about women which is generally omitted from standard American histories. She is concerned not only about women, but about the white American male's denigration of blacks, Native Americans and the natural environment, topics she includes here from time to time. The result is an intensely personal view of American history which, though meaningful to its author, will not readily find a responsive audience. Sochen sets up little thematic structure, seldom preparing her readers for the direction of her thought.

Walters, Ronald, ed. *Primers for Prudery: Sexual Advice to Victorian America. Englewood Cliffs, New Jersey: Prentice-Hall, 1974. 175p.*

Similar in intention to the book by the Hallers, Ronald Walter's book has selections from 19th-century sex manuals, medical journals, and homemaking guides that not only reflect Victorian attitudes about sex, but also show the connection between sexual mores and the economic, social and cultural forces of the time.

BIOGRAPHY

Douglas, Emily Taft. *Margaret Sanger: Pioneer of the Future.* New York: Holt, Rinehart and Winston, 1970. 274p.

Douglas has written a readable account of Margaret Sanger's life covering the full span of her career until her death in 1966. Unlike the book by David Kennedy, *Birth Control in America,* which covers only the years until 1940 (thus giving the impression that Sanger's career stopped then), the Douglas book includes those crucial post-war years when the Birth Control Movement made gains once more. The war interrupted Sanger's progress after she opened her first clinic in 1916. Always viewing contraception in human terms — a woman's right to control her pregnancies, a child's right to enter the world wanted — Sanger was infuriated by the legal and political opposition which continuously distracted her from the humane focus of her work. She was therefore disheartened, after battling Comstock Laws, state legal restrictions and the Catholic Church, to be stopped on the way to making international progress by the ugly nationalism of governments at war. Within the context of theories about "racial suicide," foreign countries banned the spread of information about birth control.

After the war, as before, Margaret Sanger made trips to Japan, China and India, organized international conferences, and lived to see sympathies toward her cause change once more. Her most notable achievement may well be her direct connection (through support and funding) with the development of the birth control pill.

Emily Douglas makes the subject of her biography come alive by providing interesting details and anecdotes to illustrate the zeal and crusading spirit of Margaret Sanger. Although the lack of footnotes in this book may irk scholars, it is a good selection for undergraduate and general readers.

Fetherling, Dale. *Mother Jones, the Miners' Angel: A Portrait.* Carbondale, Illinois: Southern Illinois University Press, 1974. 263p.

Mother Jones is a unique figure in women's history. On the one hand she was a radical who worked as a paid organizer and freelance agitator for the United Mine Workers, yet she was also a life-long opponent of woman suffrage. Mother Jones's activities reflect the history of labor in America, particularly the mine workers. When she was thirty-seven, she lost her husband and four children during a yellow fever epidemic, moved to Chicago and worked as a seamstress until she was made homeless by the Chicago fire of 1871. She became involved with the Knights of Labor at that time and never again settled into a home. She devoted the last half of her life traveling from one troubled part of the country to another on behalf of the trade unionists. She was on the scene at the Haymarket Riot, the Virden and Ludlow Massacres, the Pullman Strike, and the Anthracite Strike of 1902.

There is much that is inconsistent in her speeches and writings; for instance, Fetherling tries to decide whether or not Mother Jones was a socialist. She attended the organizing meeting of the I.W.W. and believed in the collective ownership of the means of production. But this concept was not at the heart of her thought. Economic betterment for the worker and protective laws for child laborers were her concern. She left theorizing to others, occupying herself more directly with the workers' problems — housing conditions, hours of labor, and the exploitive company store.

Her verbal style was memorable, and she gained fame for saying things that, had they come from a man and not an elderly woman, would have landed her in the hospital. She enjoyed turning a phrase, referring to all miners, for instance, as "slaves of the caves."

As for her place in labor history, Fetherling sees Mother Jones as the human element, "a folk heroine whose inspiration reached down to those people who were unimportant in name or wealth or title but all-important in numbers." Since for her the economic fight was the most vital one, she failed to see the importance of the feminist movement. Essentially, she spent her life working for a working-class ideal — for the possibility of a man to earn enough comfortably to support a wife who can then be free to stay home to care for children.

Kennedy, David. *Birth Control in America: The Career of Margaret Sanger.* New Haven: Yale University Press, 1970. 320p.

This is not a definitive biography of Margaret Sanger. We do not get a full analysis of her life and times. Instead, Kennedy focuses his study only on her career between 1914 and the beginning of World War II when she gave up leadership in the Birth Control Movement. More accurately, this work is a history of that movement, its relationship to other social developments of the period, and most specifically, Margaret Sanger's leadership, which in Kennedy's view, led to both great success and to some failure for the Birth Control Movement in America.

Kennedy tells us just enough about Margaret Sanger's early history so that he can trace influences on her career: her overburdened mother and demanding father; her antipathy to her Catholic training; her early association with Emma Goldman and other Greenwich Village radicals; and finally, the influences of Freud and especially Havelock Ellis on her attitudes about sexuality.

In long chapters, Kennedy explains the historic setting against which the birth control proponents struggled. He describes the heritage of 19th century attitudes toward the family, feminism, and sex; the positions of the various denominations; and finally, the positions of both the American medical and legal professions. The strength of the opposition which faced the reformer was overwhelming. The Comstock laws which forbade the use of the mails for the dissemination of birth control information, and the position of the American Medical Association which did not recognize contraception as a medical responsibility are but two examples.

Kennedy has organized his book so that the supportive data illustrate how the combined forces of the establishment met Margaret Sanger head-on. He is a believer in the "historic moment," and feels that Sanger was perfectly suited by temperament and ability to fight under severe opposition, and that she was uncomfortable in situations that were accommodating. Ultimately, Kennedy thinks, Sanger removed herself from the movement when times became quiescent, when she was not able to exercise her combative and unyielding disposition.

Though he does not deny her credit nor diminish her contribution to social history, Kennedy is clearly out of sympathy with Margaret Sanger and seeks to diminish what he considers to be her inflated reputation. He makes several references, for example, to her ongoing "battles between her head and heart," occasions on which he felt her emotions took over when reason would have served better. This seems harsh criticism of a leader who fought well against the powerful opposition Kennedy so skillfully describes.

Lerner, Gerda. *The Grimké Sisters from South Carolina: Pioneers for Woman's Rights and Abolition.* **Boston: Houghton Mifflin, 1967. 479p.**

The Grimké sisters, two of the most extraordinary women in American history, were Southern women who took leadership in the antislavery movement. In this biography, Gerda Lerner deals effectively with major questions about their lives: How was it possible for two wealthy Southern girls to break away from the traditions of South Carolina in the 1820's? Did Angelina's marriage to Theodore Weld, a gifted abolitionist organizer and orator, in effect bring an end to their brilliant public careers? And what was the nature of the relationship between the sisters throughout their lives?

Sarah, thirteen years older than Angelina, felt thwarted by not receiving an education and by the milieu of Charleston, which she found unsuitable for a single woman with a restless and inquiring mind. She left for Philadelphia for reasons having more to do with unresolved feminism than with antislavery. Angelina, always more righteous and confident, followed eight years later in 1829 because she hated and protested the slavery system. The sisters gradually became involved with the abolitionist movement, having spent the years before 1835 living quietly within Quaker circles. Their identification with antislavery came only after Angelina wrote a letter to Garrison which was printed in the *Liberator,* and her famous *Appeal to the Christian Women of the South* calling for the abolition of slavery. By this time, the sisters and the Philadelphia Quakers had become disenchanted with each other, and the Grimkés followed the course of radical abolitionism, eventually serving as the first female agents of that cause. They spoke out publicly against slavery and ultimately for the rights of women.

Their close association with Theodore Weld led to his marriage to Angelina. Almost immediately, domestic cares and responsibilities retired them from the forefront of movement activities. Although it is a fact that Angelina had four pregnancies in quick succession and Weld aspired to farming, Lerner provides still other reasons for their virtual withdrawal from leadership in the antislavery movement. Weld had been comfortable in it when it was young and the issues clear, but had no taste for later ideological splits and factionalism. Angelina's new role as wife and mother narrowed her sphere to that of other 19th-century women with domestic responsibilities. Periods of poor health coupled with an urgent need to prove herself qualified for the traditional female role forced her to move into a private, non-political life.

This life included Sarah who had lived with Angelina for many years and contued to do so even after the Welds' marriage. Though intellectually tough and politically astute, Sarah depended on Angelina for emotional support. Angelina, more attractive and a better speaker, had led the way to abolitionism. The dependence was reversed, however, after the arrival of Angelina's children whom Sarah effectively helped to mother.

The Grimkés and the times in which they lived have been vividly brought to life in this articulate and comprehensive account by Gerda Lerner.

Levine, Daniel. *Jane Addams and the Liberal Tradition.* Madison: State Historical Society of Wisconsin, 1971. 277p.

In his biography of Jane Addams, Daniel Levine is primarily interested in tracing the development of her ideas over her long and productive career. Her participation in the Progressive Era was far-reaching and included such causes as housing reform, child-labor legislation, progressive education, labor organizing and the treatment of immigrants.

Her search for ways to improve society led her to a commitment to feminism and ultimately to pacifism. She saw the suffrage movement as an attempt to extend ''natural'' female concerns into the wider community. Care for children led naturally to child-labor laws. Housekeeping led to housing regulation; cooking for a family led to concerns for pure food supplies. It seemed an extension of all she believed in when she took up the cause of peace and became the head of the Women's Peace Party.

Levine believes that Jane Addams was a radical who operated within a liberal tradition. She believed that man was fundamentally good and that evil had a social cause which could be controlled by collective action. In expressing her social ethic, she had to combat the philosophy of individualism which had always been closely associated with American ideals. Levine points out that because Jane Addams died in 1935, she unfortunately never saw the new emphasis on social policy which Franklin Roosevelt instituted during the years of the New Deal.

Sklar, Kathryn Kish. *Catharine Beecher: A Study in American Domesticity.* New Haven: Yale University Press, 1973. 356p.

Kathryn Sklar has written an exemplary biography in which she not only defines Beecher's personality and character, but measures her impact on the lives of other nineteenth-century women and the impact of that period on Beecher herself. Sklar sees the middle decades of the nineteenth century as important to understanding the historical experience of women, for that period saw the beginning of the woman's rights movement at the same time that the cult of domesticity took hold. Sklar's study helps to explain the reasons for the apparent contradiction.

The religious revivalism of the first part of the nineteenth century was an important force in Beecher's life. Lyman Beecher, the patriarch of the large Beecher family and influential religious leader, expected his children to give themselves over to the experience of conversion. But unlike her brothers who converted and then became ministers and masters of their own households, Catherine could not submit.

Instead she began a career in teaching, an occupation that provided her with an outlet for the assertion of authority. Her aims were to enhance the teaching profession for women by bringing scientific standards to domestic education. She founded teacher-training colleges and influenced the glorification of domesticity, thereby bringing an aura of professionalism to the duties of women.

Beecher's life was filled with apparent contradictions: though childless and with no home of her own, she became an expert in domestic management and childrearing; though trying to enhance the dignity of women's lives, she was also opposed to the activities of woman's rights advocates. Sklar does a masterful job of explaining these paradoxes by scrutinizing Catharine Beecher's motivations within the context of her restricted nineteenth-century life. In order to assure women cultural supremacy, Beecher enhanced rather than diminished gender roles. She aggrandized what seemed to her to be the renunciative and nurturing capacities of women. Sklar notes that ''not until Catharine Beecher's lifetime were [women] led to accept self-sacrifice as a positive good and as the female equivalent to self-fulfillment.''

* * *

Adams, Abigail and John Adams. *The Book of Abigail and John: Selected Letters of the Adams Family 1762-1784.* Edited and with an introduction by L.H. Butterfield, Marc Friedlaender and Mary-Jo Kline. Cambridge, Mass.: Harvard University Press, 1975. 411p.

This collection contains 226 letters exchanged between Abigail and John Adams, some appearing in print for the first time. They reflect the intelligence and captivating personal style of Abigail who writes with clarity and perception.

Addams, Jane. *The Social Thought of Jane Addams.* Edited by Christopher Lasch. Indianapolis: Bobbs-Merrill, 1965. 266p.

Jane Addams has inspired a number of books by historians in recent years, indicating not only her recognized importance as a leader in the progressive movement, but also reflecting changing values in historiography. While earlier writers presented Addams as a saintly phenomenon, Lasch understands her importance in relation to social reform. He has collected in this volume excerpts from her writing which he feels best illustrate her social thought.

Blumberg, Rose. *Florence Kelley: The Making of a Social Pioneer.* New York: Kelley, 1966. 194p.

Blumberg concentrates on the influences that shaped the character and career of Florence Kelley, a leader in the reform movement against poor factory conditions and child labor. Kelley, a socialist, was one of the amazing group of women who lived at Hull House. She eventually became the Secretary of the Consumer's League, a post which enabled her to attract public support for reform.

Booth, Sally Smith. *The Women of '76.* New York: Hastings House, 1973. 329p.

A popular account of women of the Revolutionary period, this book includes biographical information about such women as Abigail Adams and Mercy Otis Warren as well as obscure figures of the period.

Davis, Allen F. *American Heroine: The Life and Legend of Jane Addams.* New York: Oxford University Press, 1973. 339p.

In writing this biography of Jane Addams, Davis claims to be dispelling myths about her created by popular writers and historians through the years. Sentimental writers have portrayed her as a saint and modern historians have relied on motivational psychology for their interpretations; for example, it has been said that she founded Hull House as a rebellion against the expectations of her family. Although the book contains some new information about Addams, Davis avoids an intellectual interpretation and thus fails to provide a meaningful perspective on her life.

Deiss, Joseph Jay. *The Roman Years of Margaret Fuller.* New York: Crowell, 1969. 338p.

Deiss covers the last four years of Margaret Fuller's life which were spent in Italy, years which included her marriage to Ossoli, the birth of her son, and finally the tragic death of all three in a shipwreck on their return to America. Deiss says that these years have not been fully explored by other biographers of Fuller, a gap filled by his book.

Evans, Elizabeth. *Weathering the Storm: Women of the American Revolution.* New York: Scribner's, 1975. 372p.

Depending primarily on letters and diaries, Evans presents first-hand accounts of the lives of women who experienced the American Revolution. It is not a well documented book, but addresses a general audience, and was timed to appear during the Bicentennial year.

Fornell, Earl W. *The Unhappy Medium: Spiritualism and the Life of Margaret Fox.* Austin: University of Texas Press, 1964. 204p.

This is a study of the phenomenon of nineteenth-century spiritualism in America. Margaret Fox, a spiritualist medium, influenced such notables as Horace Greeley and Abraham Lincoln.

Fuller, Margaret. *Margaret Fuller: American Romantic. A Selection From Her Writings and Correspondence.* Edited by Perry Miller. Garden City, New York: Doubleday Anchor Books, 1963. 319p.

Fuller, who was ridiculed and maligned by her contemporaries, has received favorable attention from scholars in recent years. In this collection, Miller has pulled together her reflections on her life from her youth in Cambridge, Mass. to her mature years in Italy. Selections are from her published work, including part of her major book, *Woman in the Nineteenth Century.* In his introduction,

Miller describes Fuller as a romantic who found her native Boston confining and stuffy and tried to resolve "the tumultuous inner strife of her Romantic compulsion" by going to Italy where she became involved in revolution. It was on her return to America in 1850 that she died in a shipwreck only fifty yards from the American shore.

Fuller, Paul E. *Laura Clay and the Women's Rights Movement.* Lexington: University of Kentucky Press, 1975. 216p.

Fuller describes how Laura Clay, a prominent Southern suffragist, dealt with the race question and cooperated with the WCTU in her work for women's rights within the South.

Goldman, Emma. *Red Emma Speaks: Selected Writings and Speeches.* Edited by Alix Kates Shulman. New York: Random House, 1972. 413p.

Goldman was a radical feminist and anarchist. Shulman has collected the documents which most sharply present Goldman's views, and illustrate the difficult and dramatic life she led.

Goldman, Emma and Alexander Berkman. *Nowhere at Home: Letters from Exile.* Edited by Richard Drinnon and Anna Maria Drinnon. New York: Schocken, 1975. 282p.

Drinnon, a biographer of Goldman (*Rebel in Paradise* 1961) co-edited these letters between Goldman and Berkman, her lover and friend. In addition to what they reveal about that relationship, the letters provide commentary on such political themes as the rise of Bolshevism and fascism and the agonies of political prisoners in Soviet Russia.

Hareven, Tamara. *Eleanor Roosevelt: An American Conscience.* Chicago: Quadrangle, 1968. 326p.

Hareven points out that Eleanor Roosevelt was a charismatic personality even though she was not brilliant and had no special training or artistic genius. In spite of these drawbacks she developed into a confident person and a leader, accomplishments which are the focus of this fine study.

Hays, Elinor Rice. *Those Extraordinary Blackwells: The Story of a Journey to a Better World.* New York: Harcourt, Brace and World, 1967. 349p.

The Blackwell family produced some remarkable women, and others married into it. Of the nine children, five were girls, and Elizabeth was the first woman doctor in America. Two of the brothers married Antoinette Brown and Lucy Stone, leaders in the nineteenth-century struggle for woman's rights. Elinor Hays sees the family as forming "a microcosm of their time in the world of rebellion and the coming to birth of a new era for women." Her book traces the family from England to America, and focuses on what it was that made them innovators.

Keller, Helen. *Helen Keller, Her Socialist Years: Writings and Speeches.* **Edited, with an introduction by Philip S. Foner. New York: International Publishers, 1967. 128p.**

Helen Keller's battle to overcome her handicaps has so absorbed her admirers that little attention has been paid to the substance of her thought. Here, Foner has gathered those writings which express her socialist views during the years between 1911 and 1929.

Lash, Joseph. *Eleanor and Franklin.* **New York: Norton, 1971. 765p.**

Lash, the first scholar to use Eleanor Roosevelt's private papers, has written a laudatory biography of the couple. He describes Eleanor in her childhood as a timid, overly protected, homely girl who was reared with bigoted attitudes about Negroes and Jews. She suffered the loss of her parents and was particularly despondent over the death of her charming, hopelessly alcoholic father. Her marriage to Franklin put her into the public arena where she rose to the occasion by accepting a public role. She lived with many problems: an interfering mother-in-law; a handicapped husband; five children who were criticized by the press; and her husband's extra-marital affair. None of these stopped her from fulfilling the obligations of her position or altered her dedication to her principles.

———. *Eleanor: The Years Alone.* **New York: Norton, 1972. 368p.**

After Franklin's death, Eleanor had to deal with the problem of sorting out her private self from her role as president's wife. At the time of his death she was writing a daily newspaper column and writing for *The Ladies Home Journal.* Afterwards, she refused to run for office, deciding to leave politics to her children. Instead, she became a member of the U.S. delegation to the United Nations and then traveled throughout Southeast Asia as ambassador-extraordinary. She was a staunch supporter of Adlai Stevenson, but was ignored by Eisenhower who never approached her during his terms in office. Near the end of her life she launched a new career as a visiting lecturer at Brandeis University and said at the time, ''When you cease to make a contribution you begin to die.''

Lumpkin, Katharine Du Pre. *The Emancipation of Angelina Grimké.* **Chapel Hill: University of North Carolina Press, 1974. 265p.**

In this fine study Lumpkin provides a careful analysis of Angelina Grimké's active career in the abolition movement and the years following her marriage to Theodore Weld in 1839. The relationship between Angelina and her sister, Sarah, is seen as rivalrous, for Sarah envied her sister's superior talents as a public speaker. The arrival of Angelina's children intensified friction between the sisters. While Angelina guiltily admitted her lack of enthusiasm over caring for small children, Sarah strove to capture their affection. Above all, Lumpkin provides valuable insights into the harsh demands imposed on the sisters and Weld by their unwavering religious convictions.

Merriam, Eve. *Growing Up Female in America: Ten Lives.* Garden City, New York: Doubleday, 1971. 308p.

Eve Merriam brings a feminist sensibility to her biographical exploration of a group of American women who lived during different periods and came from varying backgrounds. Her sources for this book are letters, diaries and auto-biographies, from which she selects excerpts to illustrate the concerns of women. She includes well known women like Elizabeth Cady Stanton, Maria Mitchell and Anna Howard Shaw, but also unknowns, including a black woman, a Jewish immigrant and a Native American.

Neidle, Cecyle S. *American Immigrant Women.* Boston: Twayne, 1975. 312p.

We have yet to see a comprehensive study of the contributions made by immi-grant women to American culture and society, but this book is a beginning. In it Neidle offers groups of biographies of women who excelled in such areas as trade-unionism, medicine and science, music, writing, and business. The strongest chapters in the book are those which deal with trade-unionists: women like Mother Jones, Rose Schneiderman, Mary Anderson and Pauline Newman. The accounts of prominent women doctors, Elizabeth Blackwell and Marie Zakrzewska in medicine and Karen Horney and Helene Deutsch in psy-chiatry, are also interesting.

Oakley, Mary Ann. *Elizabeth Cady Stanton.* Old Westbury, Long Island: The Feminist Press, 1972. 148p.

Not meant to be an ambitious biography of Stanton, this is a popular book based on several published sources. Along with her friend, Susan B. Anthony, Stanton was the inspiration for and architect of many of the ideas of the 19th-century suf-frage movement. History has proved her contention that the vote would never be enough to redress the inequities suffered by women within the society. She fought for married women's property rights, more lenient divorce laws and wrote a version of the Bible in which she tried to correct its sexist bias.

Peel, Robert. *Mary Baker Eddy: The Years of Discovery.* New York: Holt, Rinehart and Winston, 1966. 372p.

This volume, the first of a biographical trilogy of Eddy written by Peel, covers the years which led up to her founding of the Christian Science Church. Her early years were like those of other 19th-century New England women. She was the youngest of a large family that grew up on a New Hampshire farm. Though her brothers were educated, she was not; her chronic ill health prevented her from taking advantage of even the rudimentary schooling that was available. Her first marriage ended when her husband died suddenly, leaving her with an unborn child. Her second marriage ended in divorce. After that she was penniless and dependent on the largess of family members and friends. Her poor health finally led her to mind-cure under the tutelage of P.P. Quimby, and later she arrived at a spiritual discovery of Christian Science after recovering from the effects of a bad fall. She had been diagnosed as hopelessly paralyzed. At the end of this volume Eddy was living in Lynn, Massachusetts where she was becoming influential as a faith healer and religious leader.

Peel, Robert. *Mary Baker Eddy: The Years of Trial.* New York: Holt, Rinehart and Winston, 1971. 391p.

In this volume, Peel covers the years between 1876 and 1891, the fifteen years following the publication of Mary Baker Eddy's first book. She emerges from a little-known leader of a small group to a well-known leader of a religious movement. At the close of this book she is seventy years old, but her life and career continued for another twenty years.

Richey, Elinor. *Eminent Women of the West.* Berkeley: Howell-North, 1975. 276p.

Richey contends that there was something especially invigorating about western America which explains why many remarkable women had their roots there. She selects nine of them for these profiles, including Isadora Duncan and Gertrude Stein. More valuable are chapters on Gertrude Atherton, the popular novelist; Imogen Cunningham, the photographer; and Julia Morgan, the architect; the latter are lives that have not already been fully explored in other biographies.

Rogers, W. G. *Ladies Bountiful.* New York: Harcourt, Brace and World, 1968. 236p.

Today when one thinks of the sources of outside funding for artists and writers, government agencies and private foundations come to mind. In the past, such benevolence came from the good will of individuals, many of whom were women. Some were rich — Mabel Dodge Luhan, Nancy Cunard and Edith Rockefeller McCormick — but others, like Sylvia Beach who published *Ulysses* for James Joyce when no traditional publisher would touch it, sacrificed what little money she had and gave over her energy and influence to the artist she believed in. Rogers gives an interesting account of a group of twentieth-century patrons, providing descriptions of their relationship with artists, and of their motivations as supporters of the arts.

Wiley, Bell Irvin. *Confederate Women.* Westport, Conn.: Greenwood, 1975. 204p.

The letters and diaries of three Southern women of high position, Mary Boykin Chesnut, Virginia Tunstall Clay and Virina Howell Davis, provide Wiley with the material for this study, in which he describes in detail the tragic hardship of the Civil War. Their writings reveal how women competently managed complicated households during catastrophic times. Wiley's evidence supports Anne Scott's thesis (*The Southern Lady*) that the War and Reconstruction weakened the patriarchy in the South when the vanquished males returned to find that their women had successfully managed farms or plantations during their absence.

Wilson, Dorothy Clarke. *Stranger and Traveler: The Story of Dorothea Dix, American Reformer.* **Boston: Little, Brown, 1975. 360p.**

Dix, a nineteenth-century reformer, found her life's work in improving the inhumane conditions in which the mentally ill had been kept. Wilson writes in a popular style, presenting her material as a novelist, excluding footnotes.

Woodhull, Victoria and Tennessee Claflin. *Woodhull & Claflin's Weekly. The Lives and Writings of Notorious Victoria Woodhull and Her Sister Tennessee Claflin.* **Edited by Arlene Kisner. Washington, New Jersey: Times Change Press, 1972. 63p.**

In this regrettably brief book, Kisner has assembled excerpts from the writings of these sisters. As advocates of free love, they were looked upon as scandalous by most previous writers. Kisner's feminism puts them in a more favorable light.

ANTHOLOGY

Cott, Nancy F., ed. *Root of Bitterness: Documents of the Social History of American Women.* **New York: Dutton, 1972. 373p.**

Nancy Cott has assembled a superb collection of documents which deal with the social history of American women from the Colonial period to the twentieth century. The fifty selections reveal what roles women have been expected to play at various times in history, and how they have reacted to changing social pressures.

Friedman, Jean E. and William G. Shade, eds. *Our American Sisters: Women in American Life and Thought.* **Boston: Allyn and Bacon, 1973. 354p.**

The stated purpose of this anthology is "to bring together for the student a wide variety of scholarly essays on women in American history in a form available for use as supplementary reading for American history survey courses or courses on women's history." Readings are organized chronologically around four topics: women in Colonial America; the Victorian image; the Progressive impulse; and the illusion of equality. Selections include "The Lady and the Mill Girl" by Gerda Lerner, "The Cult of True Womanhood" by Barbara Welter, "The 'New Woman' in the New South" by Anne Firor Scott and "Charlotte Perkins Gilman on the Theory and Practice of Feminism" by Carl Degler. The editors have provided useful introductory material and notes.

George, Carol V. R., ed. *"Remember the Ladies": New Perspectives on Women in America.* **Syracuse, New York: Syracuse University Press, 1975. 201p.**

These social history essays which have never before been published examine history for evidence of women's experience. The three sections in the book consider: 1) the growth of feminist thought from 1600 to 1800; 2) aspects of the "cult of true womanhood" in the nineteenth century; 3) issues other than suffrage that have concerned women over the last sixty years.

Hartman, Mary S. and Lois Banner, eds. *Clio's Consciousness Raised: New Perspectives on the History of Women.* New York: Harper Torchbooks, 1974. 253p.

The papers included in this collection were originally presented at a conference titled ''New Perspectives on the History of Women'' sponsored by the Berkshire Conference of Women Historians and held in March, 1973, at Douglass College, Rutgers University. They reflect the new direction in which historians of women's history are moving, i.e., away from biographical studies of leaders and from the uncritical use of the ''male oppression model'' in explaining women's roles toward an attempt to combine a new concern about women with the methods and insights of social history. As a result, the papers deal with women as a group, not outstanding public figures, but people who shared common experiences. Some of the papers included are: ''The Fashionable Diseases: Women's Complaints and Their Treatment in Nineteenth-Century America,'' by Ann Douglas; ''Puberty to Menopause: the Cycle of Femininity in Nineteenth-Century America,'' by Carroll Smith-Rosenberg; ''Voluntary Motherhood: The Beginnings of Feminist Birth Control Ideas in the United States,'' by Linda Gordon; and ''The Feminization of American Religion: 1800-1860,'' by Barbara Welter.

Hogeland, Ronald W., ed. *Women and Womanhood in America.* Lexington: D.C. Heath, 1973. 183p.

In this anthology, Hogeland presents readings which illustrate the nature of ''womanhood'' and the roles women have played throughout three centuries of American history. About a third of the pieces are primary documents and the rest represent some of the best recent scholarship in women's studies.

Selective writings include works by Cotton Mather, Harriet Martineau and Charlotte Perkins Gilman among others. Essays by contemporary scholars which are already regarded as classics include Gerda Lerner's ''New Approaches to the Study of Women in American History'' and ''The Lady and the Mill Girl''; Barbara Welter's ''The Cult of True Womanhood, 1820-1860''; and Alice Rossi's ''Equality Between the Sexes: An Immodest Proposal.'' The writings have been so well selected that the book should have interdisciplinary uses — as helpful to the teachers and students of history and literature as it is to the social scientist.

Kraditor, Aileen S., ed. *Up from the Pedestal: Selected Writings in the History of American Feminism.* Chicago: Quadrangle, 1968. 372p.

Kraditor has brought together a superb collection of documents which trace the history of American feminist thought from 1642 (the writings of Anne Bradstreet) to 1966 (the National Organization for Women's Statement of Purpose). In her introduction, she raises the fundamental question of why it is that the seventy-year battle waged by earlier feminists failed to bring about real emancipation for women. She concludes that autonomy for women has not been possible because they have been locked into spheres defined by their sex; that while men have always been thought of as male humans, women are thought to be human females; that until the basic assumptions about the structure of the family are challenged, options for women will be only theoretical.

Lynn, Mary C., ed. *Women's Liberation in the Twentieth Century.* **New York: Wiley, 1975. 139p.**

The focus here is on the role of women between the time the suffrage amendment was passed to the present time. Early essays included are by Emma Goldman, Charlotte Perkins Gilman and Margaret Sanger, and recent ones are by Betty Friedan, Alice Rossi, Caroline Bird and Shulamith Firestone.

Rossi, Alice, ed. *The Feminist Papers: From Adams to de Beauvoir.* **New York: Columbia University Press, 1973. 716p.**

In selecting the documents for this anthology, Rossi has combined her skills as a sociologist with her interest in history. The result is an excellent collection of readings which trace feminist thought from the late eighteenth century to the mid-twentieth century. In addition to a general introduction, Rossi provides analytical material before each entry, placing the writers within the context of their times. Excerpts are long, providing substantial material for analysis.

Schneir, Miriam, ed. *Feminism: The Essential Historical Writings.* **New York: Random House, 1972. 360p.**

Schneir understands the contemporary feminist movement to be unfinished business, a continuation of a progression of ideas that began in the eighteenth century with the writings of Mary Wollstonecraft and Abigail Adams. Included are excerpts spanning the years between 1776 and 1929, containing mainly writings by American feminists, but also works by George Sand, John Stuart Mill, Engels, Ibsen and Virginia Woolf.

Scott, Anne Firor, ed. *The American Woman: Who Was She?* **Englewood Cliffs, New Jersey: Prentice-Hall, 1971. 182p.**

Anne Scott says in her introduction: "Poets and novelists rarely overlook women. Historians almost always do." This omission has made it necessary for Scott, a scholar and teacher of women's history, to provide an appropriate selection of readings about women as a supplement to standard textbooks in American history. Her aim is to examine vital roles in which women have clearly established a history — education, work, reform movements and family life — and show how changes in these areas relate generally to the changing role of women in the society. Scott is concerned here with the hundred years between the end of the Civil War and 1970, and includes excerpts beginning with passages from *The History of Woman Suffrage* and ending with the "Red Stockings Manifesto."

Sochen, June, ed. *The New Feminism in Twentieth-Century America.* **Lexington, Mass.: D.C. Heath, 1971. 208p.**

Sochen has brought together feminist writings from three periods: the nineteenth-century suffrage movement; feminism in the 1910s; and the revival of feminism in the 1960's. Though the third section is the longest, the second is more valuable, for it contains writers not often anthologized — Floyd Dell, Max Eastman and Margaret Sanger.

Welter, Barbara, ed. *The Woman Question in American History.* **Hinsdale, Ill.: Dryden, 1973. 177p.**

Welter says she has compiled this anthology because "scholarly books and articles on women in American history are not easy to find... Only a handful of historians have actually done research in primary materials relating to women in this country's history, and written about it." She has selected writing by scholars such as Andrew Sinclair, Aileen Kraditor, Eleanor Flexner, Carl Degler and Christopher Lasch who write about women within the broad context of social history.

Law and Politics

Books dealing with law and politics are considered together here. The accounts of the trial of Angela Davis bring together themes that are relevant to many of the other books — how women have been treated within the legal system and how they aspire to effect change, sometimes through traditional political careers and at other times by radical activism.

Leo Kanowitz, Karen DeCrow and Ellen Switzer point out how the law has been used to discriminate against women. For example, protective laws, which were originally passed to spare working women from abusive treatment are now used to keep women out of better paying jobs.

The authors of books on politics describe how women are making strides within the existing political system or working outside of it. Political activists of the 1960's like Susan Stern and Diana Oughten were radicalized by the war in Viet Nam and sought instant change by drastic and often destructive means. Within party politics, women are just beginning to learn how to acquire power. Kirsten Amundsen, Jeane Kirkpatrick and the Tolchins document how women are working for their own candidacies rather than for the election of men.

Hilda Scott, in her study of women in socialist Czechoslovakia, draws conclusions that have implications for those who see socialism as a panacea for the kind of discrimination against women that characterizes Western countries. Scott proves that sex-role stereotyping will not be cured by economic and political ideology alone, but by educational programs designed to eradicate it.

Aptheker, Bettina. *The Morning Breaks: The Trial of Angela Davis.* New York: International Publishers, 1975. 284p.

There are at least three notable accounts of the trial of Angela Davis — her own description in her autobiography, the book written by Mary Timothy who was a jury woman at the trial, and this book by Bettina Aptheker who was Davis's friend and active supporter throughout the trial. The other two accounts tend to be circumspect: Davis uses great control in writing about personal feelings;

Timothy attempts to be an impartial observer; but Aptheker is emotional and exuberant in her description of the dramatic events of which she was a part.

She tells us, for instance, that the concern for Angela Davis's freedom became the rallying point for a coalition of 120 national and regional organizations representing every conceivable political and social movement in the progressive spectrum. She details the overwhelming task of preparing Davis's defense. Paramount in the preparation was gathering background information on the hundreds of potential jurors. The Davis case involved racism, Communism, the role of women in society, academic freedom and the war in Vietnam. A jury member on the conservative side of any of these issues might have condemned Angela Davis. Aptheker describes the difficult process of jury selection and provides absorbing behind-the-scenes accounts of the trial itself, from its occasional moments of frantic worry to its ultimate vindication of Davis.

All of the books about Davis's trial provide a locus and a series of insights into some important issues of the 1960's. They describe the substantive social and political questions raised by the trial and raise other questions about the jury system and about the law itself.

Kanowitz, Leo. *Women and the Law: The Unfinished Revolution.* Albuquerque: University of New Mexico Press, 1969. 312p.

Leo Kanowitz wrote his book in the years just preceding the women's movement when he could rightly claim that no one was paying much attention to sex-biased legal inequities. He identifies certain representative areas of the law in which sex-based discrimination has been or is now present — property, divorce and employment — and examines the sociological conceptions and misconceptions which underlie the legal disenfranchisement of women. He finds, for example, that many discriminatory laws were based on the desire of lawmakers to protect women, a philosophical position which has been frequently debated by those concerned with the Equal Rights Amendment. Labor movement people felt the Amendment would cancel much of the legislation they fought so hard to obtain. On the other hand, feminists felt that this legislation has done more to keep women out of jobs than to protect and improve the ones they have.

Kanowitz's attempt here is to identify areas of sex-based discrimination for the purpose of stimulating courtroom and legislative reform. He calls for a national examination of sex-roles and their implications and an opening up of opportunities for all Americans — men and women — to participate fully in American life. Despite these aims, he was not in favor of the passage of the Equal Rights Amendment at the time he wrote this book. He feared that people would work long and hard for an amendment which, finally, would not make any difference because he felt the courts would still see functional differences between men and women.

Timothy, Mary. *Jury Woman: The Story of the Trial of Angela Y. Davis.* San Francisco: Glide, 1975. 276p.

This book is as much the story of the author's experience as a jury member as it is an account of the trial of Angela Davis. As one of a large number of potential jurists, Mary Timothy felt certain that she would be rejected by the prosecution on the grounds that her husband was a practicing attorney and her son a registered conscientious objector. She was therefore surprised when she was found acceptable, but apprehensive about being in a position to judge the guilt or innocence of another human being.

Like many other Americans, Timothy learned her notions about courtroom procedure from popular culture. She anticipated the drama of a murder trial, but was unprepared for the tedium and physical hardship that characterized many weeks of sequestered jury life. Jurors were discomforted by standing in lines for hours in poorly ventilated rooms and by sitting around for an undetermined length of time cut off from the outside world. Timothy felt dehumanized by such treatment and offers suggestions that would eliminate some of the rigors of the situation.

Much of the fascination of her book is her commentary on the realities of her experience — her own reactions to key moments in the trial as well as her narration of the trial itself. Timothy reveals how she and the other jurors concluded that the evidence did not support the prosecutor's contention that Davis was guilty of conspiring in murder. The jury found the defendant not guilty on all counts. When the trial was over, she met Davis at a celebration party and asked why Davis and her lawyers wanted her on the jury. "There were lots of reasons," she was told, "but the most important one was — you liked your children."

Mary Timothy liked that answer. It told her, as little else about the trial did, that she was a person, that she would not automatically condemn someone whose lifestyle differed from her own, and that she could be trusted to listen to and accept explanations of behavior that did not square with established cultural patterns.

*   *   *

Abzug, Bella S. *Bella! Ms. Abzug Goes to Washington.* New York: Saturday Review Press, 1972. 314p.

Written in diary form for the year 1971 and against the background of the Nixon administration and the War in Vietnam, this political autobiography gives the flavor of that time and gives a sense of the qualities of Bella Abzug — that high-spirited, tough-minded, former congresswoman from New York who tried to form a new coalition of the powerless, poor ethnics and women. Abzug's book gives a day-to-day sense of how power operates in Washington.

Amundsen, Kirsten. *The Silenced Majority: Women and American Democracy.* Englewood Cliffs, New Jersey: Prentice-Hall, 1971. 184p.

As a political scientist, Amundsen is acutely aware that women's general lack of equality in the society is based on their lack of power. In this study she discusses how institutional and ideological sexism have assured the status quo, and then offers a vision — and strategies — for change.

Babcock, Barbara, Ann Freedman, Eleanor Holmes Norton, Susan Ross. *Sex Discrimination and the Law: Causes and Remedies.* **Boston: Little, Brown, 1975. 1092p.**

This is a text book for teaching law courses on women and the law. It grew out of the need for a collection of material that deals with such matters as: the relationship between Constitutional law and feminist history; employment discrimination; sex role discrimination in the law of the family; women and criminal law; and the laws governing women's rights to control their reproductive capacities. The information gathered here is valuable not only to students of the law, but to investigators interested in any one of the subjects covered.

Chamberlin, Hope. *A Minority of Members: Women in the U.S. Congress.* **New York: Praeger, 1973. 374p.**

This book contains brief biographical sketches of the eighty-five women who have been senators and representatives in the U.S. Congress throughout history. They range from Jeannette Rankin, the first woman to achieve high elected office, to the numbers of women who took over their husbands' duties after they were widowed.

Chisholm, Shirley. *The Good Fight.* **New York: Harper and Row, 1973. 206p.**

Shirley Chisholm was the first black woman to run for president. She waged her 1972 campaign with practically no money and no organization. The fight did, however, provide her with the opportunity to speak on issues from her own unique perspective; her book describes the campaign with interesting comments about the times and the personalities who were then making news.

_____. *Unbought and Unbossed.* **Boston: Houghton Mifflin, 1970. 177p.**

In this biography which emphasizes her political career, Shirley Chisholm speaks out on such issues as abortion, her relationship with militant blacks, and her reasons for choosing to work within the conventional political system.

DeCrow, Karen. *Sexist Justice.* **New York: Random House, 1974. 329p.**

DeCrow, a lawyer and the past president of NOW, presents general discussions and specific cases to show how the law has been used to the disadvantage of women. In the name of ''protection,'' for instance, women are prevented by law from running an elevator at night when the pay is higher, but are permitted to clean offices at 3 A.M., when the pay is lower.

Gruberg, Martin. *Women in American Politics: An Assessment and Sourcebook.* **Oshkosh, Wisconsin: Academia Press, 1968. 336p.**

Gruberg's book is part political essay and part reference book. As a sourcebook it gives information about women in all of the states who have been active in politics. His essay concludes that women have been relatively powerless in American government. He says, ''Women are discriminated against in every field where they try to compete with men, especially in politics, where virtually every woman who has achieved high political office has succeeded because of her close association with a successful male politician.''

Jaquette, Jane S., ed. *Women in Politics.* New York: Wiley, 1974. 367p.

This is a collection of essays by academic writers who try to explain women's negligible effect on political systems. American politics is discussed in the first half of the book and the role of women in the politics of foreign countries in the second.

Josephson, Hannah. *Jeannette Rankin, First Lady in Congress: A Biography.* Indianapolis: Bobbs-Merrill, 1974. 227p.

The author writes effusively about Rankin, but does not provide psychological insights or a historic perspective that make Rankin and the times in which she lived come alive.

Kanowitz, Leo. *Sex Roles in Law and Society: Cases and Materials.* Albuquerque: University of New Mexico Press, 1973. 706p.

Essentially a text for law school courses on women and the law, this book is also useful for students of history and the social sciences who are interested in the relationship between the law and social change. Kanowitz focuses on how the assignment of sex roles has led to legal inequities. He supplies legal cases and social science articles which make the point that men as well as women become victims when the society ''arbitrarily assigns roles on the basis of sex.''

Kirkpatrick, Jeane J. *Political Woman.* New York: Basic Books, 1974. 274p.

Kirkpatrick interviewed fifty women state senators and representatives from twenty-six states. By analyzing their personal and professional styles, she tries to determine how they overcame a hostile environment in order to achieve political goals.

Lamson, Peggy. *Few Are Chosen: American Women in Political Life Today.* Boston: Houghton Mifflin, 1968. 240p.

About women in public life Lamson says: ''There seems no way to get around this dichotomy between men and women. To do her job successfully in public office a woman must occasionally appear unfeminine. But to do the same job successfully a man may under no circumstances appear unmasculine.'' She drew this conclusion after interviewing the ten women who are the subjects of this study, such notable women as Margaret Chase Smith, Frances P. Bolton, Esther Peterson, Constance Motley and Martha Griffiths.

McCarthy, Abigail. *Private Faces/Public Places.* Garden City, New York: Doubleday, 1972. 448p.

Abigail McCarthy cannot be dismissed as merely the wife of a politician who ran for the presidency. On one level, her concerns had to revolve around the comings and goings of Eugene McCarthy, but on a deeper level, her fine intellect and sensitivity provided her with her own life and experience. She says about herself: ''For those of us whose lives have been defined by others — by wifehood and motherhood — there is no individual achievement to measure, only the experience of life itself.'' She reviews the essential moments of her married life, giving her readers a valuable account of politics as she viewed it. McCarthy's ill-fated campaign led to the end of their marriage, and Abigail McCarthy had to adjust her identity, this time to be the central character in her own life. This book was the beginning of that new direction.

Powers, Thomas. *Diana: The Making of a Terrorist.* **Boston: Houghton Mifflin, 1971. 225p.**

Like Susan Stern, Diana Oughten became radicalized throughout the 60's, convinced that only a violent revolution could bring sanity to a country gone mad by its involvement in an unjust war. Unlike Stern, Diana Oughten cannot tell her own story, for she was killed in 1970 while preparing a home-made bomb.

Scott, Hilda. *Does Socialism Liberate Women? Experiences from Eastern Europe.* **Boston: Beacon Press, 1974. 240p.**

Although this study deals exclusively with Czechoslovakian women, the conclusions Scott draws from her work have political relevance for all women. She was interested in seeing if a socialist form of government brings with it equal status for women, and found that sex-role stereotyping goes beyond political systems. As in Western societies, the improvement of women's role must begin with the education of children and the determination to raise them free from the crippling strictures of a sexual caste system.

Stern, Susan. *With the Weathermen: The Personal Journal of a Revolutionary Woman.* **Garden City, New York: Doubleday, 1975. 374p.**

Susan Stern tells the story of her radicalization from an upper-class American college girl to an SDS organizer, a Weatherman and a militant feminist. It is one story of growing up in the 1960's.

Switzer, Ellen. *The Law for a Woman: Real Cases and What Happened.* **New York: Scribner's, 1975. 246p.**

Through case histories, the author tries to explain to women their legal rights in marriage and the family, work, education, housing, credit, and many other areas in which they have been discriminated against. Switzer also includes information about the rights of children and a section which gives information about law schools in the United States.

Tolchin, Susan and Martin Tolchin. *Clout: Womanpower and Politics.* **New York: Coward, McCann & Geoghegan, 1974. 320p.**

The Tolchins have written a popular account of the ways in which American women have begun to be effective in getting and using political power. By combining the use of personal interviews with their investigative reporting, they show how women are learning to organize and make use of informal networks, just as men have always done.

Life Styles

This section deals with books offering insights into the lives of women whose experiences differ widely. Margaret Mead, one of the most famous and successful women in America, is represented here, as well as accounts of underprivileged women — immigrants, the elderly, welfare mothers and hillbilly women. Much of Mead's career has been devoted to the investigation of the lifestyles of other women. Her description of her own life reveals how she prepared for her unique career. At the same time the experiences of disadvantaged women are at once distinct from and relevant to other groups of women in America. Like most women, their primary concern is for their families, but unlike middle-class women whose fundamental needs are met, they face each day worrying about survival.

Ets, Marie Hall. *Rosa: The Life of an Italian Immigrant.* **Minneapolis: University of Minnesota Press, 1970. 254p.**

Non-fictional accounts of the lives of immigrant women are rare and this book is all the more exceptional because of Rosa Cavalleri's ability to vividly recall past experiences. She left northern Italy in 1884 among the wave of immigrants who came to America, and spent most of her remaining years in Chicago. Marie Ets, a social worker, met Rosa at a settlement house shortly after World War I. Over thirteen years Ets took notes as Rosa narrated anecdotes about her childhood in a silk producing village near Milan and about her adult life in the slums of Chicago.

Like the other female peasants in her village, Rosa began working in the silk mills when she was six years old. She obeyed her foster mother who collected the eight cents a week Rosa earned. At fourteen Rosa was pushed into marriage to a man she despised. ''I would not let you marry one of those boys who like you so much,'' her foster mother said. ''They would let you have your own way. You need someone to control you. You need an older man to make you meek and save you for heaven in the end.''

Rosa followed her husband to the iron mines of Missouri where her disastrous marriage soon ended. No longer able to tolerate his drunken abuse, she fled to Chicago where she eventually remarried.

Despite a life filled with hardships brought on by poverty, ignorance and menial work, Rosa retained buoyancy and a love of life. She loved America, for she felt that it had taught her ''not to be afraid.''

Kahn, Kathy. *Hillbilly Women.* **New York: Avon, 1972. 131p.**

Kathy Kahn has collected oral testimonies from nineteen women who live near the coal mines and in the milltowns of Southern Appalachia. They live with hardships brought on by poverty, squalid working conditions and continuous worry. ''It's a bad life being a miner's wife,'' said one woman. ''It's bad for everybody in the family. When you're setting at home, waiting on him to come back to you, and not knowing if he'll make it, you feel like you're in a grave.''

Other women describe appalling working conditions in the cotton mills where they breathe unhealthy dust that can lead to brown lung disease and endure ear-shattering noise. ''None of us that's worked there for some time can hear as well as we used to,'' a worker complained. ''It's impaired our hearing so bad, we go home and have to turn everything up loud so's we can hear it. It really has made our hearing worse.''

Kahn shapes her book into a celebration of a group of women who live out their lives with strength and pride, who endure grueling jobs while raising large families. Some even become union leaders. Kahn hopes that individuals and government agencies will begin to care enough about these misunderstood and often maligned women so that their lives will be made easier.

Howard, Jane. *A Different Woman.* **New York: Dutton, 1973. 276p.**

This autobiographical odyssey was spurred by Jane Howard's mother's sudden death, which left her feeling no longer a child but a thirty-six-year-old woman who had to sharpen her sense of herself. In it she journeys westward from New York through the Midwest, which was her home, to the far West, dropping in on dozens of women. She finds out what it is like to be married to a dying man, how it feels to be an unmarried mother, what might be the satisfactions of remaining single for the sake of a successful career — and casts these reflections as possible alternatives for herself.

While the book explores a good many lives, we are left to draw our own conclusions about these lives and to sort out the author's relationship with her mother.

Mead, Margaret. *Blackberry Winter: My Earlier Years.* **New York: William Morrow, 1972. 305p.**

No list of prominent living American women would be complete without the name of Margaret Mead. Her reputation was established in 1928 with the publication of her first book, *Coming of Age in Samoa,* and enhanced by her many subsequent contributions to anthropology. But the pleasure one takes in her autobiography lies in the clues it provides us to her success. Indeed she anticipates this curiosity, organizing her book around questions one would like to ask, and answering them in ways appropriate to a public testament, a recitation of the forces that brought her to prominence.

Among these forces are a family background that allowed her to become strong, independent and, most of all, free of prejudice. The family was a close-knit group, with the adults respectful of the young and concerned about their education. The four children, of whom Margaret was the eldest, were educated at home by their grandmother until they were ready for high school.

The recognition of her grandmother's influence is the occasion of her discussion of another aspect of the forces that molded her, the ties of genealogy. We hear a great deal in the book not only about her grandparents but her own granddaughter. Indeed she makes an engaging point about how one measures the human unit of time which she defines as "the space between a grandfather's memory of his own childhood and a grandson's knowledge of those memories as he heard about them."

At times she displays a surprising lack of candor in describing her feelings about what must have been the emotional low points in her life, including three broken marriages and several miscarriages. In spite of the claims she makes for her developed ability for self-appraisal, for being clear-eyed about the major decisions in her life, she is remarkably unforthcoming about these events, explaining that she has always had trouble remembering unhappy times. As a child she used to project the mischief she created onto her brother, remembering him as the guilty one. Whether in later life she used the same technique to discharge whatever culpability she may have felt for the failure of her marriages, we cannot tell, for the accounts of her domestic life are brief and unrevealing.

In contrast she seems most honest and revealing when she discusses her sensibilities as a woman. Not a queen bee by any means, she appears to be a woman who has always been happy being a woman, and has always liked other women. Her studies of children and adolescents in her early field trips also confirm that feeling for the young she inherited from her family. As for adults, particularly those affecting her career, she allows for having experienced certain tensions, tensions she feels she has overcome.

"I came to feel that I had by now, in my field work, repaid all that the world had invested in my training — that I had, in American terms, made good. This gave me the sense that I was from now on free to do what I would do." The statement, one feels, could have only come from a person who has fulfilled her own sense of her destiny. Margaret Mead is an exceptional woman in that she had the opportunity to do so, and for having found the right expression for her particular gifts.

Mead, Margaret. *Ruth Benedict.* **New York: Columbia University Press, 1974. 180p.**

As one of a series of books published by Columbia, "Leaders of Modern

Anthropology,'' this book is only half biographical. The rest of it contains a group of selected papers written by Ruth Benedict which are less known than those frequently appearing in anthologies. It ends with a selected bibliography of her writings.

It is the biographical information provided by Margaret Mead which will be of most interest to the general reader. Like other educated women of her generation, Ruth Benedict began a career teaching in girls' schools. This choice turned out to be a false start, for she did not want to dedicate her life in this way, but preferred marriage and looked forward to the accompanying responsibilities of home and children. Her marriage to Stanley Benedict, a distinguished bio-chemist, began happily enough, but gradually led to a separation for reasons Margaret Mead does not explore, but only implies — a drifting apart for lack of shared interests. To her bitter disappointment, Ruth Benedict was never able to have children, and the time on her hands could not be filled by the usual domestic duties and volunteer activities of affluent suburban housewives, however hard she tried to fill these roles.

Although she loved to write poetry, this occupation was not the necessary outlet for her energy and brilliance. She was introduced to the field of anthropology almost by accident during a period when she was taken occasional courses at the New School in New York. Her next step was to study with Franz Boas at Columbia where she found her life's work.

Margaret Mead traces Benedict's intellectual development and describes her profound contributions to anthropology. She brings a special sensitivity to her view of Benedict, her mentor and friend, and appreciates the personal and professional problems she faced and overcame.

*　　*　　*

Institute of Gerontology. *No Longer Young: The Older Woman in America.* Ann Arbor and Detroit: University of Michigan/Wayne State Univ., Institute of Gerontology, 1975. 120p.

The papers in this volume came out of a 1973 conference on aging sponsored by the Institute of Gerontology. They focus on the problems of aging women who suffer a double handicap in a society that devalues both women and the aged. Some of the contributors are Pauline Bart, Susan Sontag and Mary S. Calderone.

Kerr, Barbara. *Strong at the Broken Places: Women Who Have Survived Drugs.* Chicago: Follett, 1974. 333p.

This book contains a series of narratives by six drug-addicted women who had reclaimed themselves and resumed their lives. All of the women came from middle-class backgrounds and had potential and opportunities, but failed to get their lives together the first time around. Their stories are part of the social history of the 1960's.

Kriesberg, Louis. *Mothers in Poverty: A Study of Fatherless Families.* Chicago: Aldine, 1970. 356p.

This is a study of the components of poverty as it exists in households headed by women. It contains research data, and the lengthy discussion about methodology makes the book less appropriate for the general reader than for the professional.

Laing, Margaret, ed. *Woman on Women.* London: Sidgwick and Jackson, 1971. 228p.

In this book of essays eleven women discuss the meaning of being a woman. One well-known contributor, Eva Figes, discusses her experiences as an abandoned wife with two small children. She decides that she would have been better off unmarried without the expectation of security.

Lichtenstein, Grace. *A Long Way Baby: Behind the Scenes in Women's Pro Tennis.* New York: William Morrow, 1974. 239p.

Lichtenstein, a reporter for *The New York Times,* followed the growth of women's professional tennis from its beginnings in 1968 and sees it as a feminist breakthrough. This book is the record of the 1973 women's tennis circuit, and it is as much about brassieres and menstrual periods, marijuana, lesbians and women-as-losers as it is about the game of tennis. Always respectful of their unique abilities, she is at first disappointed by the unraised consciousness of these athletes; Lichtenstein comes to realize that these women are jocks first and women second. Other people write analyses of the game, but Lichtenstein writes about the lives of these competing stars.

Milwaukee County Welfare Rights Organization. *Welfare Mothers Speak Out: We Ain't Gonna Shuffle Anymore.* New York: Norton, 1972. 190p.

This is an angry book written by people who are tired of having the poor treated as a political football when the truth is that practically everyone in America benefits from government welfare — only they call it farm subsidies, defense contracts, guaranteed loans or government grants. This book debunks many of the myths about the poor, stressing that most poor people in America are mothers and children. The authors hope that the time will come when the care of children will be recognized as legitimate work in this country and that those who do it will be paid for their jobs.

Literature, the Fine Arts and Popular Culture

Unlike men who have trained in all fields and have faced few obstacles to entering professions, women have been excluded historically from all but a few occupations. But in creative fields, women have found outlets for the expression of their talents without necessarily having to seek special training or permission. Women have achieved success more often in writing than in fine arts or music because writing is an isolated occupation and, like women's traditional work, it is done in the home.

There are many books which deal with female artists and their work. These books have been divided into two general categories: autobiographies, diaries and biographies of female artists whose lives and experiences reflect the experiences of women generally; and studies of the portrayal of women in fiction and in film.

The authors of studies of women in fiction analyze literature to support a variety of theses about women. For instance, Carolyn Heilbrun illustrates the feminist theory of androgyny through an analysis of characters in fiction; Jane Rule explores the attitudes of lesbian novelists by examining their fiction; Patricia Spacks describes aspects of female psychology through an analysis of characters in literature and the women who created them.

Film critics tend to be more like-minded when analyzing the portrayal of women in the movies. They all point out that the image of women has become increasingly misogynistic since the 1940's, a period when autonomous women were portrayed in films, and that in this present period of heightened awareness of women's issues, the portrayal of women in current films is, so far, more denigrating than ever.

The biographical section of this chapter contains descriptions of the lives of women who have made contributions to literature, the fine arts and popular culture. Because biographical detail is the most fruitful source of information about female experience, many of the lives have been described at length.

These books reveal fascinating glimpses of how women have managed the essential ingredients of their lives — careers, marriage and motherhood. For example,

Dorothy Thompson, after two failed marriages to sophisticated men, found happiness with a man whose earthiness and simple tastes were in marked contrast to her own worldliness. Isadora Duncan, who was driven by the need to express her art, was expected to sacrifice her own identity to meet the needs of the men in her life. Sylvia Plath, who drove herself toward an unrealizable perfection in her life and art, was shattered by her broken marriage and her other unfulfilled dreams.

Most of the biographers of these women express no feminist point of view or even a sensitivity to women's problems when they interpret the lives of their subjects. Clues about essential female experiences have had to be picked out of the masses of biographical detail offered. Although biographers are quick to acknowledge other important qualities that formulate a human being (i.e., race, social class, level of education), they often overlook the most basic distinction of all: sexual gender. What was the ideal of womanhood that women were asked to fulfill and what did it cost them to fulfill or depart from it? Those books that come closest to answering these questions are included in the section on biography.

BIOGRAPHY

Chicago, Judy. *Through the Flower: My Struggle as a Woman Artist.* **Garden City, New York: Doubleday, 1975. 226p.**

The feminist art movement has had its most notable success in California where the Women's Building, an old Los Angeles mansion converted by women artists to the expression of female experience, has received wide attention and public interest. But such expression is a recent phenomenon, for the art world has been dominated by men who hold that acceptable art has a masculine theme and that its execution is based on skills and craftsmanship that are male prerogatives.

To be a female artist confronting male dominance in art schools, museums and galleries has been an ego-crushing experience for many women artists. In her book, Judy Chicago describes how she emerged from the stranglehold of conforming to male standards. Her developing sense of female worth has led to what in effect has become a female aesthetic. She has found ways to identify and legitimize the hidden content in women's art, and has helped to build a community of women artists who can offer training and support to their younger colleagues. Her book is an articulate account of these important accomplishments, and includes many photographs which illustrate how female experience has become the subject matter of beautiful and exciting art.

Edwards, Anne. *Judy Garland.* **New York: Simon and Schuster, 1975. 349p.**

In his eulogy at Judy Garland's funeral in June, 1969, James Mason said, ''She was the most sympathetic, the funniest, the sharpest and the most stimulating woman I ever knew.'' The thousands of other people who paid tribute to her that day testified that she was also one of the most talented and compelling performers America has ever known. Her electrifying effect on audiences inspired a cult of worshippers who created a Garland mystique. The major problems for Garland's biographer are to separate the myths about her life from the truth, and to explain why this gifted and successful woman's life was characterized by anguish and a life-long addiction to drugs that resulted in her death at forty-seven.

To answer the riddle of Garland's life, Anne Edwards depends largely on the testimony of friends and family. She also relies on Garland's own interviews and commentaries in spite of the fact that she was known to exaggerate and lie habitually about her past. The resulting portrait is that of a victimized woman who was exploited first by her stage-struck mother, then by Louis B. Mayer, the powerful head of the Metro-Goldwyn-Mayer Studio, and finally by the many men in her life.

Garland's show business career began when she was two years old, the youngest of three daughters trained for vaudeville by their mother. Lured by the movie industry, the family moved from Minnesota to Southern California in the 1930's, an era in which the child star was in vogue. Eventually Garland was offered a contract by MGM and was thus brought into a structured, patriarchal setting which profoundly affected the rest of her life.

Her adolescence offered little opportunity for growing up. It was a period of instant gratification in which good performances led to immediate rewards and everyday decisions were made by others. She was undereducated and overworked. Her weight problem became the focus of attention and she began taking amphetamines in order to curb her appetite. Garland later blamed Louis B. Mayer for introducing her to drugs.

By 1950, Garland's career at MGM was over. The studio would no longer tolerate the erratic work habits brought on by her instability. A chronic insomniac, she had become increasingly dependent on sleeping pills and alcohol as well as on amphetamines in her desperate attempt to manage her work life. Her private life was also unmanageable. Two marriages had already failed, and her third to her manager, Sid Luft, was also failing. Under these circumstances she launched her new career as a concert performer.

She appeared at the Palladium in London and the Palace in New York to wildly enthusiastic audiences who saw Garland as a suffering heroine who defied convention. Her fans identified with her vulnerability and longed to protect her.

In spite of such adoration, Garland still could not prevent her life from slipping away from her. Unaccustomed to managing money or other practical matters, she was continually in debt and was driven to earn still more money. She taxed what was left of her shattered health by performing in concerts throughout the world and eventually died in London from a drug overdose.

Although Garland's great talent and career separate her life from the experiences of most other women, her responses to certain problems are familiar. She depended on one man after another to integrate her life. With each new marriage (there were five in all) she hoped that a new central focus would somehow protect her from the strain of her life as an entertainer and from her own vulnerabilities. No relationship could assume such a heavy burden, and Garland was inevitably disappointed.

Frank, Gerald. *Judy.* **New York: Dell, 1975. 716p.**

About his book Gerald Frank says, "It is the only biography of Judy Garland written with the complete cooperation of her immediate family ... they have exercised no editorial control over what I have written." This helps to explain Frank's kind treatment of them in contrast to Anne Edwards who blamed the family for allowing Garland's destruction of herself to go unchecked. Factual material in the two books is much the same but Frank's lengthier work allows him to describe in greater detail the complexities of the Garland personality.

He vividly recaptures moments of her legendary performances and points up her lightning quick mind and mordant wit. Most of all, Frank communicates that Garland felt terror and helplessness in facing her problems in spite of years of psychotherapy and occasional hospitalization.

Like Edwards, Frank describes the dissolution of most of Garland's close relationships — several failed marriages, her breaks with her sisters and with her mother. Garland's rejection of them all points up the unrealistic demands she made on others, a pattern which allows Frank to see her as much the victimizer as the victim.

Friedman, Myra. *Buried Alive: The Biography of Janis Joplin.* **New York: William Morrow, 1973. 333p.**

In the 1960's popular culture heroes of American youth did not come out of Hollywood and the motion picture world; they came from the world of rock music. In this biography, Myra Friedman, who worked for Janis Joplin during the height of the singer's short career, captures the qualities of the rock music culture and describes how it contributed to Joplin's destruction.

Joplin grew up in Port Arthur, Texas, a river town in the southeastern corner of the state. In adolescence she was overweight and scarred by acne. Feeling out of place in the feminine role, she chose to be "one of the boys" throughout high school and began the habits of hard drinking and use of foul language that later became her trademarks. Her professional singing began when she was a student at the University of Texas, a period when she also began to use heroin. Joplin went to San Francisco where she was invited to join the group, Big Brother and the Holding Company, and became successful instantly.

Friedman provides an excellent description of the rock music industry, a business that goes beyond musicians and audiences and includes managers, publicists, equipment managers, groupies and rock journalists. The latter, a power bloc which can establish stars overnight, was responsible for the instant fame of Janis Joplin who had "made it" even before she ever produced a recording.

Stardom created new anxieties for Joplin and provided more opportunities for the self-destructive course she was on. She worried that her new found fame would not last, and spent her time with other reckless people who drank heavily, used hard drugs and were sexually indiscriminate. Though her death from an overdose of heroin was ruled accidental, it was, her biographer feels, a suicidal act.

Friedman understands Joplin's behavior to be the result of arrested adolescent development. The singer's sense of her own deprivation made her unresponsive to any needs but her own and she became a victim of her own self absorption.

Friedman has done a skillful job of portraying Joplin and the milieu in which she functioned and of providing some answers to the important question of why Joplin was unable to protect herself from outside harm and from herself. The pressures felt by a popular entertainer who must depend on public approval for a sense of identity are unbearable. Only a stable private life can begin to protect the popular star, but the style of life allows for no privacy. The same dilemma occurred in the lives of other popular female entertainers who died prematurely from drug overdose, like Judy Garland and Marilyn Monroe.

Guiles, Fred Lawrence. *Norma Jean: The Life of Marilyn Monroe.* New York: McGraw-Hill, 1969. 341p.

On the surface there are a number of similarities between the lives of Marilyn Monroe and Judy Garland. Both grew up around Hollywood, achieved popular success, suffered precarious mental health and drug dependencies, and died prematurely from overdoses. But unlike the biographies of Garland which bring their subject to life, this book about Marilyn Monroe does not explain the woman, only the superstar she became.

We are told of her underprivileged start in life, born out of wedlock to a woman whose frightening mental illness duplicated the fate of her own parents. Monroe spent a period of her life in an orphanage, then lived with family friends, and finally entered an early marriage which soon ended in divorce. She drifted into the movies at Twentieth Century-Fox and was eventually molded into the sex symbol everyone now remembers.

To a large extent before her death and certainly since, a mystique was built up about the star. Some say Marilyn Monroe was potentially a great actress, a woman of deep sensitivity and empathy who could create great roles. Guiles states, however, that some of her scenes were replayed forty times before the director was satisfied, that she was incapable of abstract thought, that things had to be explained in the most concrete terms before she understood a part. Her marriage to Arthur Miller perhaps adds to the legend that she had untapped dramatic talents. But like most of the other important happenings of her life, the marriage is not fully explained in this book. Guiles writes that Miller knew that he would be a caretaker, but was still surprised by what this meant — counting out sleeping pills, staying up during her nights of insomnia, and most difficult for him, being so busy filling her needs that he could not do any of his own work. But little information about other qualities of their relationship is provided.

Marilyn Monroe remains an enigma in this book. Guiles never explains whether or not she believed in her own Hollywood image, and if not, whether she thought she knew what she wanted from life.

Hellman, Lillian. *An Unfinished Woman: A Memoir.* **Boston: Little, Brown, 1969. 280p.**

Lillian Hellman has said about these memoirs that she never intentionally set out to write her autobiography. Her original intention was to pull together previously written magazine articles into a collection. In doing so she discovered that significant past relationships and experiences led to her development, and that she finds she is "unfinished," having spent too much time searching after "truth" and not enough time enjoying the pleasures of life.

The origins of this book help to explain the selectivity which characterizes Hellman's writing. Instead of a fluid narrative of her life, she provides fragments which highlight key friendships and extraordinary moments in her history.

Her friendship with Dashiell Hammet covered thirty years, beginning after most of his books had been written, but before Hellman's own work had begun. This relationship was the most formative one of her life, and his death in 1961 was a profound loss to her. Her friendship with Dorothy Parker was also important, and Hellman provides amusing and poignant anecdotes about her friend.

Hellman is highly selective about what she considers to be the great historic moments of her time. The fight for women's rights was "stale stuff" by the time she grew up, for she had outdistanced the "flaming youth" of the 20's by having already slept with men, and had even had an abortion. Her great historic moments came in the 30's when she went to Spain during the Civil War and in 1944 in Moscow when she was asked to join the Russians on their march to Berlin.

Hellman leaves much unsaid. She speaks about her taste in people, in books, her love of nature, but we do not really come to know her. It is characteristic of her to avoid discussing the everyday experiences of her life, for she is interested only in the significant ones.

Hobhouse, Janet. *Everybody Who Was Anybody: A Biography of Gertrude Stein.* **New York: G.P. Putnam's, 1973. 244p.**

There was perhaps no more enticing time and place in modern history than Paris in the decades before and after the First World War. It was a vital time for creative people. Picasso and Matisse were stirring up the art world, and Gertrude Stein was setting new standards in literature which eventually influenced writers like Sherwood Anderson and Ernest Hemingway. The weekly salon presided over by Stein attracted artists and writers who had gravitated to Paris, and Stein eventually knew "everybody who was anybody." She is perhaps better remembered for her influence on others and for being one of the great personalities of her age than for her own literary achievements.

Janet Hobhouse recaptures the feeling of this era in her readable biography of Gertrude Stein. She has relied on the Stein autobiographies and on biographical accounts by others for her information, and her book brings the period to life as much by its excellent photographs as it does by the skillful retelling of a fascinating life.

Stein's early years centered around her relationship to her brother, Leo. They were inseparable growing up in California, and Gertrude later followed Leo to Harvard where they both studied with William James. Just before she was to graduate from Johns Hopkins Medical School, Gertrude again followed Leo, this time to Paris where they established a household. The Steins shared a passion for the experimental art that was appearing, and together they built up an impressive collection that drew the curiosity and admiration of a growing circle of friends.

Stein severed her close tie to her brother when Alice Toklas arrived in Paris. For the rest of Stein's life, the two women lived a mutually gratifying relationship that simulated marriage. Stein's role was that of the ''great man'' and Toklas assumed all responsibility for running a well-ordered household.

Stein's literary output, much of it unpublished during her lifetime, included prose, poetry, opera libretti and her curious book called *The Autobiography of Alice B. Toklas.* A kind of literary joke, it was written as though Toklas were describing Stein, a device which allowed Stein to dispense with the pretense of modesty facing writers of autobiography and to praise herself shamelessly. The book made many of her contemporaries angry. Some felt they were poorly represented and others resented Stein's exaggerated sense of her own importance within artistic circles. Nevertheless, the book became a sensation and was read by thousands of people who had never before read Stein's other, more difficult prose.

Stein was convinced of her own genius, an appraisal not adequately explored by her biographer. Hobhouse is more comfortable examining Stein's friendships, particularly the reciprocal influences between the writer and the painters she admired. One hopes that any future biographer of Stein will evaluate her literary achievement and will analyze the key relationships in her life — her early attachment to Leo and her lesbian relationship with Toklas which was clearly based on a male chauvinist ideal.

Keats, John. *You Might as Well Live: The Life and Times of Dorothy Parker.* **New York: Simon and Schuster, 1970. 319p.**

> ''These be the things I shall have till I die
> Laughter and hope and a sock in the eye''

Dorothy Parker wrote verses memorable for their bright wit and characteristic mixture of world-weariness and hilarity. Some of her short stories are even better than the verses. Given her gifts, says Keats, it is ''a pity that she could not have gone to the typewriter more often, but then, if she had, she might not have been Dorothy Parker.''

Keats faced difficult obstacles in uncovering Parker's life. No collection of her papers exists and little biographical information is provided in her published writing. Nevertheless, he pieces together her life and approaches his study by questioning why she never achieved happiness despite her literary success, large earnings and wide circle of friends.

Keats sees Parker's childhood as sad and lonely. Her mother died when she was an infant, and her father remarried a woman who at best ignored her and at worst tormented her by sending her to a strict Catholic school, an atmosphere intolerable to her temperament and training. Parker's situation improved when she was sent away to a fine boarding school, but she never overcame a lifelong feeling of deprivation.

In the 1920's, a time when successful careers for women were rare, Parker achieved commercial fame as a writer at *Vanity Fair* (the precursor of *Vogue*) and as a Hollywood screenwriter. In spite of her outward appearance of success, she was not content. Keats describes the intensity of her life which was characterized by hard drinking and sexual promiscuity. But more needs to be said about her relationship to the metiers of Hollywood and literary New York which were controlled by men whose misogyny was a trademark. Parker gained acceptance and admiration by taking on a foul-mouthed, wise-cracking tomboy role, but one wonders about her real feelings about her role and about the men who accepted her.

She is probably best remembered for her part in the circle of New York writers who met regularly at the Algonquin Hotel. As self-styled wits and raconteurs, their reputation may be overblown: Keats finds them provincial and given to self-aggrandizement. He does, however, appreciate Dorothy Parker, whom he considers, in spite of her slim output of three books of poetry and two collections of short stories, a first-rate writer.

Milford, Nancy. *Zelda.* New York: Harper and Row, 1970. 424p.

The private lives of Zelda and Scott Fitzgerald have fascinated observers of American literature and the life style of the American twenties. But while much has been made of Scott, this best-selling full biography is the first to focus on Zelda and the degree to which her reckless and self-destructive life also epitomized that period her husband dubbed ''the jazz age.'' The story has often been told, most notably by Fitzgerald himself, about how heavy drinking and peripatetic party-going sapped his creative energy, but what Milford reveals was Zelda's own fierce desire for creative expression and how her failures helped to destroy her. She painted but not ''seriously.'' She studied ballet with a ferocious intensity but had to stop with the onset of mental illness. She wrote many stories, some under Scott's name so that they would fetch more money, but the lack of credit for her work was less painful than the fact that her life seemed to provide her husband with material for his work. Witness *Tender is the Night,* a novel about madness and human destruction.

Zelda spent the last years of her life moving between her mother's house and a mental institution where her schizophrenia was periodically treated with insulin therapy. She died in 1942 when the wing of the hospital in which she was living was wiped out by a sudden fire.

This biography has been used in women's studies courses where it has been effective in illustrating a number of issues that have been of concern to feminists: recognition for women; competition in marriage; and loss of youth. Certainly Zelda Fitzgerald led a life more colorful and tragic than most, but aspects of it are illustrative of problems shared by many contemporary women.

Moffat, Mary Jane and Charlotte Painter, eds. *Revelations: Diaries of Women.* New York: Random House, 1974. 411p.

The editors see the activity of diary-writing as a form of expression that has engaged women in particular. Men, who traditionally have involved themselves in the work of the world, have been less inclined to pour out their feelings on paper, but are more likely to be issuing directives when they write — memos and reports. But "for women," the editors write, "the form has been an important outlet ... partly because it is an analogue to their lives: emotional, fragmentary, interrupted, modest, not to be taken seriously, private, restricted, daily, trivial, formless, concerned with self, as endless as their tasks." Above all, they say, women diarists express loneliness, sometimes stemming from the conflict they feel over their duties to others and what they feel they owe to themselves; sometimes as the result of physical isolation as with Anne Frank, or from psychological alienation as with Fanny Kemble.

For this book, the editors have assembled fragments from the diaries of thirty-three women who lived in different countries and in different periods in history. The principles of selection were based not only on what revelations the writers made about themselves and other women, but on the literary quality of the writing. Many of the diarists included are famous women — Louisa May Alcott, George Sand, Ruth Benedict, Dorothy Wordsworth and Virginia Woolf; but some are not well known, like an American woman living in Alaska who describes how she delivered her baby alone during an Arctic winter: "I have never seen a child born. I always felt inadequate to help and was too modest to want to be a spectator. I have never seen anything born — not even a cat ... I am no longer afraid, yet I do wish someone were with me to help me take care of the child..."

In the current search by historians and literary critics for evidence of authentic female experience, such revelations from diaries by women are a rich and vital source of information.

Nin, Anaïs. *Diaries.* Edited and with introductions by Gunther Stuhlmann. New York: Harcourt, Brace and World, 1966-1976. 6 vols.

Anaïs Nin was born in France in 1903, the daughter of Joachim Nin, a Spanish musician and Rosa Culmell, a singer of Danish and French extraction. After her parents separated, her mother brought the three children to New York where Nin attended school irregularly, preferring to read literature on her own. She began the custom of keeping a diary as a child. For over half a century she wrote in her journal her feelings about life, her perceptions about other people, and most of all, her awareness of herself. Although she produced essays and fiction, Nin considered the diaries her lifework, her "most natural, most truthful" writing.

The decision to allow them to be published was an extremely difficult one for Nin to make. Stuhlman, her editor, wrote, "The sheer bulk of material, with its burdensome secrecy, the emotional weight of its content, the overwhelming significance of the diaries in shaping and creating her own life, undoubtedly had begun to exert increasing pressure on Anaïs Nin."

She had not expected to become a cult figure, but the *Diaries,* which started to appear shortly before the emergence of the new feminist movement, came to be viewed as the articulate expression of the spirit of all women.

She did not write like a man, but instead created themes from her sense of femininity — intuition, nurturance, sensuality and compassion. "What I have to say," she writes "is really distinct from the artist and art. It is the woman who has to speak. And it is not only the woman Anaïs who has to speak, but I who have to speak for many women. As I discover myself, I feel I am merely one of many, a symbol. I begin to understand women of yesterday and today. The mute ones of the past, the inarticulate, who took refuge behind wordless intuitions, and the women of today, all action, and copies of man. And I, in between...."

Plath, Sylvia. *Letters Home: Correspondence 1950-1963.* **Selected and edited with commentary by Aurelia Schober Plath. New York: Harper and Row, 1975. 500p.**

From the time she left home as a freshman at Smith College until her death in London in 1963, Sylvia Plath wrote almost seven hundred letters to her mother. Aurelia Plath's decision to publish these letters has come as her reaction to the growing cult which worships her daughter, more it seems for the morbid aspects of her life and death than for her art. She would wish her daughter's fame to rely more on the positive aspects of her being — her perseverence and dedication to writing, and her achievement as an artist.

In part, this book does achieve that aim, for one does get through the letters a narrative of the development of a gifted young woman who set specific tasks for herself and went on to accomplish them. But one cannot help but approach the book in an investigatory frame of mind, looking for clues to help explain a suicide. What accounted for Plath's psychological instability, the hard-driving need to succeed? What, moreover, can be learned about her experiences as a woman that can help explain the lives of women in general?

Plath was born in 1932, the daughter of educated parents who took immediate delight in her beauty and precocity. Her father, a professor of entomology at Boston University, established an autocratic household which Aurelia took pains to comply with, and she tells us that a happy household was maintained in spite of Otto Plath's unreasonable demands. Otto died when Sylvia was eight from a long-neglected diabetic condition. The family, which included her mother's parents and her younger brother, then moved to Wellesley where her mother still lives.

Plath went to Smith as a scholarship student, where she excelled at all of her studies and sent off hundreds of stories and poems, many of them published during these undergraduate years. In spite of constant recognition, Plath set more and more goals for herself, and in spite of temporary set-backs invariably achieved them. After her junior year, she spent a month in New York working at *Mademoiselle Magazine,* a period in her life which has been immortalized in *The Bell Jar.* Exactly like Esther in the novel, Plath suffered a collapse after the New York experience, and made a serious attempt at suicide by taking an overdose of sleeping pills. Her recovery involved shock treatment and several months of intensive therapy until she was ready to complete her studies at Smith.

After graduation she went to Cambridge University on a Fulbright Scholarship and spent what were undoubtedly the happiest two years of her life. While there she continued to write stories and poems and was still publishing occasionally. Among her other goals was her need to make a brilliant marriage, and when she met the British poet, Ted Hughes, she felt she had met her counterpart. They married, and together they threw themselves into the hard routine of serious writing, and they began to receive ever widening recognition, Hughes even more than Plath. They tried to live in America for a year when Plath got a teaching job at Smith. But it became clear to her that teaching literature was robbing her of the time and the inspiration to do her own creative work. The couple moved back to England, and within three years had two babies. Money problems, the hardship of the English climate, and the intensity of their work tore away the fabric of this ''perfect'' marriage, and Ted Hughes ultimately betrayed his wife by leaving her for another woman. Plath tried to go on alone, caring for her children and writing so intensely that she was producing a poem a day. The pressures she had experienced ten years before were back again, and one morning, in the midst of the most bitter winter England had known in 150 years, Plath died of gas poisoning in the kitchen of her flat.

Earlier in her life Plath had said, ''I was terrified that if I wasn't successful writing, no one would find me interesting or valuable.'' She seemed to feel the same way about managing a successful marriage and about homemaking. She needed constant recognition and drove herself to achieve continuing perfection. Some of these drives can be explained by the early loss of her father and by her position as a scholarship student at a school where she mingled among the rich, but there are some unanswered questions about her life and death.

Plath's letters home provide some answers. In particular, her letters dramatize the dilemmas of growing up female in the 1950's when no one questioned the necessity of marriage and children for women, and when careers had somehow to be wedged into one's life. What is unsatisfying about this book is that we get just half of the correspondence. One wonders about what Aurelia Plath wrote back to her daughter, what expectations she set up that could not be met. Plath was clearly keeping up appearances for the world, and for her mother in particular. Aurelia was totally unprepared for the ruination of the Hughes's marriage when last she saw her daughter in England. The book ends with this heartbreaking comment by Aurelia, the only reference she makes to her daughter's death: "Her physical energies had been depleted by illness, anxiety and overwork, and although she had for so long managed to be gallant and equal to the life-experience, some darker day than usual had temporarily made it seem impossible to pursue."

Sanders, Marion K. *Dorothy Thompson: A Legend in Her Time.* **Boston: Houghton Mifflin, 1973. 428p.**

At the height of her career in the 1930's, Dorothy Thompson was one of the best known journalists in America. As a correspondent living in Europe during the politically tumultuous years of the 20's and 30's, she became increasingly involved with reporting the international crises that eventually led to World War II. She was an astute observer and with the help of politically sophisticated friends became an influential and impassioned commentator against fascism, in strong sympathy with the European Jews imperiled by a Germany gone berserk.

In her biography of Thompson, Marion Sanders approaches this dynamic life with a sharper sense of Thompson as a woman than as a political critic. We are told where Thompson was living at any given month of her life and what general opinions she held, but Sanders gives no systematic analyses of her ideas. She is more interested in the emotional content of Thompson's life and the panache of her existence which included several elaborate homes and an international set of friends whom she entertained in great style. In spite of her peripatetic life, she married three times and had a child by her second husband, novelist Sinclair Lewis. Aside from her marriages, she intermittently had emotionally and sexually involved relationships with women throughout her life.

The passion and drama of her life is all the more remarkable when contrasted with her start in life as the daughter of a Methodist minister from up-state New York. She was the oldest of three children and had a happy childhood until she was eight, when her mother died from the complications of an abortion. Sanders tells us that the abortion had been performed by Mrs. Thompson's own mother, and that the resulting death "left Dorothy with a deepened aversion for her grandmother and may have helped shape the concern for women that would one day find expression in the suffrage movement and in her writings." Her involvement with women's rights began in college where she joined the Syracuse Equal Suffrage Club, and continued after graduation in her work as a suffrage organizer in western New York, not far from Seneca Falls. With the encouragement and influence of a wealthy friend, Thompson turned to journalism as a natural outlet for her particular talents — a quick mind, an amazing memory, and the ability to assimilate herself into new surroundings.

She left for Europe for the first time in 1920 with a friend who also aspired to write for newspapers, and by the following year managed to land a job in Vienna working for the *Philadelphia Ledger.* Her insatiable appetite for information, along with her charm and stupendous energy, brought her into touch with important people and made her a successful journalist. She was married for a short time during the early twenties to an Austrian writer who grew apart from her and the life she led and sought a divorce.

Later in the 20's while still in Europe, Thompson met and married Sinclair Lewis who was by then an extremely successful author, but hard-drinking and demanding of others. This union between two people who both required admiration and attention caused H.L. Mencken to comment when asked about the future of the marriage, ''No telling. Red will drink and Dorothy will talk until they both go *mashuggah.*''

Mencken was right. The marriage was far from compatible. One factor complicating their relationship was the fact that Lewis's best writing had already been done, while Dorothy Thompson was to go on to achieve even greater success in her career. She became a columnist for the *Herald Tribune* and *The Ladies' Home Journal,* and found continuing opportunities to travel away from her difficult husband.

Although she had no trouble filling her time with her work and her efforts to rescue and sponsor refugee Austrian and German friends, Thompson was lonely after her second marriage failed. When she met Maxim Kopf, a minor Austrian painter, she was immediately attracted to him although his earthiness and lack of sophistication were in marked contrast to the earlier men in her life. They soon married, and she enjoyed nine happy years with him until his death. After 1950 her professional as well as her personal life went into a decline.

She had been dropped as a columnist from the *Herald Tribune* at the beginning of the 40's because she had supported Roosevelt. The liberal *New York Post* had taken her on after that until her criticism of Zionism caused them to discontinue their association, since their circulation depended on Jewish readers. Dorothy Thompson got caught in the middle of the Palestine conflict. Although a long-time partisan of Jews, she could also see the potential danger in the creation of Israel. But such reservations were interpreted as anti-semitism in the late 40's.

In 1961 Thompson died on her last visit to Europe. In her later years her world-fame had all but disappeared. For emotional support she looked to her son, Michael, whom she had neglected throughout his childhood. Sanders describes the adult Michael as not very stable, and as an actor not able to earn a living. His wife and children became Thompson's absorbing interest during her last years, almost the only time in her life when individuals took precedence over world events and her excitement over participating in those happenings.

Seroff, Victor. *The Real Isadora.* New York: Avon, 1971. 480p.

Victor Seroff attempts in this absorbing book to reveal the truth behind the legends that surround the life of Isadora Duncan. He disapproves of previous biographies which were written by those who knew the dancer only during the latter part of her life and were heavily influenced by her autobiography, *My Life.* This was a book written shortly before her death at a time when she was under considerable pressure from her publisher to sensationalize her experiences, as if they were not sensational enough in themselves.

In trying to put Duncan's life into a more meaningful perspective, Seroff, a musician as well as a writer and loyal friend, appraises her life in terms of her art and her contribution to dance. His problem — and a problem it is for the reader as well — is that her triumphs happened, were acclaimed, but were never to be seen again, not even on motion picture film, which was available in her lifetime.

Born in California in 1878, the youngest of four children whose father deserted when she was a baby, Duncan grew up in near poverty. In spite of hardship, the family took on a creative life of its own, inspired by the mother who earned money by giving piano lessons. The children all performed, and Isadora Duncan seems always to have danced. Recognizing her talent, her family sent her to New York where she joined the Augustin Daly troupe and took her first trip to Europe, where she eventually moved with her family. In London and Paris she had little trouble meeting influential people — aristocrats and established figures in the arts — but her popularity did not prove financially profitable until a theatrical manager arranged a series of performances first in Budapest and then throughout Germany where she was widely acclaimed.

In Hungary she was forced to make a choice between art and love. Her first lover, an actor, insisted she retire from the stage and devote herself completely to him. Duncan, never conventional even in small ways, severed the relationship, albeit at the expense of a bout of severe depression and a need for complete rest. Like many a male artist, she had been inconvenienced, disappointed and poor for the sake of her art; unlike a man, she had been asked to give it up.

And give up too her greater ambition, that of founding a school where a thousand pupils would be trained in her style, and thenceforth go out and train thousands of others. The idea became a lifelong desire which she first attempted to satisfy in Germany. Unfortunately the school she established there was left to be run by her sister, Elizabeth, who seized control while Duncan toured. She tried to establish other schools in other European countries, but recurring wars and political crises consistently denied her her dream.

Her personal life was also ultimately disappointing. She had long affairs with two extraordinary men, each of whom fathered a child, but the affairs proved compromising of her talents and aims, and her children died tragically. In spite of her proclaimed anti-marital convictions, she later married Sergei Essenin, a wildly tempestuous Russian poet who could not live outside his country, and eventually not even within, for he committed suicide a few years after his separation from Duncan.

The great love of her life was Gordon Craig, a gifted theatrical designer who had by the time he met her already fathered eight illegitimate children and was himself the illegitimate son of the actress Ellen Terry. Craig saw in Isadora and her art the same ideals he sought, ideals involving their mutual sense of the interrelationship and staged possibilities of drama and dance. Despite his relationship with another woman, Duncan was totally committed to him during the course of their affair, supplying him with funds and taking sole responsibility for the support of their daughter. But the affair inevitably ended because of the clash of their similar temperaments and their primary commitment to their irreconcilably demanding work.

After Craig, Duncan met the millionaire, Paris Singer, who provided her with luxuries. He remains a shadowy figure in this biography, but Seroff makes it clear that he never really touched her soul, as had Craig. In any case, he was the father of her son, Patrick, who, with his half-sister, Deirdre, died in a drowning accident in 1913.

It was an accident from which the dancer was never completely to recover. Seroff describes a recklessness that all but overcame her after this terrible loss. She raced around in fast cars and attracted a coterie of unsavory companions who took advantage of her generosity and good will. However, she did return to performing and her continuing quest for a school. It brought her to post-revolutionary Russia where she had already danced and made an impression upon traditional ballet and its tight, prescriptive movements. Yet the school she was promised went unsupported, and her connection with Communist Russia so damaged her reputation in the West that when she returned to France shortly after she could barely support herself, certainly not another school. She danced infrequently in her last years and was penniless at the time of her death.

Her death was as dramatic as her life had been. She went out for a ride in a chauffeur-driven sports car, and when the fringes of her long scarf got caught in the spokes of an open wheel, she was killed instantly, her neck broken, her face crushed. The last words she was heard to speak to friends as she waved good-bye were, "Adieu, mes amis. Je vais a la glorie."

One must be grateful to Victor Seroff for his conscientious recreation of a talented artist whose exuberance and sense of expectation only made her vulnerable to life's complexities and potential for catastrophe. Duncan, one feels after reading this life, had more to lose than most, and lost it all.

Sorell, Walter. *Three Women: Lives of Sex and Genius.* **Indianapolis: Bobbs-Merrill, 1975. 234p.**

In this trio of essays, two of which are devoted to European women, Alma Mahler Werfel and Lou Andreas-Salomé, Walter Sorell provides an illuminating chapter on Gertrude Stein. He raises questions which have only infrequently engaged her biographers — Why was she so indifferent to the death of her father? Why did she so completely reject her brother Leo, considering how close their relationship had been? Why in her writing did she show such disdain for conventional language?

Sorell understands her rejection of the male members of her family as the result of an overpowering desire to get on with her own life and its needs, serious writing and homosexual attachment. As for her rejection of English rules of grammar, Sorell understands this to be the natural outcome of her ultimate aim in writing, the description of what she called "the continuous present," capturing with words on paper a moment in time, much like the impressionist painters had been doing on canvas. For Stein, the author feels, normal sentence structure was restrictive, an acknowledgement of and dependence upon the past.

Sorell is open about Stein's homosexuality, a fact of her life which biographers have been awkward about approaching, partly because the subject was taboo, partly out of deference to Alice Toklas while she lived. Sorell sees Stein's disdain for the male explicit in much of her writing, and particularly in her last work, the libretto for an opera about Susan B. Anthony called *The Mother of Us All.* Her depiction here of Daniel Webster as an overbearing and tyrannical man is taken by the author as evidence of the unresolved feeling of Stein toward her father.

Taken by itself, this essay may appear an excessively psychoanalytical interpretation. But since fuller biographies of Stein ignore the important questions about Stein's life that interest Sorell, it must be acknowledged that he fills a gap and, indeed, makes a valuable contribution to our understanding of an important modern figure.

Steegmuller, Francis, ed. *"Your Isadora": The Love Story of Isadora Duncan and Gordon Craig.* New York: Random House, 1974. 399p.

Victor Seroff's book gives one a sense of all the events in Isadora Duncan's life juxtaposed against her indomitable will to succeed in the expression of her art. Steegmuller accomplishes something else. By examining the never before published letters and diaries of Isadora Duncan and Gordon Craig, he presents not so much a biography, but a penetrating analysis of the relationship between two extraordinary people. Steegmuller is cautious about commenting on the effect these two gifted people had on one another. Since they are so articulate, this sense of them can be drawn from the writings themselves. In them Duncan is generally buoyant, loving and warm, and Craig is overwhelmingly egocentric. Duncan needed to combine her art with the love of a man. Craig had little commitment to anyone but himself.

They met in Berlin in 1904 when Duncan had already begun to astound her audiences. To give a sense of her effect on people, Steegmuller quotes from critics who found her dances fascinating, "each one a mobile sculpture, a piece of music in its imagery, a poem in its rhythm." Craig was a theatrical producer whose head was filled with multiple schemes and plans: his own theater; an international theater magazine; individual state productions; book illustrations; and a series of posters of Duncan as she danced. He was earning no money, and Duncan supported him from the start. Craig's intractibility is stressed by Steegmuller who points out that Craig was so unwilling to make compromises with co-workers that very few of his projects were ever staged. George Bernard Shaw commented, "Gordon Craig has made himself the most famous producer in Europe by dint of never producing anything."

By the time Duncan and Craig had met, he had already fathered eight illegitimate children, most of them supported by his mother, the actress Ellen Terry. His appeal to Duncan was immediate and profound, for as well as astonishing good looks, he possessed a romantic and unconventional air which Duncan found irresistable.

There were frequent and long separations because of Duncan's tours, and letters reveal the intensity of her love for him. When pregnant with their child, she moved to a remote seaside house in Holland where she lived alone, the object of disapproval from her mother and the rest of conventional society. Although she experienced severe depression and even attempted suicide, her letters to Craig generously avoided any mention of her true state of mind:

> I am so glad to be alone myself, and think of you. Just the difference between you and other people is that you are Beautiful and they are not. With you all is transformed to wonder and loveliness — with other people things suddenly lose their light and become commonplace — so if I'm not with you I'd a thousand times rather be alone — when I am truly with you just the same.

Craig was busy with his projects and felt that children were solely the mother's responsibility. He gave no thought to supporting their child; on the contrary, he was impatient for Duncan to regain her strength after her confinement so that she could earn funds to finance his projects as she had promised.

Years later, after the death of Duncan's two children, Craig showed himself at his worst. He had been a distant parent but took the position that Duncan was to blame for the tragic drowning.

> She let them be looked after by governesses ... Never could they have died as they did die with their MOTHER watching. She simply failed to watch — and I believe her grief loses its worth since it was her own fault.

Long before the tragedy their personal involvement had ended. Duncan could not cope with all of the demands of supporting her mother, her child, the school, the expenses of her house, and Gordon Craig and his projects as well. For Craig, life was relatively simple; all of his energies were expended on himself and the production of his art. He made sacrifices, to be sure, but not nearly of the kind and number made by Duncan who keenly felt the conflict between duty and desire.

Toklas, Alice B. *Staying on Alone: Letters of Alice B. Toklas.* New York: Liveright, 1973. 426p.

Alice Toklas has been called "a person in her own right," a term reserved usually for the wives of presidents or other men of high achievement. But her relationship to Stein can most readily be understood within the terms of that overworked phrase, for Gertrude Stein and Alice B. Toklas functioned as a married couple, Stein being the "great man" and a male chauvinist at that, Toklas the devoted wife who took care of all the details of their domestic life, and even typed Stein's manuscripts.

The letters in this collection were written by Toklas to her friends over the years following Stein's death in 1946. Her bereavement is intense. 'Gertrude's memory,'' she writes, ''is all my life — just as she herself was before.'' Toklas's immediate concerns are with preparing Stein's manuscripts and letters which were to go to Yale, and she spends many months absorbed in the practical details in winding up Gertrude's life and death. Gradually, however, Toklas became caught up in the everyday matters of her own life — moving from one flat to another, buying a new Hoover, tracking down a satisfactory recipe for gazpacho.

Like so many other women who have lived within a subordinate role, Toklas was gifted, her intelligence and wit coming through in her comments about people. Speaking of her friend, Harriet Levy, who had published her first two books when she was eighty, Toklas says, ''And the worst is she can write. It's that she has nothing to say which is a thousand pities as it's nearly always the other way round.''

It is a criticism that cannot be made of Toklas. She has much to say about her long and satisfying life and her loyalty to an admired friend. And she can write, as these letters demonstrate.

Toklas, Alice B. *What Is Remembered.* New York: Holt, Rinehart and Winston, 1963. 185p.

These memoirs offer Alice Toklas's reflections over more than fifty years of her life — the years immediately preceding her life in Paris with Gertrude Stein to the years after. Like all writers of autobiography, she is selective about what she includes, and most particular about how she herself wants to be remembered. She sees herself as a background person, one who served Stein, and what she stresses in this book are the people she met and the places she visited. As a girl, she had met the author of *Ben Hur,* Lew Wallace, to whom she refers as ''my first author.'' Although Toklas may have been a less renowned person than Stein, she is never dull or undiscerning, and can always be counted on to make a penetrating and witty comment. Of Allen Stein, Gertrude's nephew, she said, ''Both Matisse and Picasso had painted portraits of him, the greatest distinction he was to know.''

Much of what Toklas includes in these memoirs has been incorporated into more recent biographies of Stein, so that if one turns to this book after having read the others hoping to learn more about the relationship between them, the book will be disappointing. One should read it for the pleasure of knowing Alice Toklas, even if it includes only what she would want the world to know.

*   *   *

Hellman, Lillian. *Pentimento.* Boston: Little, Brown, 1973. 297p.

Pentimento is Lillian Hellman's second volume of memoirs. *An Unfinished Woman* appeared in 1969 and *Scoundrel Time* in 1976. The title is a painting term used to describe the original lines that sometimes show through the paint on an old canvas, indicating that the painter changed his mind. Hellman says about the people described in her book, ''The paint has aged now and I wanted to see what was there for me once, what is there for me now.'' Her portraits include recollections of significant friends like Julia, her wealthy childhood friend who risked and then lost her life rescuing victims from the Nazis.

Mellow, James R. *Charmed Circle: Gertrude Stein and Company.* New York: Praeger, 1974. 507p.

Mellow's book provides no new point of view or fresh literary analysis of Stein and her work. Like Janet Hobhouse in her biography of Gertrude Stein, Mellow focuses on Stein's relationships with family members and friends and minimizes discussions of her literature. He does, however, talk about Stein's lesbian relationship with Alice B. Toklas, a subject avoided by earlier biographers out of deference to Toklas while she lived.

Secrest, Meryle. *Between Me and Life: A Biography of Romaine Brooks.* Garden City, New York: Doubleday, 1974. 432p.

Romaine Brooks, a lesbian artist, lived in Paris at the same time as Gertrude Stein, though she maintained a separate social circle. In this biography, Secrest captures the texture of the times, and Brooks herself, who could never escape the effects of a tormented childhood. Instead of offering a refuge from the pain of her life, Brooks's works of art reflect those agonies.

Seyersted, Per. *Kate Chopin: A Critical Biography.* Baton Rouge: Louisiana State University Press, 1969. 246p.

One of the responsibilities of literary criticism is the recovery of forgotten or neglected books of quality; for feminist critics the search is vital for it is leading to the recognition of books which authentically depict female experience. Kate Chopin's *The Awakening* is such a book. Banned during the author's lifetime, it is now recognized as an important classic of American realism which introduced a heroine whose struggle to establish and preserve her autonomy ultimately led her to suicide. Seyersted played a major part in rediscovering Chopin. His book, at once biography and criticism, traces the author's development as a writer and provides insights into her novel and short stories.

Tufts, Eleanor. *Our Hidden Heritage: Five Centuries of Women Artists.* New York: Paddington, 1974. 256p.

Tufts surveys five hundred years of art to reveal the existence of women artists. Because the scope is so broad, only three Americans are featured in this book: Sarah Peale, Edmonia Lewis and I. Rice Pereira. Handsome photographs of the works discussed accompany the text.

CRITICISM

Donovan, Josephine, ed. *Feminist Literary Criticism: Explorations in Theory.* Lexington: University of Kentucky Press, 1975. 81p.

Feminist literary criticism has evolved from the women's liberation movement, and brings to the study of literature a new political point of view similar in intent to a Marxist approach. In both cases, the "new criticism," that is, the critical position that a book must be evaluated for its internal contents and style alone, is rejected in favor of an approach that judges a book according to a preconceived doctrine. For feminists, that approach is the evaluation of female characters to see whether or not they are authentic, and if not, to see how badly they fall under the sexist stereotype of women as submissive and dependent beings.

The approach is a problematic one since few autonomous female characters exist in the history of literature. Does this mean that one rejects most of what has been written? Another problem which can come from a political reading of literature is that questions of style become submerged beneath the overriding philosophical concerns. This is a heavy price to pay as can be seen when one looks at State Art of the Soviet Union where dullness and mediocrity replace the poetic imagination for the sake of party line.

These issues and many more are discussed in the five essays that comprise this excellent book which offers an overview of the state of the art of feminist literary criticism. It begins with a bibliographic review by Cheri Register who has pulled together the existing feminist criticism found in such scattered places as introductions to books or from *Female Studies,* the women's studies course lists published by Know Inc. and the Feminist Press. Donovan has also included two theoretical essays, one by Dorin Schumacher, the other by Marcia Holly; a look at Virginia Woolf's criticism in an essay by Barbara Currier Bell and Carol Ohmann; and finally, a piece by Carolyn Heilbrun and Catharine Stimpson called, "Theories of Feminist Criticism: A Dialogue."

It was the intention of the editor to bring together some of the best critical thinking representing this new approach to literature in the hope that a feminine aesthetic could eventually be developed. In her conclusion to the book, Donovan discusses her belief that there is a female culture which must be retrieved because "there are truths and probabilities about the female experience that form a criterion against which to judge the authenticity of a literary statement about women." Clearly, the study of women's history is the essential first step in establishing a female aesthetic, for how can one hope to evaluate the significant or the beautiful in the perceptions of women unless one has an understanding of the truth about women's lives?

Earnest, Ernest. *The American Eve in Fact and Fiction, 1775-1914.* Urbana: University of Illinois Press, 1974. 280p.

Earnest's thesis is that the American woman has had far more variety and vitality in her make-up than is generally recognized, and that an inaccurate image has been generated by the way she has been treated in literature. He is concerned here with the years between the Revolutionary War and World War I, and uses diaries and other autobiographical accounts written by women as a basis for comparison.

He is most persuasive in his examination of 19th-century fiction, particularly the portrayal of women by such influential writers as Henry James and William D. Howells. Earnest sees the women in their fiction as unsophisticated, inactive, sexless and self-absorbed, epitomized by Daisy Miller, the James creation who has been seen as representative of the American girl. By contrast, Earnest proves through primary sources that real women engaged in physical exercise, were well-read, and possessed a worldliness denied them by the novelists. He quotes Dr. Elizabeth Blackwell to support the position that passion in women was considered legitimate, and is inclined to believe that Jennie Jerome is a more legitimate prototype than the prudish and provincial heroines of 19th-century literature.

Ellman, Mary. *Thinking About Women.* New York: Harcourt, Brace and World, 1968. 240p.

This is a book that defines and examines the stereotypes that have been used to describe female writers. Ellman illustrates, for example, how women have been accused of passivity, formlessness, piety, irrationality — in short, of not writing like men. With the recent interest of feminist critics in establishing criteria for a female aesthetic, one can forget that it was only a short time ago that women writers were taking seriously such harsh criticism by male critics. Particularly in American writing, where male writers have dominated and a male ideal been insisted upon has the ideal of being ''womanish'' been condemned. (Witness Hawthorne's derisive comments on ''the scribbling women'' of the 19th century and the renown of Hemingway's novels in the 20th). This is a point of view with which Ellman attempts to conjure. Writing in the late sixties, Ellman is a precursor of the current and urgent interest in the problems facing women writers.

Haskell, Molly. *From Reverence to Rape: The Treatment of Women in the Movies.* New York: Holt, Rinehart and Winston, 1973. 388p.

Like Marjorie Rosen in her book, *Popcorn Venus,* Molly Haskell takes an historic view to see how women have been portrayed through the years. She tries to limit her discussion to the treatment of sexuality by the film-makers, and presents the thesis that the portrayal of women has steadily deteriorated from their image as steadfast virgins to their presentation as whores. Again, like Rosen, Haskell is faced with the huge job of organizing masses of material into a coherent discussion. This involves summarizing hundreds of movie plots, commenting on the individual work of actresses, directors and screen-writers, and arriving at some conclusions from this vast array of material. Despite these problems, Haskell has written a critically astute book which documents her view that the image of women in films has declined over the years.

Although the image of the ''new woman'' as the sexually exciting flapper or vamp was introduced in the 20's, the central convention of womanhood during this period was the eternal virgin. Stars like the Gish sisters and Janet Gaynor portrayed impeccably moral women who hid their strength behind a facade of innocence and dependence. The popularity of their style is documented by the fact that women stars outnumbered their male counterparts throughout the 20's.

By the 30's, sex queens like Pola Negri, Mae West and Jean Harlow became popular, and though more explicit about their sexuality, they were still portrayed essentially as heroines, not villainesses, and they were women who possessed brains and wit. At the same time, the eternal virgin was still an active convention. Even Scarlett O'Hara, who defied all other moral expectations, obeyed the sexual rules. Haskell sees her as ''in many ways, a forerunner of the career woman, with her profession-obsession (the land), her business acumen, her energy that accumulated steam from sexual repression.''

At the end of the thirties and into the forties, a new film genre was gaining enormous popularity, the ''woman's film.'' Everything in these films revolved around what was happening to the female star, played by such strong actresses as Bette Davis and Joan Crawford, and the themes centered around the hardship of life and love and the sacrifices demanded of these women for the sake of their true love, or more often, for their children. The heartbreak involved with giving up illegitimate children was a recurring theme. Although the ''woman's film'' is still occasionally being made today — *Play it as it Lays, Diary of a Mad Housewife* — they are empty of positive values and portray women who are numb with despair and feelings of alienation.

The 40's introduced a new kind of melodrama in which women were not so much acted upon by the forces of fate as they were actively treacherous, hardboiled, and even homicidal. Stirred on by neurotic envy, greed or lust, women in such films as *Double Indemnity* (Barbara Stanwyck) or *The Maltese Falcon* (Mary Astor) killed for gain. Haskell sees this period as the beginning of the steady denigration of women in films to the present day when they are assaulted and brutalized in films as a matter of convention (*Clockwork Orange, Straw Man, Frenzy*).

The fifties was a time of turmoil for the motion picture industry because of the threat of television and the competition from foreign filmmakers. Some of the stars who came into fashion during this time were Marilyn Monroe, Audrey Hepburn and Doris Day, each creating distinctly different images of women, and each becoming obsolete as tastes changed and the male-dominated films came into fashion. Haskell makes the point that sturdy John Wayne survives from decade to decade while female stars disappear.

Haskell calls the ten years between 1963 and 1973 ''the most disheartening in screen history'' where women are concerned because directors who before then had been discreet about their misogyny (Stanley Kubrick's *Lolita*) were becoming overt. Violence was replacing romance, and actresses needed only to be curvy, not intelligent, and certainly never strong. There is a paradox in that as women came closer to claiming their rights and achieving independence in real life, the more loudly did films glorify machismo (*Dirty Harry, Deliverance*).

She ends her study by commenting on the absence of films which show women showing mutual support. "Where, oh where," she says, "is the camaraderie, the much-vaunted mutual support among women? It was there, without advertising itself, in the twenties: among Griffith's women, with Clara Bow and her college pals; in the thirties, among the gold diggers; ...in the forties, with Bette Davis and her female costars; even in the fifties, with Marilyn Monroe and her millionaire-hunting friends. But where, in the movies and out, are their modern equivalents?"

There is something of the anthropologist in a film critic like Molly Haskell who looks back on the world of motion pictures as if they were foreign lands inhabited by unfamiliar beings. We might think that we are at home in the world of films because we have all experienced them, but Haskell shows that "there are two cinemas: the film we have actually seen and the memories we have of them." By taking a hard look at how women have been treated in the movies, she brings a new interpretation to them, as if she were resurrecting a lost civilization.

Heilbrun, Carolyn G. *Toward a Recognition of Androgyny.* New York: Knopf, 1973. 189p.

Any serious discussion of sex-role stereotyping will sooner or later lead to the question of what is truly masculine and what is feminine in our gender-conscious society. In the introduction to her book, Carolyn Heilbrun writes, "I believe that our future salvation lies in a movement away from sexual polarization and the prison of gender toward a world in which individual roles and the modes of personal behavior can be freely chosen. The ideal toward which I believe we should move is best described by the term *androgyny.*"

To uncover the manifestations of this androgynous ideal, Heilbrun applies her considerable skills as a literary critic and explores classical drama, religious literature, Shakespeare, and, finally, the modern novel which has seen the rise of the woman as hero, particularly in the writings of Jane Austen, the Brontë sisters, George Eliot, Henry James, E. M. Forster and D. H. Lawrence. Heilbrun rightly points out differences between the feminist novel with its angry tone and polemic intent, and books which contain characters who embody both male and female characteristics. In *Wuthering Heights,* for example, Heilbrun shows that when Catherine denies her identity with Heathcliff, she sinks to her death within the conventional feminine life that she has deliberately chosen, and that Heathcliff's masculine side develops into a brutality and violence which become a hideous exaggeration of masculinity.

Major evidence for the androgynous ideal is found in both the art and the personal style of the Bloomsbury group which, to Heilbrun, exemplifies the creative possibilities of that ideal in which a writer like Virginia Woolf can say, "Some collaboration has to take place in the mind between the woman and the man before the act of creation can be accomplished."

Although Heilbrun's discussion of androgyny has sometimes been misunderstood — she is not talking about bisexuality, for instance, but rather social behavior free of sex-role prescriptions — her androgynous ideal has gone on to influence other feminists searching for a reasonable future for the relationship between the sexes.

Mellon, Joan. *Women and Their Sexuality in the New Film.* New York: Horizon Press, 1973. 255p.

Like the other critics who have looked for a positive image of women in films, Mellon finds that the contemporary film portrays women not only as unable to achieve, but as emotional cripples who are self-hating and demoniacally sexual. She attributes this distortion to the deterioration of bourgeois values which has led to the end of the image of women as prim, sexless and domestic. Instead, women have become fair game for the violence previously reserved for the "loose" woman, and Mellon points out that there now is an "ambivalence towards women in both the society and in the films: if they did not perform sexually they were not truly arousing; if they did, they threatened male adequacy and command."

Her conclusions apply to films directed by women as well as by men, and to foreign filmmakers as well as Americans. Mellon points, for instance, to the portrayal of Lila in the film *The Heartbreak Kid* (1972) directed by Elaine May in which her own daughter, Jeannie Berlin, plays a major role. Lila is a Jewish girl from the Bronx whose new young husband finds her so disgusting that he dumps her on their honeymoon in favor of a beautiful blond Wasp from the Mid-West. Lila talks with her mouth full, spits when she talks, and has to be reassured about her lovemaking — "Is it what you thought it would be like? Exactly or better?" Who can blame anyone for rejecting such a woman? Mellon sees her portrayal as vicious, and indicative of the anti-female attitudes prevailing in most films. She says, "Lila is so gross that her body and its carriage are used by May to revolt us all. It is a conception born of a considerable self-hatred of women, Jews, and, at some level, her own daughter." She concludes that although May can register what the society has done to women, she has no vision of how these circumstances can be changed, nor does she seem to desire a better life for women.

Mellon devotes a great deal of attention to the work of such prestigious foreign directors as Bergman, Bertolucci and Rohmer, and uncovers their anti-female biases. She finds it paradoxical, for instance, that at a time when women are expressing concerns for their autonomy, and are acting upon these needs, Bergman continues to envision women as being hopelessly bound to their own physiology, and hating themselves for their animal needs. To her credit, Mellon, in her determination to focus on what they are really saying about the sexuality of women, rises above the cult-worship enjoyed by these directors.

In a chapter that may take some readers by surprise, Mellon praises the work of Mae West in her early films. In spite of some vulgarity and tawdriness, West is thoroughly comfortable about her own sexuality, and though she uses it to her advantage with men, she is anything but self-hating and masochistic, a state of mind considered "natural" by contemporary directors and performers.

Rosen, Marjorie. *Popcorn Venus.* **New York: Coward, McCann and Geoghegan, 1973. 448p.**

Kitsch criticism, the study of popular culture, is almost always entertaining, and when employed by an astute critic, it can be revealing and provocative. For example, George Orwell made some discerning comments about the British when he interpreted their popular taste for crime stories and "penny dreadfuls."

In her book, Marjorie Rosen has assigned herself the difficult task of interpreting several decades of the American experience by examining the ways in which women have been portrayed on the motion picture screen. The job necessarily calls for a broad knowledge of that media as well as reliable critical acumen. It also calls for a sound knowledge of American social history. Rosen is weak in the latter, and this shows up in odd ways such as her use of improper terminology — "suffragettes" for the American suffragists, and the redundant prefix when she talks about "profeminists" and "promilitants." But she is considerably more at home when she discusses films and the world they create. "As long as movies exist," she says, "so does the danger that we will surrender ourselves unquestionably to their instant make-overs and portable ideals... Movies are escape. And we annoint the actresses embodying our fantasies as deities, our Popcorn Venuses."

She organizes her investigation of the portrayal of women in films by showing how women were being depicted in successive decades: flappers and vamps in the 20's; Rosie the Riveter in the 40's; Marilyn Monroe and other mammary types in the 50's, and so on. Her chapter on the 30's, a period which produced some fine films with women in strong roles contains some good observations. Questioning the historic truth of this positive portrayal of women, Rosen says "It was a belated distortion of the truth of woman's social role. In the name of escapism, films were guilty of extravagant misrepresentations, exuding a sense of well-being to the nation in general and women in particular. In fact, precisely the opposite was true." To prove this point, Rosen includes government labor statistics, descriptions of contemporary events, and the plots of the books people were reading.

She is at her best, though, when she describes individual films, the actresses who starred in them, and how they created stereotypes about women. She has boundless enthusiasm for her subject, but of the sort that is often expressed in that attention-getting prose style usually associated with the advertising world. For instance, in introducing her chapter about the films of the 40's she says: "On December 7, 1941, the Japanese bombed hell out of Pearl Harbor, Johnny got his gun. America mobilized. And social roles shifted with a speed that would have sent Wonder Woman into paroxysms of power pride."

Readers may find that a little of such peppy prose goes a long way, so that reading the book straight through may be a chore. However, taken in part, it is a fine reference book which brings useful commentary about and some excellent descriptions of the images of women in the history of the American film.

Rule, Jane. *Lesbian Images.* **Garden City, New York: Doubleday, 1975. 245p.**

Jane Rule is a Canadian writer and academic who happens to be a lesbian. In this book, she presents a survey of the attitudes other writers have had toward their lesbian experience, and she measures these attitudes against her own.

In discussing such writers as Gertrude Stein, Willa Cather, Radclyffe Hall and Elizabeth Bowen, Rule gets at the reality of lesbian experience not through questionnaires or other sociological techniques, but through literature. She is interested in how these writers interacted with their culture — how they were influenced by religious and psychological concepts and by their own personal experience — and how this was presented in their fiction. Although concerned with literary people, the book is not literary criticism; instead it is an attempt to understand lesbianism within the context of a culture which has long held it in contempt.

In two long, introductory chapters, Rule tries to trace the history of attitudes toward lesbians. That task is hampered by the lack of information about homosexual women, a fact Rule acknowledges to be the result not so much of women living outside the law, but beneath it. Beyond fragments of Sappho's poetry, not much is known about women loving women in Greek life. There are conjectures, but few facts, about homosexuality and prostitution being part of early religious ceremonies. In Jewish history, all homosexuality was considered a crime because it stopped procreation, a situation Jews could not afford. Christianity inherited the Jewish negative attitude toward homosexuality and assumed additional sanctions against all unmarried sexual activity. To this day, homosexuality is considered a sin by most organized religions, a circumstance that puts the religiously inclined homosexual in the position of either leading a double life or fighting within these institutions for reforms.

In a chapter on attitudes of psychiatrists, Rule contends that the profession has simply translated from moral into medical language the taboo against homosexuality. Although Havelock Ellis had an enlightened attitude, Freud tended to ignore his work, and proceeded to see things only within the framework he himself established. Rule goes over the Freudian notion that the clitoris is an inferior male organ, the theory which led to the idea of the vaginal orgasm. Its implication for the lesbian is, of course, that homosexual activity is incomplete and infantile. Rule also takes issue with Helene Deutsch and Charlotte Wolff whose interpretations of sexual behavior were codified by Freud, and concludes that so damaging have the professionals been in interpreting sexual behavior that the field of psychiatry should be off-limits for anyone trying to understand the nature of lesbian experience.

By discussing various writers, Rule is able to present different ways in which they have handled their homosexuality. For instance, Radclyffe Hall, Gertrude Stein and Willa Cather all desired to be men, and by adapting male dress as Hall did, or by living the role of a husband, these women were admitting that men are superior to women. At the other extreme was Ivy Compton-Burnett who, Rule explains, was a private lesbian living what was probably an asexual life in platonic devotion to another woman.

With so much current fiction and non-fiction being written with lesbian themes, the chronicling of the lesbian sensibility ought to be less of a problem for future historians and literary critics. Rule anticipates this in the concluding chapters of her book which offer an analysis of some of the literature written in the last decade. In all, Rule's book is a valuable contribution, for it brings a sensitive and mature point of view to its subject.

Spacks, Patricia Meyer. *The Female Imagination.* **New York: Knopf, 1975. 326p.**

This book, literary criticism of a very high order, evaluates feminine psychology as it appears in novels, autobiographies and literary criticism by women writers. Spacks examines the writings of those women who best typify that quality of mind she calls ''the female imagination'' and isolates recurring themes that have engaged the minds of British and American women writers over three centuries.

In her opening chapter, called ''Theorists,'' Spacks analyzes works by Virginia Woolf, Mary Ellman and Kate Millett, women writers who have written about being women writers. The content, style and tone of their writing is examined, then undercut to reveal what, in Spacks's opinion, they have all unconsciously attempted to conceal about their feelings about being women writers, most particularly their feelings of anger. In the cases of Woolf and Ellman, Spacks finds that while they deal with anger in others, their own is evaded or denied, a phenomenon she finds recapitulated in her Wellesley students who fail to recognize themselves in the female characters they read about in the fiction she has assigned. In the case of Millett, Spacks insists that anger has at once set the tone and destroyed the effectiveness of *Sexual Politics,* the author's sympathetic responses having been reduced to the point where she can only care for other angry women.

Other chapters nicely describe female fictional characters in the work of Jane Austen, the Brontés, George Eliot and Virginia Woolf as well as more recent women authors. Often Spacks finds their characters to be passive beings, frustrated artists, adolescents, or domestic caretakers, the prime example of the latter being Mrs. Ramsey in Woolf's *To the Lighthouse.* In an especially illuminating chapter called ''The Adolescent as Heroine,'' Spacks offers sensitive interpretations of Catherine Earnshaw in Emily Bronté's *Wuthering Heights* and Esther Greenwood in Sylvia Plath's *The Bell Jar.* These characters represent the adolescent who, with her heightened sense of self-drama and conflict, becomes an exaggeration of all women. Spacks considers Esther a lineal descendent of Catherine, for both value their inability to adjust to the adult world, and at the same time, refuse to be treated like children. With temperaments that do not allow for compromise, along with a heightened sense of their own specialness, each character moves headlong to her destruction. Of these characters, Spacks says, ''More vividly than older women in fiction, they express women's anger and self-hatred and the feeling that there's no way out.''

The Female Imagination is a well conceived and accomplished book that does what literary criticism can do at its best. It offers us insights into new and established literary achievements and a vital and relevant perspective from which these achievements can be better understood and judged.

* * *

Feminist Art Program, California Institute of the Arts. *Anonymous was a Woman: A Documentation of the Women's Art Festival: A Collection of Letters to Young Women Artists.* **Valencia, Cal.: California Institute of the Arts, 1974. 137p.**

The aim of the Feminist Art Program is to present the point of view of women artists to the rest of the art world. Half of this book contains reproductions of work by young women artists; the other half is made up of letters written by older creative women offering commentaries and advice to younger women.

Hardwick, Elizabeth. *Seduction & Betrayal: Women and Literature.* **New York: Random House, 1974. 208p.**

Hardwick has brought together a collection of essays which discuss women as characters in or writers of literature. She deals with the Brontés, Ibsen's women, and Virginia Woolf, and has essays on Sylvia Plath and Zelda Fitzgerald. In discussing the two Americans whom she calls ''victims,'' she focuses on Plath's suicide and on Zelda's tragic relationship with Scott in order to explore the self-destructive impulse in both women.

Hess, Thomas B. and Elizabeth C. Baker, eds. *Art and Sexual Politics.* **New York: Macmillan, 1973. 150p.**

The contributors to this volume address themselves to the question of why there have been no great women artists. Their conclusion is that unlike creative writers who do not require extensive training, artists must have instruction, but until recently women have been excluded from classrooms and from apprenticeships.

Leighton, Jean. *Simone de Beauvoir on Woman.* **Rutherford, New Jersey: Fairleigh Dickinson University Press, 1975. 230p.**

Leighton analyzes the novels and autobiography of Simone de Beauvoir for her views on women. She concludes that de Beauvoir expresses a considerable amount of misogyny in her works, extolling such qualities as action, power, success and domination, and deprecating the traditionally feminine qualities of passivity and contemplation.

Munsterberg, Hugo. *A History of Women Artists.* **New York: Clarkson N. Potter, 1975. 150p.**

The author presents an extremely broad survey of women artists, covering many art forms — pottery, weaving, painting, graphics, sculpture and photography — from prehistoric times to the present.

Nemser, Cindy, *Art Talk.* **New York: Scribner's, 1975. 367p.**

Nemser, an art historian and editor of *The Feminist Art Journal,* conducted interviews with twelve women artists ranging in age from thirty-four to eighty-nine. She skillfully led her subjects into revealing discussions about themselves as women and as artists. The book has many handsome photographs of the artists and their work.

Marriage and Related Issues

Traditionally, marriage has been at the center of most women's lives. Like careers for men it has provided the social role which defines women's identity. In a society in which the married couple has been the social norm, single and divorced women were pitied. Recent literature on marriage shows that this point of view is becoming dated, for a growing number of women are choosing to reject traditional marriage, finding it incompatible with personal goals.

In her book *The Future of Marriage,* Jessie Bernard makes a fundamental distinction about traditional marriage by observing that within every union there are two marriages, the man's and the woman's. She points out that the woman's marriage is more difficult than the man's because a woman has been socialized to be dependent. By not preparing for an adult identity beyond being a wife and mother, a woman finds herself bonded to a life of service. The running of a home is her focus, and serving the needs of husband and children her primary responsibility. The reactions of many women to this submersion of their own needs has been a major cause of the social movement for women's liberation that began in the late 1960's. Judy Sullivan's *Mama Doesn't Live Here Anymore* is a biographical account of how one woman resolved the conflict over her obligations to her family and the freedom she felt she owed herself.

The recent literature about marriage is as much about marital separation as it is about successful marriage. According to Robert Weiss in his book, *Marital Separation,* almost half of the marriages in America are dissolved by separation or divorce. He suggests that this phenomenon is, in part, the result of the American preoccupation with self-realization, a state of mind which is affecting women in particular. His book is designed to prepare the recently separated for the unfamiliar new status of the single life.

How to cope with living alone is a theme that comes up again and again in these books on marriage, divorce and widowhood. Authors advise women to learn how to live alone and to have expectations for themselves independent from their functions within families.

This trend toward the rejection of traditional marriage has alarmed conservatives who view the preservation of the family as a fundamental American goal. Their opposition to the Equal Rights Amendment, the legalization of abortion and gay rights reflects their desire to retain the values of traditional marriage. They would insist that women return to the home.

Bernard, Jessie. *The Future of Marriage.* **New York: World, 1972. 367p.**

When Jessie Bernard began this book in 1969, she did not expect that it might become an all but insurmountable task to accumulate and interpret the latest available research on marriage trends. She had to revise the drafts of her study over and over again to account for the radical changes in attitudes toward marriage that took place in the late sixties. These changes were reflected in the women's liberation movement, the concept of no-fault divorce, new abortion laws, improvement of contraceptive devices, a greater tolerance for homosexuality and a more general tolerance of alternate lifestyles, including communal living.

In this book Bernard examines the nature of marriage and predicts the future of the relationship. She observes that in every union there are really two marriages: the man's and the woman's. The woman's marriage is by far the more difficult because women have been socialized to be docile and dependent. Shared responsibility in marital relationships will improve the woman's marriage, not necessarily at the expense of the man's but for the mutual benefit of both partners.

Bernard believes that there will be varying styles of marriage: the traditional one with which we are familiar; short term marriages between two people; and group marriage. She predicts that the trend toward unmarried couples living together will continue and become even more common than it is today.

Bernard regards not only mainstream male sociologists but also early women's movement theorists like Dana Densmore and Shulamith Firestone as major prophets of change. It is clear that Bernard, despite an established reputation based on forty years of work in family sociology, listened to and understood younger colleagues in the field. She describes a confrontation with a younger woman who objected to what seemed to her the insensitive non-involvement of the sociologist. Bernard accepted the objection and was amazed to find how unaware she had become of the real measure of women's unhappiness in marriage. "We documented *ad nauseum*," she says of herself and her colleagues, "the dependencies of wives rather than how to overcome them. We did all this under the illusion that such formulations of research questions demonstrated our objectivity."

The observation suggests that when a full-scale history of the women's movement is written, it ought to include consideration of the impact the movement has made on people whose professions insisted that they only describe and record.

Seidenberg, Robert. *Corporate Wives — Corporate Casualties.* New York: Amacom, 1973. 177p.

In 1972, Robert Seidenberg, a psychiatrist, wrote an essay which appeared in *The Wall Street Journal* called "Dear Mr. Success: Consider Your Wife." It discussed the damaging effects that frequent and continuous moves have on the wives of corporate executives. Although the effects of mobility on immigrants and migrant workers had been examined by historians and social scientists, very few studies on the mobile middle-class had appeared. The response to Seidenberg's essay was overwhelming; he was asked to develop the discussion into a book. He describes as his thesis "that when husband and wife adhere to their traditional roles, the conventional expectations arising from these roles demand exorbitant renunciations from the women. These excessive renunciations — not personal immaturities or childhood problems — are enough to account for the grave consequences that accrue."

For the husband, geographic moves generally bring enhancements — promotions, new challenges, and the stimulation for continued success. On the other hand, wives, whose personal identity apart from the care of children is tightly connected with the community, are unable to "transfer credentials," as Seidenberg puts it. Typically, their attachment is to community institutions where they have established reputations as able workers for schools, hospitals or churches. In addition, they have built friendships with other women; the need for a confidant is particularly necessary to women, according to Seidenberg.

Uprooted wives tend to blame themselves for not adjusting, for falling short of the ideal wife and mother. Some women become dependent on drugs or alcohol and/or become suicidal. At that point psychiatric help may be sought.

As one who has treated these women Seidenberg draws certain conclusions. It is not geographic relocation itself which is at fault but the societal values which instruct women to live within prescribed modes. Middle-class women are trained to live for and through others, to seek material success and a stable suburban home. Seidenberg states the problems inherent in these aims: it is psychologically impossible to live through others, and suburban life is intellectually and culturally sterile.

The most obvious solution is for women to enter the work force and to achieve their own executive suites. He suggests the restructuring of jobs so that more people will work part-time in order to avoid increasing unemployment. Other solutions include the creation of more imaginative living arrangements. Picking up cues from the young, Seidenberg suggests communal living or dual residence. There is already a precedent, particularly with academic couples, for wives to teach in locations hundreds of miles away from their husbands' jobs, constituting a sort of professional "jet set."

More generally, society's attitudes about marriage will no doubt change so that present middle-class goals may someday seem sentimental and passé. Seidenberg has identified a problem that is serious for some, and traced it to a society whose views, he hopes, are not as unshakeable as some would think.

Seidenberg, Robert. *Marriage Between Equals: Studies from Life and Literature.* New York: Anchor Press, 1973. 340p.

Seidenberg, a classically trained psychoanalyst, criticizes traditional marriage: the "natural" order of things, with a dominant husband and a submissive wife, is an arrangement which is damaging to both partners. He understands marriage to be a difficult relationship even for wives who are content to stay at home. For women who seek a professional career, the marital relationship can be disastrous. Apart from problems within the marriage, women are burdened by social attitudes which prevent them from undertaking careers in business and the professions.

Freud defined the institutions of the Church and the Army as homosexual. Seidenberg extends this observation to most other major institutions — big business, science, law and universities. Historically, women have been excluded and in effect have been persuaded to stay at home. But "motherhood has no future," Seidenberg points out, and women should continue to insist on their rightful places in any field. Often women themselves accept the societal view. Seidenberg quotes from Dr. Judith Kestenberg who writes extensively on the psychological need for women to be submissive to men or else suffer the consequences of neuroses. He points out that she herself is leading an active and rewarding professional life.

So against great odds, and with few well-wishers, how are women to succeed in marriage and in anything else? Seidenberg offers a humanistic suggestion, requesting couples to look at one another not as "I" and "it," but as "I" and "Thou," to use Martin Buber's terms, so that people see one another beyond the terms of what services they perform for one another. He points out that men appalled at racism very often show prejudice against their own wives.

Seidenberg hopes that the single state will gain respectability and that "marriage will cease to be the unalterable imperative" that it has been. He hopes for "a climate of understanding that may allow young people to work out their destinies with passion but also with autonomy which demands the elimination of power as an interpersonal demiurge, and with love which has an authentic concern for the identity of the other and self."

Sullivan, Judy. *Mama Doesn't Live Here Anymore.* New York: Arthur Fields, 1974. 243p.

Shortly after the first flood of press accounts of the Women's Liberation Movement, when bra-burning was the distorted symbol of feminist action, the media picked up on the issue of the "run-away wife" as a symbol of the havoc the new movement was creating. In several newspaper accounts, Judy Sullivan was described as a woman who had everything — a loving husband and child, and a beautiful home — who, God knows why, turned her back on it all and moved away to New York to start an independent life. It was implied that she gave up the American dream to act out a delayed adolescent fantasy.

In telling her own story, Judy Sullivan cuts through the distortions of the press and the myths of American family life to explain her need to take control of her own life. She describes how she satisfied that need.

Her background is not atypical. Raised in a small town, she married at eighteen and had a child before she could complete her college education. While her husband worked long hours, she was stranded in a suburb and experienced the housewife's malaise described by Betty Friedan in *The Feminine Mystique*. The monotony was broken when she went back to school and earned a master's degree in art history. But the turning point of her life came when she attended a summer workshop at a black college in the South, an experience she describes as her belated entrance into the 20th century. She met bright, dedicated people and was inspired to work at something she felt was important: a book about black people in art.

After that summer she felt alienated from the life she had previously lived and made plans to leave her husband. Her decision to leave her daughter behind was painful but practical. Sullivan was leaving with limited funds and with undetermined plans.

Her story can be considered a parable of our times. It instructs women not to be pressured into marrying young, and not to bear children without thought. Most of all, it dramatizes the need for women, like men, to have expectations about life apart from their functions within families. All of these messages have been stated in women's movement literature and by contemporary social scientists. But Judy Sullivan's first-hand account rids the message of abstraction and brings us into the context of a life with which many women can identify.

Weiss, Robert. *Marital Separation.* New York: Basic Books, 1975. 334p.

Robert Weiss, a sociologist, has designed this book for professionals working in family psychiatry, marriage counseling and related fields and by those who are undergoing the trials of marital separation. Its audience should be broader; it should be read by all those who are relatives or friends of the separated, a category that might very well apply to everybody in America. In addition to its adherence to professional standards in the presentation of sociological theory and data, the book contains insights that are more usually found in novels. Weiss describes the pain and anxiety that those undergoing marital separation experience before they achieve emotional and social adjustment.

Weiss wrote this book after originating and conducting "Seminars for the Separated," a course offered under the auspices of the Harvard Medical School. He worked with the problems of bereavement; his particular interest was in the psychology of attachment and loss. He realized that during separation and divorce people undergo a pattern of common experiences; the realization of this commonality helps them to cope and adjust. His course dealt with the reasons for separation, the emotional impact on the formerly married, the relationship between separating spouses, the relationship of each with family and friends, the problems with children, the problems with establishing a new life, and legal difficulties.

Separation occurs in almost half of all marriages. If this figure seems startling it must be remembered that not all marriages dissolve during the same year. The breakdown of so many marriages in this country, Weiss suggests, may be due to American preoccupation with self-realization which leads to intense impatience with barriers. Women in particular are leaving marriages that seem stifling.

The decision to end the marriage is only the first of a long series of problems. The loss experienced after separation is invariably intense. Weiss makes an important distinction between the loss of an attachment figure and loneliness. Loneliness is experienced only after the emotional link to the former husband or wife is finally given up. "They may be angry, even furious with one another; they may hate one another for past injuries and fear one another's next outburst of rage ... But when they actually consider leaving their marriage they become almost paralyzed with fear."

The ambivalence and pain of separation apparently take two to four years to disappear. In addition to handling depression, the newly separated must deal with the external problems of handling family, friends, and the children of the disrupted marriage.

Since there is no socially endorsed response to separation, the reception of the news by family members and friends is unpredictable and characterized by embarrassment and discomfort. The newly separated will feel out of place with friends whose entire social network is with other married couples and may eventually need to establish new links with other people who are newly single.

Children's responses will vary according to age. Younger children tend to blame themselves for their parents' separation; Weiss suspects they may prefer to feel guilt rather than face their own powerlessness in controlling the conditions of their lives. Adolescents' responses are more complicated. They may feel anger and embarrassment at the disruption. Children can be a burden to the custody-retaining parent and a source of deprivation to the parent who gives up custody. However, Weiss points to statistics that prove that the children of broken homes adjust, and that boys in fatherless homes nonetheless learn their appropriate sexual identity.

Weiss concludes that "separation seems to me like being packed off to a foreign country in which one is constantly confronted by new customs and new practices, and is constantly thrown off balance by the strangeness of other's reactions." He has provided his readers with a guide-book to this foreign land.

*   *   *

Caine, Lynn. *Widow.* New York: William Morrow, 1974. 222p.

Lynn Caine thought of her husband and herself as a "classy couple." They lived in New York, sent their two children to private school and summered in New England. Martin Caine was a lawyer earning a substantial living and Lynn Caine worked in publishing while a housekeeper ran things at home. The Caines shared a taste for fine food and wine, a love of classical music and took pleasure in each other's company. Then Martin Caine was told he had cancer, a disease which killed him after fourteen agonizing months.

His widow writes about the torment of those months and about the trauma of being a widow; about grief and loneliness; financial worries; the burden of caring for children; and the stigma of widowhood. Caine wrote her book as an exercise in self-awareness and as a warning to other women. She offers advice to help other women avoid the errors she made during a frightening time in her life when her judgment was unsound.

Dash, Joan. *A Life of One's Own: Three Gifted Women and the Men They Married.* **New York: Harper and Row, 1973. 388p.**

Joan Dash examines the lives of Margaret Sanger, Edna St. Vincent Millay and Maria Goeppert Mayer to discover the relationship of their success to the nature of their marriages. Mayer, the least well known of the three, is a Nobel laureate in nuclear physics and was married to a prominent chemist. Because the couple shared the excitement of a creative scientific life, the marriage endured even though Mayer was denied academic positions wherever her husband worked. In all three of these biographical essays, Dash illustrates the familiar problems facing talented women who try to combine domestic roles with career goals.

Kessler, Sheila. *The American Way of Divorce: Prescriptions for Change.* **Chicago: Nelson-Hall, 1975. 216p.**

This is a prescriptive book for the newly separated who need emotional support as they adjust to new roles. Kessler uses assertiveness-training techniques to instruct people on how to control their behavior so they can view themselves as successful people.

Keyes, Margaret F. *Staying Married.* **Millbrae, Cal.: Les Femmes, 1975. 157p.**

Keyes, a psychotherapist specializing in marriage therapy, believes that marriage is a relationship couples should try to preserve. Crises are an important element in marriage: partners must learn ways to overcome the defenses each builds up which can threaten the relationship. Her book describes techniques toward that goal.

Krantzler, Mel. *Creative Divorce: A New Opportunity for Personal Growth.* **New York: M. Evans, 1973. 268p.**

Krantzler leads divorce adjustment seminars on the West Coast. His purpose is to offer emotional support to the newly separated and help them to evaluate and respect themselves so that they can go back to being single with self-awareness and self-esteem.

Lederer, William and Don D. Jackson. *The Mirages of Marriage.* **New York: Norton, 1968. 473p.**

The authors find that so much myth and idealism surround marriage that those in trouble cannot find the help they need until they learn to separate false assumptions from reality.

Lewis, Alfred Allan and Barrie Berns. *Three Out of Four Wives: Widowhood in America.* New York: Macmillan, 1975. 216p.

There are eleven million women in America who are widows. Apart from the trauma of bereavement, widows often endure financial hardship and the sudden loss of social status. The authors interviewed a group of them and concluded that the American culture is hostile to single women.

Lopata, Helena Z. *Widowhood in an American City.* Cambridge, Mass.: Schenkman, 1973. 369p.

In this scholarly study Lopata, a sociologist, interviewed over three hundred widows fifty years of age or more living in Chicago. She examined particular social and personal aspects of their lives in order to measure the women's adjustment to their changing status in society.

O'Brien, Patricia. *The Woman Alone.* New York: Quadrangle, 1973. 285p.

O'Brien, an investigative journalist, left her husband and family temporarily in order to explore womanhood and the single life. Through her own experiences and from interviews with single women, she learned about the problems facing single women in a society prejudiced against the woman who is alone. O'Brien concludes that everyone should plan life without expecting to marry, the vagaries of life being what they are. One should expand the possibilities of living alone — not by attending church groups or Parents Without Partners meetings — but by learning how to enjoy one's own self.

O'Neill, Nena and George O'Neill. *Open Marriage: A New Life Style for Couples.* New York: M. Evans, 1972. 287p.

Deploring the numbers of failed marriages, the O'Neills set out to prescribe a new view of marriage that incorporates the needs of modern couples. They define open marriage as: ''an honest and open relationship between two people, based on the equal freedom and identity of both partners. It involves a verbal, intellectual and emotional commitment to the right of each to grow as an individual within the marriage.'' In an open marriage, they say, couples view life as a cooperative venture and do not interfere with their partner's self expression by setting up patterns of dependency.

Peck, Ellen and Judith Senderowitz, eds. *Pronatalism: The Myth of Mom & Apple Pie.* New York: Crowell, 1974. 333p.

The editors, advocates of the child-free marriage, view parenthood as culturally compulsory, not the result of instinct or of biological necessity. In this book they include twenty-four essays, some by well known people like Gael Greene, Stewart Mott and Betty Rollin, who have chosen not to rear children. They discuss such issues as the relationship between marital breakdown and children in the family, and the responsibility of the media in promoting the glorification of parenthood.

Radl, Shirley L. *Mother's Day Is Over*. New York: Charterhouse, 1973. 238p.

Shirley Radl is a mother who loves her two children but does not love being a mother. Like other recent writers who discuss the negative aspects of child rearing, she feels that motherhood has been so glorified that women suppress the rage and guilt they feel if they do not like the role. Radl describes how children can ruin the quality of a marriage, drain a mother's energy and destroy her personal property and sense of self.

Rheinstein, Max. *Marriage Stability, Divorce and the Law*. Chicago: University of Chicago Press, 1972. 482p.

Rheinstein is concerned with ways in which the law and the society can help to prevent the mass phenomenon of failed marriages in America. He dismisses the idea of strict divorce statutes as an effective means of preventing or even reducing the incidence of marriage breakdown. Instead he advocates the discouragement of teen-age marriages, the institution of trial marriages and the availability of family life education and family counseling.

Sheresky, Norman and Marya Mannes. *Uncoupling: The Art of Coming Apart*. New York: Viking, 1972. 208p.

The authors offer a rational approach to divorce, one which avoids matrimonial warfare. They feel that the courtroom is a risky place to attempt to settle complicated break-ups by handing out swift emotional retribution for marital wrongs. The court can only dissolve the marriage, divide property and award custody of children. Couples must do the rest.

Smith, James R. and Lynn G. Smith, eds. *Beyond Monogamy: Recent Studies of Sexual Alternatives in Marriage*. Baltimore: Johns Hopkins University Press, 1974. 336p.

This collection contains essays by such experts in the fields of marriage and sexuality as Alex Comfort, Albert Ellis and Jessie Bernard who describe changes that have been occurring in monogamous marriage. They point to the effect of innovative behavior such as "open marriage," mate swapping and group marriage on traditional marriage.

Whelan, Elizabeth M. *A Baby? ... Maybe: A Guide to Making the Most Fateful Decision of Your Life*. Indianapolis: Bobbs-Merrill, 1975. 237p.

Whelan, a professional in the health field, wrote this book as the result of her own ambivalence about choosing parenthood. She presents an articulate summary of arguments on either side, information she evaluated after interviewing older couples, some with children and some without. Having no vested interest in what other people decide, Whelan is interested only in helping people to make their own decisions.

Prostitution

Surprisingly few scholarly books or first hand accounts of prostitution have been written. In the past, particularly during the Progressive Era, most books on the subject were moralistic in tone and reformist in intent. Writers were not interested in presenting sympathetic accounts of the lives of prostitutes, and few prostitutes wrote about their own lives.

However, since the advent of the women's movement, books which offer insights into the lives of prostitutes have begun to appear. Both Gail Sheehy and Kate Millett interviewed prostitutes, bringing a sense of the realities of "the life" to their books. Their books also illustrate that in the early 70's some feminists viewed prostitutes as the most oppressed women in a male-dominated society. This image was not acceptable to prostitutes themselves who were hostile to well-meaning feminists and resented their interference. What was generally agreed upon, however, was the injustice of the legal system which arrests prostitutes and not their customers.

The scholarly investigation of prostitution is just beginning. Historical studies in particular have appeared in the last few years: Judith Walkowitz's "We Are Not Beasts of the Field: Prostitution and the Campaign Against the Contagious Diseases Act, 1869-1886." Doctoral dissertation, University of Rochester, 1973-74; Ruth Rosen's "The Lost Sisterhood: Prostitution During the Progressive Era." Doctoral Dissertation, Univ. of California, Berkeley, 1976; *The Maimie Papers,* edited by Ruth Rosen and Sue Davidson. The Feminist Press, 1977.

Millett, Kate. *The Prostitution Papers: A Candid Dialogue.* New York: Avon, 1973. 160p.

> Kate Millett, long interested in creating new literary forms for the expression of feminist themes, experiments in *The Prostitution Papers* with such a form. This work originally appeared in the anthology, *Woman in Sexist Society,* edited by Vivian Gornick and Barbara Moran, in which the text ran as four columns running across two pages, a metaphor for the musical quartet which could provide, Millett says, "a four-cornered conversation encompassing very different persons, whose voices were instruments expressing their diverse experience." The

135

''four voices'' are transcripts of tapes that Millett made with two prostitutes, a feminist lawyer who defended prostitutes in court, and finally a statement by Millett herself. In this Avon edition, the pieces run consecutively, a format which loses the book's original intent. It thus becomes a series of four monologues which offer insights about prostitution from a feminist perspective.

The first speaker is J, a white woman who drifted into the life because she needed money, the only reason, she says, that anyone goes into prostitution. At the time of writing, she has given up the life in order to go back to school and is pursuing a graduate degree. With the help of a therapist she is able to acknowledge her hatred of men. She says, ''They put you down for what they have made of you.''

The other prostitute is a black woman and a former drug addict who says, ''Prostitution goes with addiction. Because it's a means of supporting a habit. Something that'll sell when nothing else will. I don't think you ever get too sick or too ragged or too ugly or too beat up to turn a trick.'' In discussing the black man she says, ''Charlie's his role model. He has no other. The white man is the *only* man. You give a black woman to a black man and she'll remind him of his mother who he wanted desperately to get away from. She's spent a great part of her time doing what he calls 'suppressing' him, that is, keeping him from being a white man.''

Millett's statement is in her inimical style — that mixture of fluid academese and feminist anger. ''Everything I've read on prostitution,'' she says, ''pisses me off ... The smug stupidity with which people are accustomed to discuss the subject is fairly outrageous.'' She blames the poor economic position of women along with the psychological damage inflicted upon them by the sex-role conditioning of the patriarchal society. As a partial remedy for the historic injustice to prostitutes, she insists that prostitution should be removed from the criminal code, for it is outrageous that the seller is prosecuted while the buyer goes free.

The relationship between prostitutes and the law is the substance of a statement by Liz Schneider who, as an attorney, has provided civil rights counsel at the arraignments of prostitutes. She was shocked and disappointed by the impossibility of establishing a relationship with the women she saw in court. Prostitutes were not used to receiving outside help and did not accept her feminist good-will. ''The distance I feel from the women when I'm in court,'' Schneider says, ''the familiarity with which they relate to the men — the clerks, the judges, the cops — is so heart-breaking to me that I don't know how to bear it.'' The prostitutes refused to talk with her about the women's movement. She found herself feeling useless and helpless within the dynamics of courtroom scenes where women were taking the blame as a kind of nod to public decorum, amid the derision and contempt of men.

Millett's book provides a perspective which is rare in the literature about prostitution: the point of view of the women involved rather than the views of social analysts. The book convinces one of the need for each disenfranchised group to do its own organizing.

Sheehy, Gail. *Hustling: Prostitution in Our Wide-Open Society.* **New York: Delacorte, 1973. 273p.**

Sheehy has written an exposé of prostitution in New York, reporting on the wide range of participants from girls on the street to high-priced call girls who work out of East Side apartments. She describes pimps and madams, the police, and the owners of the tawdry hotels catering to the street trade. Interesting facts are presented — that many young prostitutes come from the Midwest, particularly Minnesota, and that many high-priced call girls are suburban housewives earning a second income for their families.

Although feminists have tried to meet with prostitutes, the results have been disastrous. Sheehy describes a conference held in 1972 between feminists and prostitutes which almost wound up in a brawl. Sheehy says, ''Working girls see feminists in very basic, competitive, American capitalist terms. 'They're trying to butt into everything, grab the publicity and wreck our business. How many of them can make $1,000 a week lying down?' a call girl I later met summed up the prevailing attitude.''

The overriding theme of Sheehy's book is that prostitution provides the occasion for large-scale corruption in New York and other cities. While the women do all the work and face legal jeopardy, pimps and property owners rake in huge profits at little risk.

*   *   *

Benjamin, Harry and R.E.L. Masters. *Prostitution and Morality.* **London: Souvenir Press, 1965. 495p.**

Benjamin, a physician who is aware of the hypocrisy in our society about prostitution, advocates that it should be an accepted profession, not illegal. In an intelligent society, the service of sex can find a useful and beneficial place, he says. He believes that present attitudes are tightly bound up with politics and theology.

Bullough, Vern L. *The History of Prostitution.* **New Hyde Park, New York: University Books, 1964. 304p.**

Bullough has written this admittedly superficial history of prostitution in the absence of any prior, more thorough study. He hopes that his book, which covers primitive societies to the modern day, will prompt a serious study of the field. The book contains little analytical material but may be useful for its bibliography.

Winick, Charles and Paul M. Kinsie. *The Lively Commerce: Prostitution in the United States.* **Chicago: Quadrangle, 1971. 320p.**

This book, which claims to be the first serious study of prostitution to appear in America in half a century, approaches the subject from all but the most essential point of view, that of the prostitutes themselves. The authors report about pimps, madams, brothels and even clients, but seldom present a sympathetic account of prostitutes. Compounding this omission is the authors' insistence on dredging up old and tired dirty jokes about prostitutes. They claim that this technique reveals attitudes and gives sociological credence to their analysis.

Psychology

Research on the psychology of women has taken on a new vitality in response to the women's movement and the issues it has raised. Although the points of view of authors are as varied as the special areas they represent, all are interested in the fundamental question of identifying the psychological needs of women.

Feminists are challenging Freud and the value of psychoanalytic theory to women today as therapy or as theory on the nature of women. Phyllis Chesler believes that women have been socialized into dependent roles. By suppressing their natural protest against their lack of autonomy, they become depressed and are candidates for psychiatric treatment. To Chesler, mental health for women will come from independent life styles and not from therapy. Robert Seidenberg applies a similar feminist analysis to explain the significance of certain phobias suffered by women.

That socialization has damaged women is the prevailing theme of much of the new psychological literature on women. Researchers interested in achievement motivation point out that sex-role stereotyping has prevented women from attaining career success. Behaviorists believe that by undergoing assertiveness training, women can be conditioned to change their dependent and submissive roles. Whether their emphasis is on theory or practice, current researchers are providing stimulating and valuable new material on the psychology of women.

Chesler, Phyllis. *Women & Madness.* Garden City, New York: Doubleday, 1972. 359p.

Phyllis Chesler, a feminist psychologist, explores the high incidence of madness in women from a perspective which includes a study of literature and mythology as well as social science methodology. That women make up more than sixty percent of hospitalized mental patients is a symptom of the real problem, the absence of women's power over the means of production and reproduction in this society. To Chesler, women are losers. They are socialized to marry, to become the caretakers of husbands and children, nurturing everyone but themselves. To illustrate the origins and models of contemporary female personality, Chesler refers to the myth of Demeter and her daughters.

139

Demeter is the goddess of life, corn and grain. Her daughter, Persephone, is abducted and raped by Pluto, god of the underworld. In great sorrow and fury, Demeter refuses to let any crop grow until her daughter is returned to her. Ultimately, Persephone is allowed to return to her mother for most of the year, but remains with her husband during winter, when no crops can grow. Chesler comments that "while Demeter protects and 'saves' her daughter, Persephone is still denied uniqueness and individuality. Both women still symbolize the sacrifices of self that biology and culture demand of women." Chesler sees contemporary marriage as the equivalent of the powerlessness of women portrayed in the myth, and the modern mother-daughter relationship as one of abandonment, with mothers handing over their dependent daughters to the grown up world of men.

A major result of the profound denial of autonomy for women, says Chesler, is that psychotherapy has become a common form of treatment for women, and depression a major female disorder. Chesler includes interviews with hospitalized women, examines the values of the institution of private therapy, and discusses the phenomenon of sex between patient and male therapist. She concludes that the vulnerability of women will disappear only when they experience profound psychological changes leading to independence.

Deutsch, Helene. *Confrontations With Myself: An Epilogue.* **New York: Norton, 1973. 217p.**

Helene Deutsch refers to these memoirs as an epilogue to her earlier major work, *The Psychology of Women* (1944), a book she also considers to be autobiographical.

Born in Poland and educated in Vienna where she met Freud and became his disciple, Deutsch lived through times that were intellectually and politically challenging. Before her association with Freud, she was involved in the socialist cause. Some of her most vivid recollections of this period are those of the women she met in the movement. "Both of these women," she says of Rosa Luxemburg and Angelica Balabanoff, "are classic examples of the process of sublimation. Destructive impulses were harnessed to work for social justice and peace among nations." And of Bertha von Suttner, Deutsch observes that she "did not resemble in the least one's image of the gentle, peace loving woman... Her struggles for peace were a reaction formation against her own aggressiveness."

The descriptions are typical of the kind one may expect of a psychoanalyst of Deutsch's training. They tend to be reductive, to ignore the other sources of human motivation and to trivialize the aims and efforts of the women she knew. Another problem with her book, perhaps due to the fact that it was written when she was eighty-nine, is its selectiveness, its inclination to emphasize certain memories that fascinate her rather than to provide us with a systematic narrative and interpretation of her long life. She includes, for example, certain memories of her childhood because she was surprised that they had not come up in the course of her analysis.

Nevertheless, her book describes most vividly her association with Freud and her move to America. Until the 1930's when she left Vienna because of the Nazi threat, she worked with Freud first as his pupil and then as his associate in the training of other analysts. Leaving Freud, who ultimately went to London, was a difficult separation for Deutsch. Although she continued her work upon her arrival in Boston, her career did not seem to her to have the same intense focus, and she eventually chose a life of rustic peace on a farm she and her husband bought in New Hampshire. When her husband died she withdrew from her work at the Boston Psychoanalytic Institute and called herself ''a stranger with a 'brilliant' past.''

The strength of this book is Helene Deutsch's analysis of old age. Since she highlights her total career in ways that interested her at the time of the writing, one gets a limited view of what was undoubtedly a dynamic and dramatic life. But her reactions to old age are truly moving. She acknowledges her loneliness since the death of her husband, and sees it as ''a hunger to fill my depleted existence with the past.'' As further justification for writing this kind of book during advanced age, she discusses how ''the inner mechanisms geared to the future must be given up, and [that] this further clears the way for the return of the past.''

Franks, Violet and Vasanti Burtle, ed. *Women in Therapy: New Perspectives for a Changing Society.* **New York: Brunner/Mazel, 1974. 441p.**

Most of the contributors to this anthology believe that women have traditionally been treated by psychotherapists as incomplete or derivative males. The editors, disputing such an approach, have set out to explore the contemporary status of psychotherapy and its response to the changing role of women in today's society. Accordingly, the largest sections of the book deal with cultural influences on therapist and patient, patterns of problematic behavior in women, and the range and effectiveness of modern methods of treatment.

The book attempts to cover a great deal of material; thus it may seem superficial to the professional and confusing to the general reader. But the issues dealt with here are important and responsibly discussed. Included in the volume, for example, are illuminating examinations of what women expect of themselves, and men of them; the prejudices and preconceptions patients have regarding the sex of their therapists; and the problems that are increasingly affecting women — depression, phobias and alcoholism.

Suzanne Keller writes the concluding chapter as a summary and a criticism of the assumption that women are altogether repressed. In effect she draws up a balance sheet, weighing the advantages many women enjoy — economic security, relief from the pressure to achieve, and the ability to express themselves emotionally — against detriments to their mental health — decreased autonomy, constraints upon personal development, ignorance and lack of training, and categorical subjugation to men. Not unexpectedly, her conclusion is that ''the female role exchanges autonomy for security.''

In spite of this general finding, Keller wisely suggests that therapists ought to resist the temptation to discover more universal conceptions of womanhood, that if they wish to be effective they must be sensitive to the needs of individual women, taking into account their age, class, educational level and style of life.

Mander, Anica Vesel and Anne Kent Rush. *Feminism as Therapy.* **New York: Random House, 1974. 127p.**

The authors worked in women's groups in the San Francisco area and developed the process of consciousness raising into what they describe as one of the healing arts. For political reasons, they reject Freudianism and other traditional approaches to psychotherapy, finding them male-dominated and capitalistic. They believe that since our culture has taught women to be distrustful of one another, women must now be encouraged to be mutually supportive. In short, feminism for the authors has become a vital form of therapy.

In addition to what now may be called classic consciousness-raising sessions wherein participants are conditioned to listen to and learn from other women, the authors have promoted transactional analysis meetings. By role-playing, women gain insights into such key relationships as mother-daughter and husband-wife.

The book derives from deeply held feminist convictions and offers descriptions of treatment which evolved from the women's movement. Such therapy exposes women to companionable and supportive peers and opens up to them the possibility of making choices free from daunting preconceptions of their place in the world.

Miller, Jean Baker, ed. *Psychoanalysis and Women.* **Baltimore: Penguin Books, 1973. 415p.**

Like other important fields in the human sciences, psychoanalysis has felt the impact of the women's movement. In her excellent anthology, Jean Baker Miller brings together sixteen fine essays on women written by well-known analysts, with the intention of allowing us to see the past and present state of the art.

In her own concluding essay, "New Issues, New Approaches," Miller observes that "the field has always been in a state of tension with the society in which it exists." She notes with interest that the papers contained in her book have been written at times when the "woman question" has been particularly acute: the twenties; the period during and immediately after World War II; and again beginning in the late sixties.

Modern-day feminists have accused analysts, and rightly so, Miller feels, of assuming a submissive role for women by viewing them as the less important sex. Accordingly, treatment has often involved the process of helping women accept and adjust to their roles as wives and mothers, with little regard for personal fulfillment. Both the treatment and the attitude that informs it are commonly laid at the feet of Freud and his "phallocentric" theory of women, his idea of penis envy and its implication that women see themselves as lesser beings, unfinished males.

The writers within this anthology challenge Freud's maxim that anatomy is destiny. They explore the possible bases for the construction of a new psychology of women, one that takes closer account of cultural conditioning and the interrelationships between biology and psychology.

Miller divides her book into three sections: "Pertinent Pioneers"; "The Emergence of New Evidence"; "Present Problems and Some Future Possibilities." The first part contains well-known essays by Karen Horney, Clara Thompson and, among others, a brilliant piece by Gregory Zilboorg. Zilboorg provides a convincing explanation for the reasons for man's fundamental hostility to women, and for the failure of psychoanalysis to account for this phenomenon. He calls upon a knowledge of history and anthropology, particularly including the writings of Lester Ward, to support his theory that in a period preceding recorded history women had been in a position of supremacy. He says "that it is the discovery by man of his paternity that made him assert himself and perform the revolution of dichotomizing the woman from her high biological position of privilege and punitive maternal authority." Zilboorg believes, therefore, "that it is not penis envy on the part of woman, but woman envy on the part of man, that is psychogenetically older and therefore more fundamental."

Representative of those included in the section on "New Evidence" is Robert Stoller whose concern has been with the biological bases of human psychology. By observing physiologically imperfect females, he has concluded that hermaphrodites, if considered female by their parents, will identify as female, and male if their parents think of them as such. He offers what could be the last word on the subject of penis envy: "If Freud had treated a woman without a vagina, I think he would have seen that the only thing a woman wants more than a penis is a vagina. It is only when a woman has normal genitalia that she can afford the luxury of wanting a penis."

The third section of the anthology contains papers by analysts having a discernible feminist bias. Of these, Alexandra Symonds and Robert Seidenberg deal with phobia in women, presenting points of view which depart from classic interpretations of anxiety. More women than men, they find, fall victim to phobia, agrophobia in particular. Their revisionist view of this illness is that it is symptomatic of sex role conflict, that women, usually after marriage, become excessively dependent, that their lives become constricted often to the point where they become immobile, and cannot leave their homes. Calling this condition "the trauma of eventlessness," or "existential agrophobia," Seidenberg argues that in addition to the orthodox explanation of trauma, defined as "a startling experience, a shock with lasting effects," there is another possibility — the absence of stimuli. A life devoid of even the possibility of challenge can be just as damaging to the ego, he feels, as one of the more usual assaults from without.

The papers brought together in this volume are uniformly stimulating and readable, appealing to both the professional and lay reader. Like Freud, the writers are innovative and erudite, bringing to their interpretations not only persuasive reasoning, but a knowledge of mythology, literature and anthropology. In all an excellent collection.

Mitchell, Juliet. *Psychoanalysis and Feminism.* **New York: Pantheon, 1974. 456p.**

Juliet Mitchell wrote this book in reaction to feminists who discredit Freud and his psychoanalytic theories. She thinks that a rejection of Freud and psycho-analysis is fatal for feminism, for she interprets his theories not as a recommendation for, but as an analysis of a patriarchal society. Since the understanding of self is a fundamental aim for feminists, Mitchell believes that Freud's discoveries of the unconscious mind and the theory of infantile sexuality are essential tools for personal growth. Instead of Freud, Reich and Laing have become increasingly prominent as psycho-political ideologists to feminists, and Mitchell argues against their philosophies in terms of what is best for women. She also takes issue with individual feminists — de Beauvoir, Friedan, Figes and Millett — and tries to show that their arguments against Freud have been aimed at a debased notion of his theories, and not at his genuine concept of psychoanalysis.

Mitchell has written a book dealing with complicated material in a style that puts great demands on her readers. Those who can survive the challenge of her prose will benefit from her learned analyses.

Strouse, Jean, ed. *Women & Analysis: Dialogues on Psychoanalytic Views of Femininity.* **New York: Grossman, 1974. 375p.**

In this anthology, Jean Strouse provides a valuable resource for readers interested in the relationship between psychoanalytic thinking and feminist awareness. Concerned that Freud and others have been dismissed by contemporary feminists, Strouse attempts to clarify and to put into historic perspective the body of thought presented by psychoanalytic writers from the 1920's to the present. She says in her introduction, ''I have tried to select articles and writers that represent the development and variety of psychoanalytic views, and deal with the significant concepts involved in analytic thinking about women: biological determinism, passivity, masochism, penis envy, bisexuality, the female castration complex, childbearing, dependency, the social and cultural roles of women, and the development of sexual identity.''

The structure she employs in accomplishing these goals is to present the writings in pairs. So, for instance, she asked Juliet Mitchell, Elizabeth Janeway and Margaret Mead to write new essays in response to Freud's three theoretical pieces about women. This proves to be an ingenious device, for not only does it get to the heart of the issues she wishes explored, but it provides a responsible method of putting those issues into a context that is most helpful to contemporary students of the field.

*   *   *

Bardwick, Judith M. *Psychology of Women: A Study of Bio-Cultural Conflicts.* New York: Harper and Row, 1971. 242p.

Bardwick views the development of individual identity as inextricably linked with sex-role socialization. Society prefers the male role; the female therefore has conflicts about identity and is unsure about the nature of personal achievement. Bardwick states that changes in traditional role divisions are essential to the healthy psychological development of women.

———, ed. *Readings on the Psychology of Women.* New York: Harper and Row, 1972. 335p.

In this anthology, Bardwick offers a potpourri of essays which either directly or indirectly deal with the psychology of women. Most of the articles have appeared in print before, although there is one by Alice Rossi, ''The Roots of Ambivalence in American Women,'' which has not. The book covers such topics as the development of sex differences, socialization, the women's liberation movement, women and their bodies, women and mental health. Since the readings cover such broad fields, the book is useful to those looking for introductory material on the psychology of women.

Bloom, Lynn Z., Karen Coburn and Joan Pearlman. *The New Assertive Woman.* New York: Delacorte, 1975. 230p.

The women's movement has generally stressed not only the need for social changes but the need for women to change within themselves. A fundamental disadvantage for many women is that they have been conditioned to be non-assertive. The authors of this book have developed a training course which teaches women how to gain and then to accept power in interpersonal relationships. Such strength has been thought to be unfeminine, and the authors show how women can be taught to overcome that feeling through exercises.

deCastillejo, Irene Claremont. *Knowing Women.* New York: Putnam's, 1973. 188p.

The author, a Jungian analyst, describes women as psychologically different from men: a woman's mind operates at a level of ''diffuse awareness'' very different from the ''focused consciousness'' of men. She interprets our male-dominated society as imbalanced, for it expresses the values inherent in the male psychology while ignoring the female.

Denmark, Florence, ed. *Who Discriminates Against Women?* Beverly Hills: Sage, 1974. 143p.

Most of the papers in this collection were delivered at meetings of the American Psychological Association in 1972. Each deals with a particular source of discrimination against women — parents, men, other women and institutions. Together they reiterate the difficult position of women in the society, particularly those who aspire to independent lives.

Group for the Advancement of Psychiatry. Committee on the College Student. *The Educated Woman: Prospects and Problems.* **New York: Scribner's, 1975. 188p.**

The college-educated woman faces dilemmas which, though not new, are at least discussed today in new ways. This book offers guidelines for women who aspire to careers as well as marriage. Among its recommendations are: more open definitions of femininity and masculinity; an emphasis on individual autonomy rather than an adaptation of sex-role stereotypes; more women in faculty positions to act as role models.

Hammer, Signe. *Daughters and Mothers: Mothers and Daughters.* **New York: Quadrangle, 1975. 175p.**

Inspired to a large extent by Nancy Chodorow's essay, "Family Structure and Female Personality" found in the anthology *Woman, Culture and Society,* Signe Hammer explores the relationship between mothers and daughters. She shows the inextricable connections in the lives of generations of women. Through informal interviews she evokes discussions that illustrate the dependency among women influenced by cultural expectations.

Horney, Karen. *Feminine Psychology.* **Edited and with an introduction by Harold Kelman. New York: Norton, 1967. 269p.**

Horney, an eminent European psychoanalyst who died in 1952, is known primarily for her theoretical differences with Freud. Human behavior, according to Horney, is determined culturally as well as biologically. Women really envy the superior opportunities that society offers men which to Horney is the real meaning of the concept of "penis envy." In this book, Harold Kelman, the editor, has brought together Horney's writings on feminine psychology, some of which have never before appeared in English translation. Included here are essays on such subjects as frigidity, the problem of monogamy, maternal conflicts, feminine masochism and the neurotic need for love.

Kent, Patricia. *An American Woman and Alcohol.* **New York: Holt, Rinehart and Winston, 1967. 184p.**

For both men and women, alcoholism is an individual reaction to stress. But in this book, Kent examines the situations most stressful to women — the search for approval and a sense of belonging. Kent writes a straightforward account of why some women become alcoholic, and then offers suggestions for overcoming the addiction.

Mednick, Martha, Sandra Tangri and Lois Hoffman, eds. *Women and Achievement.* **Washington, D.C.: Hemisphere, 1975. 447p.**

The contributors to this excellent volume are mainly psychologists concerned with the question of achievement motivation in women. Their papers reflect current research and theoretical concerns in a growing field which had formerly focused entirely on the psychology of men. Such topics as sex-role socialization, attitudes toward success, and the effects of job discrimination are discussed by Inge Broverman, Valerie Oppenheimer, Matina Horner and Helen Astin in valuable articles containing excellent bibliographies. The book is a fund of information for professionals and advanced students interested in the social psychology of women and in motivational theory in particular.

Osborn, Susan M. and Gloria G. Harris. *Assertive Training for Women.* Springfield, Ill.: Thomas, 1975. 204p.

Assertive training, an approach that is growing in popularity among those in the mental health field, deals directly with overt behavior rather than with unconscious thoughts and feelings. Many feel that it is particularly appropriate for treating women who have been socialized to be submissive and dependent. Although primarily intended for professionals, this book presents materials in a nontechnical style and will be useful for the general reader.

Phelps, Stanlee and Nancy Austin. *The Assertive Woman.* San Luis Obispo, Cal.: Impact, 1975. 177p.

The authors submit that there are three ways in which people react to life's situations — passively, aggressively, or assertively. They explain why the last is best, and then offer a manual by which women can diagnose their responses to various situations and learn how inappropriate reactions can be faced and changed.

Sherman, Julia. *On the Psychology of Women: A Survey of Empirical Studies.* Springfield, Ill.: Thomas, 1971. 304p.

This book is a review of the literature on the psychology of women collected before the new emphasis inspired by the women's movement shifted the direction of research toward motivational theory. Sherman's book emphasizes biology because the author feels that the reproductive cycle is inexorably connected to psychological response. Nevertheless she does not ignore social causes of behavior. The bibliographic information collected here is invaluable; this is a vitally important book for the researcher.

Ulanov, Ann Belford. *The Feminine: In Jungian Psychology and Christian Theology.* Evanston, Ill.: Northwestern University Press, 1971. 347p.

The author explores various aspects of the feminine as a style of consciousness not restricted to women alone, but common to men as well. She feels that the suppression of the feminine has been detrimental to Western modes of thought for both sexes, and suggests that the androgynous psyche is the next step toward a psychological ideal.

Rape

Until the 1970's the issue of rape received little serious attention from the general public. At most it was a legal matter and of little concern to the medical or psychiatric professions. Within the last few years, however, feminists have heightened public awareness of the crime and have proved that rape is a potential threat to all women.

The New York Radical Feminists, a group to which Susan Brownmiller belonged, began to understand the dimensions of the crime when consciousness-raising sessions revealed that rape experiences were widespread and not rare, isolated incidents. This first revelation led the group to uncover other myths about rape — that women victims want to be raped, that they cannot be raped against their will, and that women often make false accusations.

Brownmiller then spent several years investigating other aspects of rape such as its occurrence throughout history, the motivations of the rapists and preventive measures for the future protection of women. She builds a powerful feminist case to prove that rape is ''a conscious process of intimidation by which all men keep all women in a state of fear.''

The work of Brownmiller and other feminists has had a dramatic effect on public and professional awareness of the severity of the rape problem. Hospital staff and legal authorities in growing numbers of communities are treating rape victims with sensitivity instead of with the suspicion or indifference that often characterized earlier treatment.

Brownmiller, Susan. *Against Our Will: Men, Women and Rape.* New York: Simon and Schuster, 1975. 472p.

Susan Brownmiller redefines rape from a feminist perspective as ''nothing more or less than a conscious process of intimidation by which all men keep all women in a state of fear.'' She does not arrive at this conclusion impressionistically or out of anger alone. Her book is the result of solid research; she presents factual material which includes: concepts of rape and punishmen in history; contemporary information about perpetrators of rape; descriptions of victims of rape in

149

contrast to what their image may be; and some recommendations for the elimination of this crime.

Brownmiller hypothesizes about the relationship between rape and the patriarchy. Forcible abduction (bride capture) appears to her to have been the earliest form of the protective, conjugal relationship. Women became property, and any outside violation of their bodies became a threat to their mate as property-holder. It is Brownmiller's contention that this frame of reference continues to the present time. There is little societal concern about the effects of a personal assault on the mind and body of a woman, and much concern about the male requirements of virginity, chastity and the rights of the marriage contract.

Brownmiller gathers considerable data on the effect of war on women. Rape is inevitable when men are bonded together in a gigantic male-only club in positions of power which enable them to give vent to their natural contempt for women. She draws information from records of the Battle of Culloden, both World Wars, and Viet Nam, all proving that conquering armies rape women as a bonus for their victories. That sex is unavailable in other ways has been disproved; American soldiers in Viet Nam had a ready and inexpensive supply of prostitutes at the same time that they raped and murdered women.

It is in connection with her discussion of the Vietnamese War that one of the prevalent themes of Brownmiller's book first becomes clear — the parting of the ways between the old Left and the new feminist movements. Before her identification with feminism, Brownmiller was involved with the anti-war movement. She left that movement because the abuse of women in the war was never taken seriously.

Brownmiller documents the sexual abuse of women throughout history: the pogroms in Europe; the Mormon persecutions; modern African revolutions; and in this country, the treatment of Native American women and of Black slave women.

Modern-day rapists, those Brownmiller refers to as "police-blotter rapists," are most typically nineteen years old, live in lower class neighborhoods, and represent a violence-prone ethic. They are not the timid, sexually warped characters the popular culture would have us believe. Much of Brownmiller's information is based on a sociological study done by Menachem Amir, *Patterns of Forcible Rape* (1971). It is the first study to draw a profile of a typical rapist. One of Amir's findings was that in 43% of the cases he studied, the victim was attacked by two or more men. For Brownmiller, this is evidence that there is an ideology of rape. She borrows from Lionel Tiger the principle of male bonding, and interprets gang rape as "proof of a desire to humiliate the victims beyond the act of rape through the process of mass assault."

Since the typical rapist comes from the lower socioeconomic level of society, it comes as no surprise that a high proportion of black males are involved. In a chapter discussing questions of race, Brownmiller returns to her theme of the clash in values between the old Left and the new feminism. In researching the black female experience of rape, Brownmiller visited the Schomburg Center for Research in Black Culture. The librarian in charge told her that if she were really serious about her subject, she would have to start with the historic injustice to black men. ''That must be your approach,'' said he. Said she, ''that has been your approach sir. I'm interested in the historic injustice to women.''

No issue has separated liberals more than the issue of inter-racial rape. Brownmiller is not unsympathetic to the notion of ''the rapist as victim.'' She simply is more interested in woman as victim and points out that rape is to women what lynching has been to blacks.

New York Radical Feminists. *Rape: The First Sourcebook for Women.* **New York: New American Library, 1974. 283p.**

This book is the result of the Speak-Out and the Conference on Rape organized by the New York Radical Feminists in 1971. Susan Brownmiller was part of this group, and her major work on rape, *Against Our Will,* was inspired by her participation.

Rape has become a feminist issue newly defined as ''sexism carried to its logical conclusion.'' Talking about rape experiences in consciousness-raising groups led women to realize that personal experiences of forced sexual acts were in fact widespread and serious incidents affecting all women in a sexist society.

After the issue was recognized, the radicalization process set in. The New York Radical Feminists organized a speak-out which included rape testimonials. The effect of the meeting was to break down the myths about women rape victims which society had created — that women cannot be raped against their will, that women really want to be raped, and that women make false accusations. The testimonies helped to clarify a new body of information about rape and to establish a clear history of the problem.

The book offers a feminist analysis of rape with a particularly fine chapter by Florence Rush on the sexual abuse of children. She sees their subjugation as an effect of a male dominated society and therefore as a feminist issue. Most of the abused children are female and their assaulters are male. Other chapters include an analysis of the rape theme in popular fiction written by women, and its treatment in motion pictures. After examining books by Jacqueline Susann, Ayn Rand and Grace Metalious, the Feminists conclude that current cultural belief insists that a rape victim must be punished. She may become pregnant, turn to prostitution, or commit suicide. Blatant misogyny is found in such films as Kubrick's *A Clockwork Orange.*

After dealing with the popular culture, the New York Radical Feminists discuss the New York rape laws. Until 1974, rape victims had to corroborate their testimony with proof of penetration, identification, and lack of consent. In other words, the burden of proof made the victim's testimony the central object of inquiry, not the rape incident itself. In addition, the court system proved itself biased against women by allowing their past sexual conduct as admissible evidence.

The last step in this chain of growing awareness and analysis of rape is its prevention and eradication. Feminists believe that only a social revolution which eliminates sexism will accomplish the latter. In the meantime, the New York Feminists have helped women by establishing rape crises centers, advocating better emergency treatment in hospitals, teaching self-defense and lobbying for changes in the law. By determining rape to be a feminist issue and not only a legal or medical matter, the New York Radical Feminists have brought long overdue attention to a problem of concern to all women.

* * *

Amir, Menachem. *Patterns of Forcible Rape*. Chicago: University of Chicago Press, 1971. 394p.

This landmark sociological study, emphasizing the social characteristics of both offenders and victims, offers new information about the incidence of group rape and the relationship between alcohol and rape. Amir collected data on all cases of forcible rape in Philadelphia over a two-year period and provides the first systematic and exhaustive study of the crime. Susan Brownmiller and others acknowledge their debt to his study.

Burgess, Ann Wolbert and Lynda Lytle Holmstrom. *Rape: Victims of Crises*. Bowie, Maryland: Robert J. Brady, 1974. 308p.

In 1972 the authors, one a psychiatric nurse and the other a sociologist, established the Victim Counseling Program, a rape crisis intervention service at Boston City Hospital. Their book describes that program, offering insights into the needs of victims, the background of offenders, and the function of the crisis center. They point out the inadequacies of most existing community services for rape victims and give a practical account of how they can be improved.

Horos, Carol. *Rape*. New Canaan, Conn.: Tobey, 1974. 130p.

With information based largely on Amir's findings in *Patterns of Forcible Rape*, Horos combines the new knowledge of who commits rape and why with practical information: how to avoid rape; methods of self-defense; and how to organize a rape crisis center.

Lynch, W. Ware. *Rape! One Victim's Story*. Chicago: Follett, 1974. 230p.

In the style of the investigative reporter, Lynch has drawn a composite portrait of four women recently raped by typical offenders. His book dramatically illustrates the viciousness of the crime and the unsympathetic way in which victims are treated by the authorities.

MacKellar, Jean. *Rape: The Bait and the Trap*. With the collaboration of Dr. Menachem Amir. New York: Crown, 1975. 154p.

Basing her material on the data collected by Amir, MacKellar discusses the implications of his findings. She tries to separate myth from fact and suggests how the crimes can be prevented in the future.

Medea, Andrea and Kathleen Thompson. *Against Rape.* **New York: Farrar, Straus and Giroux, 1974. 152p.**

This is a short, readable book directed to all women as potential rape victims. The authors offer a survival manual explaining how to recognize and avoid dangerous situations, how to train for self-defense, how to overcome feelings of guilt if raped, and how to cope with the legal entanglements involved in a rape case.

Russell, Diana E.H. *The Politics of Rape: The Victim's Perspective.* **New York: Stein and Day, 1975. 311p.**

Russell, a sociologist, interviewed ninety victims of rape to learn about the crime from the victim's point of view. Because the law has mistreated victims, blaming them and excusing the perpetrators, Russell believes that society should become aware of and sensitive to the effect of rape on victims.

Religion

The changing relationship between women and organized religion is one of the most radical aspects of the women's movement. Feminist theologians of all denominations are challenging traditional patriarchal views which have relegated women to subservient positions. Perhaps the most dramatic evidence of change is the departure of many thousands of nuns from convents to secular life. Writing in 1967, Sister M. Charles Borromeo described the changing image of nuns from cloistered childlike women to "the new nuns" who are seeking lives of social relevance. Writing in the 1970's Mary Griffin and Nancy Henderson are outspoken in their criticism of church hierarchy, raising objections to the low status of women within the Church.

Mary Daly, who is in the mainstream of American feminism, brought specific charges against organized religion. In 1968, armed with formidable knowledge and feminist anger, she challenged Catholic traditions that had been accepted for centuries, hoping that the Church would accommodate the rights of women. Since then her theological position has gone beyond such expectations in favor of a new religion that will have a feminist structure. But for other religious women of all faiths, the feminist impulse is moving them to work for change within existing structures, and their books are challenging many traditional views.

Borromeo, Sister M. Charles, ed. *The New Nuns.* **New York: New American Library, 1967. 216p.**

In the middle 1960's "new nuns" emerged from the strict contemplative life to participate in the larger community. That began a process of liberation that preceded the more general movement for women's liberation in America. It was also the preface to the mass departure of nuns from the convent, a phenomenon that has since involved the editor of this volume.

The essays in this book deal with two general topics — changes in nuns' personal style and changes in their relationship to church bureaucracy. The editor dismisses the traditional simple and childlike image of nuns made popular in a film like *The Bells of St. Mary's.* Many nuns have had sophisticated educations and are as complicated as other intellectuals.

155

The most conspicuous change has been nuns' abandonment of traditional garb in favor of ordinary street clothes. Although this trend met with general approval by those who worked with the sisters as well as by the nuns themselves, in some cases modernization led to extreme psychological discomfort. Nuns were suddenly women who had to think about worldly matters like fashion and figures, after having obliterated such concerns over the years. Some older nuns have chosen to remain in habits.

Less visible changes have also occurred. The loosening of strictures of convent living has made possible the greater participation of nuns in the larger world such as working in the inner cities, and in protest movements.

The rapid changes that have been advanced by sisters in the Catholic Church have provided an interesting and important chapter in the social history of American women.

Griffin, Mary. *The Courage to Choose: An American Nun's Story.* Boston: Little, Brown, 1975. 214p.

Since 1965 over 40,000 nuns have left their orders in America making up a part of the women's movement which may be quieter but no less radical than the activities of the most vociferous feminists. Mary Griffin left the Order of the Blessed Virgin Mary after living more than twenty-five years in a convent. She describes the gradual process which led her from a total commitment to a religious life to an increasing involvement with the cares of the outside world.

Life within the walls was depersonalized and anti-intellectual. Names were taken away from entering postulants and new ones prescribed. Clothing was uniform, and all conversation had to be directed away from such individualizing characteristics as nationality, social position, or levels of education. The sin of intellectual pride had to be recognized, and the possession of knowledge had to be suppressed for the sake of "one life in God." The sisters were reminded "that it was better to practice than to be able to define compassion." The hierarchical organization of the convent led to an atmosphere of childishness where young sisters were made to feel dependent and in need of approval. Mary Griffin spent World War II removed from the realities of world politics, a situation she now finds incredible when she compares it with her active participation in anti-war efforts in the 1960's.

Vatican II began the liberalizing process for nuns and priests and the Vietnam War radicalized them. Although the Vatican Council emphasized the necessity for the religious community to participate in the larger world, Mary Griffin notes that no women were present at the august gathering. The Civil Rights Movement also increased the participation of nuns and priests in the world. Like other members of the religious community Mary Griffin marched to Selma, and like other feminists she soon saw that women in this country were oppressed by men.

According to Griffin nuns represent more than 100,000 women ripe for the philosophy of liberation. Historically they have been free from competing both for and with men. She predicts that the ordination of women priests is inevitable and that increasing numbers of nuns will live within a variety of life styles outside of convents. Many are already living within mixed groups in inner city dwellings. Leaving the Church will be even more typical than it is now; people will stay three to five years and then pursue their religious commitments outside their vows.

In other words a new ethos is developing; Christians will no longer flee the world, but build for the here and now. The Berrigan brothers represent the new religious in the extreme, but in the future radical Christian communities will emerge which will continue to fight for peace and justice. Mary Griffin believes that women will make up the leadership as well as the ranks of these new dedicated groups.

Henderson, Nancy. *Out of the Curtained World: The Story of an American Nun Who Left the Convent.* Garden City, New York: Doubleday, 1972. 276p.

Personal narratives of the lives of former nuns have always had a special appeal for readers. Catholics and non-Catholics alike are curious about convent life, about the mystery of the cloistered world, about the daily life of the convent — what nuns wear, what they eat, what their relationships are like. Books like Monica Baldwin's *I Leap Over the Wall* and Kathryn Hulme's *The Nun's Story* have accordingly become best sellers.

They have also become period pieces now that the role of the Catholic nun has changed so rapidly over the last ten years. Even when Nancy Henderson entered an order in the early sixties, there were signs of decline: only four postulants entered instead of the large numbers of earlier years. Her book describes this transitional period when traditional convent life gave way to the changing expectations of women.

Nancy Henderson grew up in the Mid-West and was educated in parochial schools. As a bright, idealistic youngster, she was guided toward a religious vocation and when she arrived at the convent at the age of eighteen she fully expected to be educated and trained to serve in a mission in Africa. Instead she found herself buried in a morass of rules and physical work. When, after several years, she began her formal education in a nearby Catholic college, her intellectual curiosity and need for personal achievement found a reasonable outlet. The outside world began to seem a more likely place for a young woman of her nature and ambitions.

The traditional convent created a climate in which day-to-day life did not allow for the expression of sympathy or affection between individuals. Being forced to forsake all personal feelings had unhealthy effects, for some of the sisters developed nervous habits — facial tics, odd gaits and peculiar tones of voice. The discouragement of intellectual pride — a sin according to Catholic doctrine — robbed the author of any sense of accomplishment she might have felt when she did exceptionally well at school. Even more difficult for her perhaps was the childish role imposed upon her because of the hierarchy within the order and its relationship to Catholic priests. When priests visited, they brought the sisters ice cream, like favorite uncles bringing sweets to children.

Henderson left the convent in order to pursue personal goals. Her reactions to the restrictions of convent life were typical, for many other women also left the Church during the 1960's.

*   *   *

Culver, Elsie Thomas. *Women in the World of Religion.* Garden City, New York: Doubleday, 1967. 340p.

Culver surveys the extent of women's participation in the Church from pre-Christian times to the present to illustrate the long history of male monopoly of religious leadership. She finds that women have been uniformly discriminated against in the past and documents the new trends which are leading to ordination for women within some religious denominations.

Daly, Mary. *Beyond God the Father: Toward a Philosophy of Women's Liberation.* Boston: Beacon Press, 1973. 225p.

Daly considers this book a sequel to *The Church and the Second Sex* and an illustration of the radicalization process she has undergone since the publication of her first book. Here she dismisses the male God and constructs the basis for a feminist religion.

_____. *The Church and the Second Sex.* With a New Feminist Postchristian Introduction. New York: Harper and Row, 1975 (c.1968) 229p.

Mary Daly is a highly trained Catholic theologian who has written a strong indictment against the Church for treating women as the inferior ''second sex.'' Her intention in the original edition of this book was to examine the gross inequities inflicted upon women by traditional Catholic theology in the hope that a new effort would be made to provide a rational and fair place for women within the structure of the Church, including the priesthood. In the new edition, Daly has provided an introduction which indicates her startling move away from the Church and traditional Christianity to her new position as a radical feminist who has thrown aside her ties with a patriarchal authority.

Doely, Sarah Bentley, ed. *Women's Liberation and the Church: The New Demand for Freedom in the Life of the Christian Church.* New York: Association Press, 1970. 145p.

Each of the contributors to this volume is a woman with a commitment to her faith who feels a particular grievance over the subordinate position of women within organized religion. Together their essays present an overview of the ways in which Christian feminism can identify and then work to correct the historic relegation of women to the unimportant functions of religious life.

Eermarth, Margaret Sittler. *Adam's Fractured Rib: Observations on Women in the Church.* Philadelphia: Fortress, 1970. 159p.

The author places the question of the role of women in the church against the activities of the women's movement, and points the way to the inevitable active participation of women in all denominations. Although her particular base is with the Lutheran Church, she discusses the religious role of women in the context of Catholicism as well as in the major Protestant sects.

Gearhart, Sally and William R. Johnson, eds. *Loving Women/Loving Men: Gay Liberation and the Church.* San Francisco: Glide, 1974. 165p.

The authors, active Christians and gay liberationists, have brought together five essays which take a hard look at the relationship between organized religion and the gay community. They point out the contradictions between the Christian message of love and the patriarchal, masculinist tradition of those within the church who hold power.

Hageman, Alice L., ed. *Sexist Religion and Women in the Church: No More Silence!* New York: Association Press, 1974. 221p.

The essays in this volume grew out of the Lentz Lectures at the Harvard Divinity School, delivered in the academic year 1972-73. The contributors are theologians who explore sexism in religion as it occurs throughout the Protestant, Catholic and Jewish religions. They express feminist concerns; the strongest voice among them is that of Mary Daly whose essay is called, "Theology after the Demise of God the Father: A Call for the Castration of Sexist Religion."

Harkness, Georgia. *Women in Church and Society: A Historical and Theological Inquiry.* Nashville: Abingdon, 1972. 240p.

A historical and theological discussion of women's role in religion written by an ordained minister of the United Methodist Church, this book is a gentle feminist discussion.

Heyer, Robert J., ed. *Women and Orders.* New York: Paulist Press, 1974. 104p.

The seven contributors to this collection address themselves to the theological and sociological consequences of the dictum of the Catholic Church which limits the ordained priesthood to celibate males.

Meer, Haye van der. *Women Priests in the Catholic Church?* Philadelphia: Temple University Press, 1973. 199p.

Father van der Meer is a Dutch Jesuit who has taken a new look at the possibility of the ordination of women in the Catholic Church. He points out that most of the opposition has been based on Jewish rabbinical tradition, a misreading of St. Paul and a belief in ignorant biological and psychological concepts about women. His own view is that God created whole persons, and that sexual inequality is the result of the failure of people to deal with one another as whole persons.

Plaskow, Judith and Joan Arnold Romero, eds. *Women & Religion: Papers of the Working Group on Women and Religion, 1972-73.* Chambersburg, Pa.: American Academy of Religion, 1974. 210p.

The papers in this volume have been gathered for the purpose of serving as an introduction to women's studies in religion. Some of the essays included are: "Phallic Worship: The Ultimate Idolatry," by Elizabeth Farians; "A Feminist View of Abortion," by Jean MacRae; and "Is Sexism a Sign of Decadence in Religion?" by Leonard Swidler.

Priesand, Sally. *Judaism and the New Woman.* New York: Behrman House, 1975. 144p.

Sally Priesand is the first woman ever to have been ordained a rabbi. She explores in this book the reasons why Jewish law has so obviously discriminated against women while at the same time held them in an honored and respected position. She explores historic aspects, including biblical concepts, the structure of the synogogue and the community, prominent Jewish women in history, the stereotype of the Jewish mother, and offers suggestions for a continuing rise in status for the Jewish woman today.

Ruether, Rosemary. *New Woman/New Earth: Sexist Ideologies and Human Liberation.* New York: Seabury, 1975. 221p.

This book contains a series of theoretical essays which examine "the relationships between sexism, racism and capitalism and how these ideologies and ideas have developed the society's ideas on women." Ruether also studies the Judeo-Christian tradition's image of women which has led inevitably to their inferior position.

————, ed. *Religion and Sexism: Images of Woman in the Jewish and Christian Traditions.* New York: Simon and Schuster, 1974. 356p.

Like Mary Daly, Rosemary Ruether is a highly respected feminist theologian who believes that organized religion has been a major factor in the development of women's inferior role in culture and society. She has brought together for this anthology essays which, she says, "attempt to give ... a glimpse of the history of this relationship of patriarchal religion to both feminine imagery and to the actual psychic and social self-images of women." The contributors, scholars of Jewish, Catholic and Protestant historical theology, write on such topics as: "Canon Law and the Battle of the Sexes," "Women and the Continental Reformation," and "Images of Women in the Talmud."

Tavard, George H. *Woman in Christian Tradition.* Notre Dame, Indiana: University of Notre Dame Press, 1973. 257p.

Tavard, a Catholic theologian, examines the Old and New Testaments as well as recent Christian thought to see what religious models have been offered to women. His focus is always theological and historical, although he is not unsympathetic to the feminist position.

Sex Roles

The subject of sex roles has provided important areas of investigation for working scholars in many of the academic disciplines. Psychologist Eleanor Maccoby explores the unsettled question of inherent differences between the sexes. Anthropologists Michelle Rosaldo and others question whether women are naturally inferior to men, why women in most societies accept a subordinate standing, how women do exercise power, and whether or not societies exist in which women are the equal of or even superior to men. Sociologists Marcia Millman, Joan Huber and others point out that women's participation in the world has been largely neglected by traditional sociologists, and they offer recommendations for new areas of research and for social policy changes. John Money, a professor of medical psychology and pediatrics, is researching gender identity in order to understand the interaction of hereditary endowment and environmental influence.

The identification of inherent differences between the sexes is obviously difficult to research since culturally imposed differences continue to develop in individuals. Even so, the pursuit of such investigation goes on over the objections of some feminist scholars who feel that the discovery of possible differences will be counterproductive to the aims of women. Alice Rossi, herself a feminist, has stirred up a controversy by the publication of an article, "A Biosocial Perspective on Parenting" (*Daedalus,* Spring 1977). She suggests that there is an "innate predisposition in the mother to relate intensely to the infant," and has observed that "Communally reared children, far from being liberated, are often neglected, joyless creatures." For other feminists who desire to see infant care shared by males and females, these speculations are unsettling. The conflict is an example of those that can result between detached scholarly inquiry and feminist or other political conviction.

Davis, Elizabeth Gould. *The First Sex.* New York: Penguin Books, 1972, 382p.

It is Davis's hypothesis that women are superior to men and that there was a time in history when they dominated men within a superior civilization. Drawing on history, archeology, mythology and science, she postulates that women are the

161

first sex. She states that it was male acknowledgement of women's greater gifts that led to overwhelming fear which led in turn to the suppression of women.

Biology also supports her sense of female superiority. Her interpretation of genetic information about the X and Y chromosomes is as follows:

> Geneticists and physiologists tell us that the Y chromosome that produces males is a deformed and broken X chromosome — the female chromosome. All women have two X chromosomes, while the male has one X derived from his mother and one Y from his father. It seems very logical that this small and twisted Y chromosome is a genetic error — an accident of nature, and that originally there was only one sex — the female.

The recent discovery that congenital killers and criminals are possessed of not one but two Y chromosomes leads Davis to state that the Y chromosome is a degeneration and deformity of the female chromosome and that "the male sex represents a degeneration and deformity of the female."

She offers no consistent data to support her conclusions. Rather, the book is a *tour de force* in which Gould delightfully picks and chooses her way through thousands of years of history. One might read the book as an antidote to the male chauvinist histories and studies which have been prevalent.

Maccoby, Eleanor Emmons and Carol Nagy Jacklin. *The Psychology of Sex Differences.* **Stanford, Cal.: Stanford University Press, 1974. 634p.**

This is a landmark book; it brings together the current scholarship on male/female differences in social behavior, intellectual abilities, motivations and aspirations. Research into sex roles seems to indicate that it cannot be assumed that no differences exist between the sexes apart from physical distinctions.

All of the chapters in this book will be of interest to psychologists and other professionals who are researchers or practitioners in the behavioral sciences. For the general reader, however, the conclusions offered in the last chapter will be of special importance. In summarizing, the authors find that some fairly well established sex differences have been measured in the following areas: girls have greater verbal ability than boys; boys excel in visual-spatial ability; boys excel in mathematical ability; males are more aggressive. The book concludes with an excellent annotated bibliography of psychological materials published between 1965 and 1973. A similar bibliography was published in Maccoby's earlier book, *The Development of Sex Differences* (1966).

Rosaldo, Michelle Zimbalist and Louise Lamphere, eds. *Woman, Culture & Society.* **Stanford, Cal.: Stanford University Press, 1974. 339p.**

According to many social scientists and general readers, this book is the most original and valuable study of women to appear in recent years. The contributors are anthropologists and other social scientists who have used their skills to study women with methods seldom tried before. The editors point out that like most other participants in society, academic anthropologists have generally viewed women as passive sexual objects, as wives and devoted mothers. The women who have written these essays are interested in questioning old biases and inquiring into areas long ignored. They all believe that anthropology has suffered from ''a failure to develop theoretical perspectives that take account of women as social actors.'' The editors summarize the general direction of questions posed by all of the contributors to this book as follows: ''Are there societies that, unlike our own, make women the equals or superiors of men? If not, are women naturally men's inferiors? Why do women, in our own society and elsewhere, accept a subordinate standing? How, and in what kinds of situations, do women exercise power? How do women help to shape, create, and change the private and public worlds in which they live?''

Only the first question can be answered briefly: in the opinion of most anthropologists, most and probably all contemporary societies, whatever their organization or methods of production, are characterized by some degree of male dominance. Answers to the other questions are approached in this book by essays on women in politics, women in domestic groups, an essay on survival strategies in an urban black community, and studies of groups of Chinese, African, and Guatemalan women, and others.

If one had to choose just one essay to read from this brilliant collection, it would have to be Nancy Chodorow's ''Family Structure and Feminine Personality,'' for in it she answers some questions that are crucial to the study of the role of women in society. She explores the mother-daughter relationship, and from it evolves a theory of personality which attempts to explain why men dislike women, and why women accept a subordinate standing in our own society and elsewhere.

It surprises Chodorow that so little scholarly attention has been given that relationship, since she feels that ''women's motherhood and mothering role seem to be the most important features in accounting for the universal status of women.'' Cross-cultural analysis proves to her satisfaction that the female personality defines itself in relation to other people, while the male, whose development is more problematic, is more independent in seeking identity. Because women raise children while fathers are absent from the home, girls take on female identity by following the example of their mothers. Boys define themselves in negative terms, rejecting their mothers as models, and rejecting what they perceive as feminine in themselves and in the outside world. In searching for an elusive masculine identity, they devalue the feminine in pursuit of the assumed superior male role. Although the mother-daughter relationship can be detrimental to the child, leading to excessive dependence, advantages do usually exist for women. The very closeness of girls' connection with women may lead to psychological security, while men may be left defensive and insecure as a by-product of independence. Chodorow concludes, therefore, that the present mode of personality development leads to social oppression for women and psychological oppression for men. She suggests that these problems would be avoided if children were to be reared by more than one adult, preferably by both men and women.

The authors of the other fifteen essays in this anthology show that anthropology has suffered from a failure to develop theoretical perspectives that understand women to be active participants in their society. They examine a wide variety of women in groups. No longer willing to dismiss women as "a vast army of the unemployed," the contributors to this volume have provided landmark studies which show that women do indeed exercise power, and that they help to shape, create, and change the private and public worlds in which they live.

* * *

Andreas, Carol. *Sex and Caste in America.* **Englewood Cliffs, New Jersey: Prentice-Hall, 1971. 146p.**

Andreas, a sociologist, examines the origins of sex-role stereotyping which have perpetuated sex roles in such major institutions as the schools, churches and the law. Her book can serve as a useful introduction to the problems and solutions of sexism in America.

Ardener, Shirley, ed. *Perceiving Women.* **London: Malaby, 1975. 167p.**

The contributors to this volume are social anthropologists who are attempting to develop a theoretical framework within which the relative invisibility and silence of women may be more easily understood. They draw their field material from unusual and diverse groups — gypsies, nuns, diplomats' wives and African tribeswomen — in order to determine how women perceive themselves and, in turn, how they are perceived by others.

Bernard, Jessie. *Women and the Public Interest: An Essay on Policy and Protest.* **Chicago: Aldine, Atherton, 1971. 293p.**

Written for undergraduates, this book offers an analytic approach to the status and problems of women in relationship to public policy. Bernard thinks that sexual division of labor violates the constitution, and that "artificial sexual allocation of function" impedes the "pursuit of happiness" mandate of the Declaration of Independence.

_____. *Women, Wives, Mothers: Values and Options.* **Chicago: Aldine, 1975. 286p.**

This is an assemblage of papers Bernard delivered at a number of professional conferences, and this collection also contains chapters from her book, *The Future of Motherhood.* The five chapters include: research on sex difference, an overview; young women and socialization; mothers at the various stages of their roles; class and race issues in connection with feminism; and the dangers today of extreme sex-role specialization. Of the current questioning of sex roles Bernard says, "I view the current restructuring of sex roles as no less epochal than the restructuring of the class system which was one of the first consequences of the industrial revolution."

Chafetz, Janet Saltzman. *Masculine/Feminine or Human? An Overview of the Sociology of Sex Roles.* Itasca, Ill.: F. E. Peacock, 1974. 242p.

This book was designed for undergraduates to be used as an overview for courses dealing wholly or in part with the sociology of sex roles.

Filene, Peter. *Him/Her/Self: Sex Roles in Modern America.* New York: Harcourt Brace Jovanovich, 1974. 351p.

Filene set for himself the task of analyzing the interaction of the sexes in order to understand how the roles of women have changed from the 1890's to the present. His book is an exploratory essay which uses the multiple approaches of history, social psychology, fiction and popular culture to discover how individuals should ideally function. In so doing, Filene traces innumerable themes — feminism, employment, child rearing, sexuality — through political, economic, intellectual and demographic history. He has been ambitious and sometimes seems overwhelmed by his material.

Huber, Joan, ed. *Changing Women in a Changing Society.* Chicago: University of Chicago Press, 1973. 295p.

This collection originally appeared as an issue of the *American Journal of Sociology.* Almost all of the articles are by women in the field who share the view that the participation of women in the changing world has generally been neglected by sociologists. Selections cover a wide range of topics and include: "Origins of the Women's Movement," by Jo Freeman; "Successful Black Women," by Cynthia Fuchs Epstein; "Marital Patterns of Female Workers," by Elizabeth M. Havens; and "Social Relations of Widows," by Helena Lopata.

Lakoff, Robin. *Language and Woman's Place.* New York: Harper and Row, 1975. 83p.

This is a good basic study of how language reflects the disparity between men and women in our society. By comparing such terms as "bachelor/ spinster" and "master/mistress" Lakoff shows that language has as its foundation the attitude that women are marginal creatures, with identities based on their relationships to others.

Lavin, Mildred H. and Clara H. Oleson, eds. *Women and Public Policy: A Humanist Perspective.* Iowa City: University of Iowa. Institute of Public Affairs, 1974. 147p.

These are the published results of a symposium held at the University of Iowa in 1973 which was concerned with the changing role of women in America and the appropriate response from academics in the humanities. The essays deal with such topics as the image of women in literature and the changing status of women in the law.

McBee, Mary Louise and Kathryn A. Blake, eds. *The American Woman: Who Will She Be?* Beverly Hills: Glencoe, 1974. 164p.

The editors have brought together essays by women who are experts in various fields. Each describes how changes in women's roles will be reflected in specific areas. Juanita Kreps discusses occupations; Anne Firor Scott writes on women in history; Patsy Mink discusses politics; and Jessie Bernard writes about women and new social structures.

Maccoby, Eleanor E., ed. *The Development of Sex Differences.* Stanford: Stanford University Press, 1966. 351p.

This excellent collection contains essays by psychologists who are concerned with the theory of sex differences. Some of the essays included here are: "Sex Differences in Intellectual Functioning," by Eleanor Maccoby; "A Social-Learning View of Sex Differences in Behavior," by Walter Mischel; and "Sex Differences and Cultural Institutions," by Roy G. D'Andrade. Maccoby has included a one-hundred-page annotated bibliography.

Malbin, Nona Glazer and Helen Youngelson Waehrer, eds. *Woman in a Man-Made World: A Socioeconomic Handbook.* Chicago: Rand McNally, 1972. 316p.

These readings were selected as material for courses on women's position in the economy and on the sociology of women. They provide interdisciplinary materials which lead to discussions of sex roles.

Martin, M. Kay and Barbara Voorhies. *Female of the Species.* New York: Columbia University Press, 1975. 432p.

This is an anthropological study of women in a range of societies including gathering and horticultural groups and the socialist and capitalist organizations of industrial society.

Matthiasson, Carolyn J., ed. *Many Sisters: Women in Cross-cultural Perspectives.* New York: Free Press, 1974. 443p.

The contributors to this anthology are all women anthropologists and sociologists who have examined the role of women in various societies. They find that the participation of women can be grouped into three categories: "societies in which women must manipulate men to achieve their own ends; societies in which women's roles are complementary to men and women have equal status; and societies in which women have a slight advantage socially by virtue of being a woman." That last category is the shortest in the book and deals only with the Onandaga, and Iroquois culture in which women control power over land and other aspects of society.

Mead, Margaret and Frances Kaplan, eds. *American Women: The Report of the President's Commission on the Status of Women.* New York: Scribner's, 1965. 274p.

The Commission was established by John F. Kennedy, with Eleanor Roosevelt as its head, to work toward the full realization of women's basic rights. This report reviews progress in education, economics and politics. In the introduction, Margaret Mead notes the growing value of paid work to women and the possibility of guaranteed income. She criticizes the American family pattern in which women have too much time on their hands.

Millman, Marcia and Rosabeth Moss Kanter, eds. *Another Voice: Feminist Perspectives on Social Life and Social Science.* **Garden City, New York: Doubleday, 1975. 382p.**

This collection contains twelve essays by female sociologists who write within their subspecialties to encourage the field to consider a broader range of theories, perspectives and social realities which relate to women. The editors indicate that because of traditional assumptions made by sociologists, important areas of social inquiry have been overlooked: women in undramatic support groups have not been acknowledged or studied; sex is not taken into account as a factor in behavior although it may be an essential variable; sociologists often assume a single society with respect to men and women in which generalizations are made about all participants when in fact experiences for women may be different from those of men.

Money, John and Anke A. Ehrhardt. *Man & Woman, Boy & Girl.* **Baltimore: Johns Hopkins University Press, 1972. 311p.**

These researchers are interested in the interaction of hereditary endowment and environmental influence on gender identity in humans. By studying young subjects, they find that it makes no difference whether a child is reared primarily by its mother or its father so long as the child learns to feel positively about its own sex. Only when either parent shows ambivalence does a problem arise.

Money, John and Patricia Tucker. *Sexual Signatures: On Being a Man or a Woman.* **Boston: Little, Brown, 1975. 250p.**

Money, a professor of medical psychology and pediatrics, has been researching gender identity in human beings for more than twenty-five years. He has tried to sort out the anatomical and biological factors that steer one toward masculinity and/or femininity from the historical, cultural and sociological influences that affect gender development. He says in this book, ''For our society today, the challenge is to decode the sex distinctions of the past that have become strait-jackets, and to keep the rest of the gender stereotypes flexible enough to meet present and future change.''

Morgan, Elaine. *The Descent of Woman.* **New York: Stein and Day, 1972. 258p.**

Elaine Morgan offers a learned and entertaining explanation of the evolutionary process and its effect on the behavior of women. Previous studies of evolution have centered only on men, and she attempts to correct this imbalance by examining essential female experiences such as the maternal relationship and female sexuality within the evolutionary framework.

Oakley, Ann. *Sex, Gender & Society.* **New York: Harper and Row, 1972. 220p.**

Oakley's interest in the housewife as a subject of study led to an analysis of sex differences. In this book she is specifically interested in cross-cultural variations in those roles.

Reed, Evelyn. *Woman's Evolution: From Matriarchal Clan to Patriarchal Family.* **New York: Pathfinder, 1975. 491p.**

Reed, a feminist, socialist and anthropologist, contends that the maternal clan system was the original form of social organization. She "traces the course of its development and the causes of its downfall," fully aware that her position is controversial among professional anthropologists.

Reeves, Nancy, ed. *Womankind: Beyond the Stereotypes.* **Chicago: Aldine, Atherton, 1971. 434p.**

This book grew out of a course on the status of women which the author, a lawyer, taught at UCLA. Half of the book is a critique of female stereotypes and the second half contains readings which refute rigid definitions of sex roles.

Reiter, Rayna R., ed. *Toward an Anthropology of Women.* **New York: Monthly Review, 1975. 416p.**

Using the tools of anthropology, the editor and contributors to this collection attempt to examine the origins of sexual inequality in modern society. They question, for example, the commonplace idea that the center of cultural development is dependent on the position of men as hunters within a society.

Safilios-Rothschild, Constantina. *Women and Social Policy.* **Englewood Cliffs, New Jersey: Prentice-Hall, 1974. 197p.**

The author, a sociologist of the family, presents an overview of problems concerning women in order to recommend social policy changes. She examines such broad areas as opportunities for education and employment, the psychology and sexuality of women and men, and the institutions of marriage and the family.

Stoller, Robert J. *Sex and Gender.* **New York: Jason Aronson, 1968. 383p.**

Stoller shows that in human beings there is a major distinction between sex and gender. The biological fact of sex is what each human is born with; however, the sense of gender identification is the result of psychological, not biological, fact. The implications, of course, are that masculinity and femininity are learned behaviors, subject to the norms of any given culture.

Sullerot, Evelyne. *Woman, Society and Change.* **New York: McGraw-Hill, 1971. 256p.**

Written by a French woman, this book is a cross-cultural study of the position of women generally. The author concludes that women are essential to the solution of such global problems as overpopulation, starvation, underdevelopment and literacy.

Thorne, Barrie and Nancy Henley, eds. *Language and Sex: Difference and Dominance.* Rowley, Mass.: Newbury House, 1975. 311p.

The editors, one a psychologist and the other a sociologist, brought their separate perspectives to the study of the relationship between language usage and patterns of sex discrimination and sex-role stereotyping. This anthology includes papers on such topics as ''The Semantic Derogation of Women'' and ''Cues to the Identification of Sex in Children's Speech.'' The one-hundred-page annotated bibliography of published sources on language and sex is of great value.

Van Vuuren, Nancy. *The Subversion of Women as Practiced by Churches, Witch-hunters, and Other Sexists.* Philadelphia: Westminster, 1973. 190p.

Van Vuuren says that by viewing women as either sex objects or as mothers, men have victimized women so that they have adopted the very traits that misogynists have accused them of having. She traces negative attitudes about women inherent in the Judeo-Christian tradition and explains why women have sought power through witchcraft and sex, often with self-destructive results.

Yorburg, Betty. *Sexual Identity: Sex Roles and Social Change.* New York: Wiley, 1974. 227p.

Yorburg, a sociologist, has pulled together existing research in the fields of biology, anthropology, history, psychology and sociology to examine the reasons for the variation in the ideals of masculinity and femininity; the extent of biological inevitability; and changing relationships between the sexes from one period in history to another.

Sexuality

In the past most serious literature about female sexuality was written from a psychiatric perspective. In fact most psychiatric literature about women deals mainly with sexuality and not with other aspects of female experience. Professionals continue to express classical Freudian views such as the belief that the clitoris is a vestigial organ related to the penis, a concept leading to the theory of penis envy. However, recent research offers far different conclusions about the nature of female sexuality. Masters and Johnson proved that no differences between clitoral and vaginal orgasms exist. Their work helped Mary Jane Sherfey to conclude that women have an intense sexual drive which historically has been suppressed for the good of family life and civilization.

Many of the new books on female sexuality are about lesbianism. Until recently, information about lesbians was found only in writings by heterosexuals or in the fictional worlds created by lesbian writers. By openly discussing their sexual preference, lesbians are clearing away misconceptions which they feel have been perpetuated by organized religion, psychiatry and the society at large.

Writers Del Martin and Phyllis Lyon are primarily concerned with combatting the social hostility facing lesbians. Their book provides a clear and honest discussion of lesbian experience. To younger women like Sidney Abbott, Barbara Love and Karla Jay who have worked in the gay liberation movement, lesbianism is a political statement. Lesbians have organized to protest their lack of civil rights, and some groups consider lesbianism to be radical feminism carried to its logical conclusion.

Chasseguet-Smirgel, Janine. *Female Sexuality: New Psychoanalytic Views.* Ann Arbor: University of Michigan Press, 1970. 220p.

The writers included in this volume represent the French point of view in psychoanalysis. As Frederick Wyatt states in his foreword, ''In their conception of the impact and scale of the overwhelming importance of the mother for the personality and later sexual adjustment of the little girl the authors tend toward the views developed by Melanie Klein and frequently promulgated by Ernest Jones. According to this position the drama of early childhood goes on very

171

much inside, consisting as it does of fantasies insinuating the usurpation of genitals and other properties of the parents' bodies, and of the guilt the child accumulates by participating in these games in his imagination.'' Topics covered include the continuing debate about penis envy, the nature of male and female fantasies, and the roots of female homosexuality.

Although the psychoanalytic interpretations contained in these essays will be of interest to the professional reader, the lay reader may find them too esoteric. Most useful for the general reader is the brief historical review of the main studies of femininity by Freud, his disciples and his opponents which the author supplies in the introduction.

Martin, Del and Phyllis Lyon. *Lesbian/Woman.* **San Francisco: Glide, 1972. 283p.**

Lesbian/Woman is an honest and thoughtful account of lives of lesbian identity. The two authors were in their late forties at the time the book was written. Their writing is not confessional, but descriptive of ''the everyday life experience of the lesbian: how she views herself as a person; how she deals with the problems she encounters in her various roles as woman, worker, friend, parent, child, citizen, wife, employer, welfare recipient, home owner and taxpayer; and how she views other people and the world around her.'' The book in no way exhibits the guilty self-image which has traditionally burdened lesbians. Martin and Lyon, who have lived together for twenty years, have accepted themselves as worthy people leading useful lives. In fact, such a positive view of themselves caused their first publisher to refuse the book.

The authors believe older lesbians have a poor self-image due to the prevailing social view of homosexuality as sinful, criminal, or deranged. Religion has had no tolerance for homosexuals and religious women have had to cope with guilt and repression. The law has been harsh and the police often raid homosexual bars and arrest ''offenders.'' The psychiatric profession has historically viewed homosexuals as misfits (cases of arrested development). Although the attitudes of these institutions are changing, most lesbians have been damaged by traditional social views.

The style of lesbian relationships has also been changing. To emulate heterosexual couples, homosexuals often developed ''butch–femme'' coupling, the ''femme'' having to act as wife, doing the domestic and supportive work of the relationship while the ''butch'' earned a living. Gertrude Stein and Alice Toklas are the classic example of this style which has been rejected by contemporary lesbians, many of whom are part of the women's movement and reject sex-role stereotyping for all women.

Before the women's movement appeared, Del Martin and Phyllis Lyon founded The Daughters of Bilitis as a social club for lesbians. They also began publishing *The Ladder: A Lesbian Review,* as a vehicle for communication. Their participation in the women's movement evolved from their earlier commitment to other lesbians. In the meantime, younger lesbians within the movement view lesbianism as a political statement whereby women seek relationships with other women as an alternative to celibacy or to demeaning sexual relations with men.

Martin and Lyon advocate a humanist point of view, a plea for lesbians to be viewed first as human beings, then as women, and then as lesbians. They are most concerned with the aspects of the external world that block tolerance. They are sure that homosexuals cannot change their orientation, although they can repress their preferences. Martin and Lyon want the helping professions to aid homosexuals in adjusting to their true natures instead of trying to change them or to root out the causes of their orientation.

For older women who have been forced to lead a secret lesbian life Martin and Lyon's support is essential. Aside from offering general reassurance, the authors give advice and inspiration to women, preferring to approach the issue of lesbianism as an individual commitment to other women rather than as an involvement in feminist politics.

Sherfey, Mary Jane. *The Nature and Evolution of Female Sexuality.* **New York: Random House, 1972. 188p.**

Mary Jane Sherfey, a psychiatrist, became interested in female sexuality when she studied premenstrual tension, a problem long neglected by men in the field. Her interest soon spread to the study of the evolution of female sexuality; this work is the result.

In the introduction, Sherfey describes the beginnings of her interest in this field during her undergraduate days at the University of Indiana. Dr. Alfred Kinsey taught a one-credit course on sex which was euphemistically entitled "Marriage." She describes Kinsey as a kind of academic sleeper, by all appearances dull and unsensational in his approach to the subject. Indeed, his scholarship had for many years been limited to the study of the gall wasp. No one realized the force in the man that would be set loose when he undertook the study of human sexuality. His enormous capacity for work (he set out to interview 10,000 people himself) along with his compassion for people and his utter incorruptibility all led him to his landmark work.

Sherfey's discovery of the inductor theory in medical literature, i.e., that the mammalian male is derived from the female was significant to the development of her thinking. She believed that the theory was ignored by everyone except the research endocrinologists who had discovered it because men unconsciously did not want it proved true. The inductor theory means that all human embryos start out as females, that male hormones appear around the sixth week of gestation and begin the differentiation leading to the human male. Sherfey sees this as a reversal of the Eve-out-of-Adam myth, and finds significant implications for psychiatry. The theory contradicts a part of Freudian theory which has generally gone unchallenged — the notion that the clitoris is a vestigial organ which did not happen to develop into a penis. Instead, Sherfey shows that it is a sexual structure of high biological destiny. Her study turned out to be "an unforeseen and surprising statement on the nature and intensity of the sexual drive in women and an explication of the biological destiny of clitoral eroticism in the functioning of the individual and the evolution of man.''

The work of Masters and Johnson led Dr. Sherfey to conclusions about the sexual capacities of women. Masters and Johnson's finding that the clitoris is the female's most erogenous zone led Sherfey and others to disprove Freud's theory of vaginal orgasm. Sherfey explores new areas when she speculates about the rise of patriarchy with its accompanying subjugation of women. She concludes that women's insatiable sexual demands had to be controlled for the good of civilization, that family life would be impossible without the forceful suppression of women's sexual demands. The young must be properly cared for, paternity established, and civilization perpetuated. She states that ''if that suppression has been, at times, unduly oppressive or cruel, I suggest the reason has been neither man's sadistic, selfish infliction of servitude upon helpless women nor women's weakness or inborn masochism. The strength of the drive determines the force required to suppress it.''

Dr. Sherfey contends, therefore, that female sexuality has been suppressed for the good of social progress, but that this suppression should not be mistaken for the inferiority of the female sexual drive — she claims quite the reverse. Other professionals disagree with her conclusions.

Stearn, Jess. *The Grapevine*. Garden City, New York: Doubleday, 1964. 372p.

Before writing this book on lesbians, Jess Stearn wrote books on prostitution, juvenile delinquency, and male homosexuality. He approaches his subjects in the spirit of investigative reporting, revealing ''the secret world of the lesbian.'' Stearn traveled around the country interviewing women who, he claimed, had confidence in him because of the success of his other book on homosexuals, *The Sixth Man*. All of the lesbians he encountered seem to him to be excessively troubled, caught between their wicked impulses and the expectations of the society.

Stearn accepts the psychiatric view that homosexuality is the result of arrested development and that such people are the doomed victims of their own weakness. Implicit throughout his descriptions of the interviews is the attitude that the women are misguided and pitiable, that if they would only try a heterosexual relationship they would probably like it. When he does acknowledge that some women find it impossible to submit to the usual female roles of supportive wives and mothers, he sees it as a threat to the continuation of the race, the same fear that grips men who worry about the effect of feminism on heterosexual women.

Wolff, Charlotte. *Love Between Women*. London: Gerald Duckworth, 1971. 230p.

Charlotte Wolff, a German psychiatrist now living in London, produced this major study of lesbians considered by some to be sympathetic, by others a perpetuation of mistaken scientific theories.

Instead of "homosexual," Wolff prefers the term "homoemotional," which she defines as "an emotional disposition which leads to close and intimate contact between people of the same sex, a contact which may or may not be expressed sexually." Wolff's appreciation of the historic subjugation of women is evident in her explanation of why laws against male homosexuality have continued to exist whereas female homosexuality has gone virtually unnoticed. "Lesbianism," she observes, "is regarded by many men as a joke, or perhaps a playful diversion, where in cases of sexual competition the male would always emerge as victor. It is the arrogance of the male which has protected homosexual women from sufering the same degree of persecution as homosexual men."

Wolff offers several explanations for the causes and nature of lesbianism. Taking up the notion perpetuated by Freud that women's sexual organs retain a masculine part, the clitoris, the author argues that "the disposition to bisexuality and therefore to homosexuality is built into every woman by nature." Her explanation is in direct contradiction to the inductor theory, the discovery by embryologists that all human embryos are at first female, with male differentiation coming later. Another conception about lesbianism that Wolff perpetuates is the belief that it makes a woman more virile and aggressive, a livelier bedpartner. But this view has been challenged by lesbian writers like Del Martin and Phyllis Lyon who argue that lesbians are no more highly sexed than so-called "normal" women.

So it is that Wolff, in spite of her apparent compassion, upholds what others consider to be distasteful myths about lesbian women, and perhaps creates another when she notes that "emotional incest with the mother is indeed the very essence of lesbianism," the idea that when some girls are pushed aside in favor of the father or brothers, lesbian impulses arise as a result of the search for the mother's affection. The possibility that lesbianism may be biological in origin is also offered by Wolff who examines a theory proposed by the East German endocrinologist, Guenther Doerner. His research seems to suggest that a disorder in the development of the sex glands in fetal life may lead to the female identifying as male, and vice versa.

Wysor, Bettie. *The Lesbian Myth.* New York: Random House, 1974. 438p.

Ten years after Jess Stearn wrote *The Grapevine,* Bettie Wysor, another journalist, produced this book. Those ten years saw a great change in attitudes about lesbians. Stearn based his judgments on interviews which he shaped to confirm his own opinions while Wysor set out to dispel the myths which people like Stearn helped to create. For all her good intentions, however, Wysor is tedious and derivative. Without acknowledging their respective books, she uses the same arguments as the lesbian writers, Del Martin, Phyllis Lyons and Jane Rule — that organized religion, the psychiatric profession and the depiction of lesbians in literature have all had harmful effects on the image of the lesbian.

She does pay her dues to another writer. Not trusting her own acumen in dealing with the lesbian in literature, she quotes widely from a book by Jeanette

Foster, *Sex Variant Women in Literature* (1956), which distills from many of the great works of literature the negative images of women and particularly lesbians which persist to this day.

The inadequacies of Wysor's book suggest that for the moment at least only those books which include subjective information about lesbianism are of special importance. In the past the lesbian experience was completely hidden, misunderstood, or deliberately distorted. The present trend in which lesbian writers are openly discussing their lives is significant and long overdue and will lead to more authentic theoretical discussions than Wysor provides.

*   *   *

Abbott, Sidney and Barbara Love. *Sappho Was a Right-on Woman: A Liberated View of Lesbianism.* New York: Stein and Day, 1972. 251p.

Abbott and Love are lesbian writers who involved themselves in gay activism after working in the feminist movement. They are filled with the exhilaration of achieving strong identities as women and as lesbians during a historically important transitional period. Before gay activism, lesbians lived with guilt and self-hatred. Abbott and Love discuss these historic problems in the first half of their book. In the second part, they describe how lesbians emerging from the gay movement have experienced the validity of their sexual identities mainly through the support groups they formed.

Bengis, Ingrid. *Combat in the Erogenous Zone.* New York: Knopf, 1973. 260p.

Bengis has written an autobiography of her sexuality, a chronicle of her growing inability to sustain intimate relationships with men. She is panicked by her vulnerability, her easily stimulated sexuality and her fury over the sexual assaults of men. She discusses what she calls ''men's vulgarization of women, and women's (my) crippled responses.'' In a mood of self protection she explores the possibility of loving women, but is inhibited by the social disapproval of lesbianism. Her problems remain unresolved at the end of the book.

Francoeur, Robert T. and Anna K. Francoeur, eds. *The Future of Sexual Relations.* Englewood Cliffs, New Jersey: Prentice-Hall, 1974. 150p.

The contributors to this collection discuss the future of sexual relations and their effect on marriage, parenthood, sex roles and social concepts of morality. Essays by such well known writers as Marshall McLuhan, Alexander Comfort and Carolyn Heilbrun are included.

Jay, Karla and Allen Young, eds. *Out of the Closets: Voices of Gay Liberation.* New York: Douglas Book Company, 1972. 403p.

When in June 1969 the homosexuals who were frequenting the Stonewall Inn in New York fought against a police raid, the Gay Liberation Movement was born. That early showing of collective support ultimately moved many homosexuals out of their secret or closet life and into an open, more integrated personal identity. This book of readings by both male and female homosexuals contains some of the early manifestoes which made strong impressions on Gay Movement people, writings like "The Woman-Identified Woman" by Radicalesbians and Rita Mae Brown's "Take a Lesbian to Lunch."

————. *After You're Out: Personal Experiences of Gay Men and Lesbian Women.* New York: Links, 1975. 296p.

The editors are aware that there are problems for homosexuals beyond the initial one of openly admitting their sexual preference. Here they discuss such practical problems as discrimination in employment, legal problems, and questions about parenthood.

Johnston, Jill. *Lesbian Nation: The Feminist Solution.* New York: Simon and Schuster, 1973. 283p.

Jill Johnston, who writes for *The Village Voice,* is a radical lesbian who says in her book, "until all women are lesbians there will be no true political revolution." Most of the articles in this book originally appeared in her column and contain topical allusions which now seem dated or obscure.

Klaich, Dolores. *Woman Plus Woman: Attitudes Toward Lesbianism.* New York: Simon and Schuster, 1974. 287p.

Klaich calls her book a social history of lesbianism. Her point of view is that of the detached observer who wishes to destroy the myths surrounding lesbianism. Her areas of investigation include an evaluation of the attitudes of mental health professionals, the lives of lesbians from the past, and information about contemporary lesbians gathered from interviews and questionnaires. In examining past and present attitudes, Klaich finds that people erroneously think of women who are lesbians only in terms of their sexuality, never as whole people.

Kronhausen, Phyllis and Eberhard Kronhausen. *The Sexually Responsive Woman.* New York: Grove, 1964. 255p.

The Kronhausens interviewed in depth four women of very different backgrounds for information about their sexual experiences, attitudes about sex, and descriptions of their relationships. The result is a book which brings acceptance and understanding to the sexual responses of women. Material in the book on lesbians is especially good.

Masters, William H. and Virginia E. Johnson. *Human Sexual Response.* Boston: Little, Brown, 1966. 366p.

Not since Alfred Kinsey's *Sexual Response in the Human Female* has there been so important a contribution to the field of human sexuality. By studying physical reaction to sexual stimulation, Masters and Johnson present physiologic and psychologic facts that were never known before, information that has helped other professionals to treat patients with problems of sexual inadequacy. Masters and Johnson have studied the effect of pregnancy on male and female sexuality, the influence of sexual activity on the heart and blood pressure, and provide evidence proving that people in their eighties are capable of normal sexual functioning. One finding which is of particular interest to feminists is that there are no measurable differences between clitoral and vaginal orgasms.

Myron, Nancy and Charlotte Bunch, eds. *Lesbianism and the Women's Movement.* Baltimore: Diana Press, 1975. 104p.

Articles in this collection first appeared in *The Furies,* a lesbian-feminist newspaper published in Washington, D.C. Taking the position that lesbianism is a political movement, writers discuss such questions as lesbian separatism, bisexuality and heterosexual privilege in society.

Nagera, Humberto. *Female Sexuality and the Oedipus Complex.* New York: Jason Aronson, 1975. 143p.

This is a classic psychoanalytic study of female sexuality by a doctor trained by Anna Freud at the Hampstead Clinic in England.

Schaefer, Leah Cahan. *Women and Sex.* New York: Pantheon, 1973. 269p.

Schaefer, a psychotherapist, interviewed thirty women about their reactions to sexual experience. She questioned them about their early sex memories, adolescent experiences, masturbatory habits, and experiences with intercourse and orgasm. She has compiled a good bibliography on female sexuality.

Seaman, Barbara. *Free and Female: The Sex Life of the Contemporary Woman.* New York: Coward, McCann and Geoghegan, 1972. 288p.

Seaman, a skillful feminist journalist who writes on scientific subjects, has brought together in this book the responsible views of scientists who have been concerned with female sexuality. She refers to the findings of such people as John Money and Mary Jane Sherfey who have established that sexuality is not to be repressed, but should be understood and enjoyed. Other topics covered are contraception, venereal disease, and medical treatment. Seaman informs women about how to evaluate the gynecologist they see.

Wolfe, Linda. *Playing Around: Women and Extramarital Sex.* New York: William Morrow, 1975. 248p.

Wolfe became interested in this subject when she began to realize that many of her seemingly happily married neighbors were having affairs. She decided to explore the subject of extra-marital sex by looking at literature and history as well as at life, and concludes that the phenomenon represents a radical break with the double standard and not so much a break with the ideal of sexual fidelity. By interviewing sixty-six women, Wolfe tries to show that changes in sexual behavior have become acceptable to greater numbers of people.

Zoltan, Anne. *Annie: The Female Experience.* New York: Julian Press, 1973. 153p.

Like Bengis's *Combat in the Erogenous Zone,* this is a documentation of a woman's sexual awareness and experience. The author, a British television personality who writes under a pseudonym, has provided a sexual autobiography which describes her intimate relationships with men.

Work

Like marriage, work defines the allocation of sex roles in the society. Traditional attitudes have prescribed that women remain at home while men earn the family living. When women do seek employment they generally find themselves in low paying jobs. Those who choose to remain at home receive little societal recognition and certainly no economic reward, even though they supposedly are fulfilling social expectations. The issue of work, therefore, has become a major topic of interest to feminists.

Many of the books deal with the role of women in the professions and management. Although the problems of uneducated women in the work force are acknowledged to be severe, academic writers are largely concerned with the ways in which women who do have advantages are kept out of rewarding jobs — to a great extent because of discrimination, but also because women have been socialized to limit their goals and are not motivated to achieve. Sociologists Angrist and Almquist describe how college women lose the opportunity to prepare for successful careers because they are preoccupied with marriage expectations; Caroline Bird describes how the business world creates obstacles for women who aspire to management positions.

When married women do attain successful careers, their lives are usually beset with practical problems. Cynthia Epstein and Ruth Kundsin examine the complexities that result from demanding and often conflicting responsibilities. They point out that busy working women must often sacrifice time with friends and other pleasurable activities. Profiles of married professional women suggest that they possess more energy and ambition than other women, who might find competing demands too hectic and exhausting. Women are learning that the career identity which has traditionally defined the male has serious drawbacks as well as satisfying rewards.

Angrist, Shirley S. and Elizabeth M. Almquist. *Careers and Contingencies: How College Women Juggle with Gender.* New York: Dunellen, 1975. 269p.

In the introduction to this book about women and careers, Jessie Bernard comments that the problems facing working wives have not necessarily intensified in recent years, although attention to them in the literature might make it seem so.

179

Juggling roles has always been necessary for married working women. The new feminism has focused a spotlight on the problems of women so that what were essentially private struggles are now public ones. This study clarifies why career choices for women are even more difficult than they need to be.

Shirley Angrist and Elizabeth Almquist, sociologists, studied a group of college women during their college years between 1964 and 1968 to observe their aspirations and to determine if they were forming career plans. What the investigators found was that unlike male students whose occupational choices narrowed as they went through school, women tended to choose a life style rather than an occupation. Because of the probability of marriage and children, women tried to remain flexible, or keep contingencies in mind, so that the single-minded pursuit of a career was unlikely. The authors also found that the women in their study tended to choose conventional ''feminine'' careers which they thought, often incorrectly, would allow them to move in and out of the job market depending on family situations — fields like teaching, nursing and librarianship. What has happened, of course, is that professional competition no longer allows for an interrupted work pattern.

This study brings hard data to bear on conclusions that have badly needed such supporting evidence. Recent feminist literature talks generally about how socialization has prevented women from achieving successful career goals; Angrist and Almquist prove how this pattern operates specifically during the college years. Their findings have practical implications for college teachers, guidance people and, most of all, for young college women. Taking the position that all women, like all men, should exploit all of the resources in their college environments, the authors believe that women should be helped to avoid blocking their own chances for reasonable career goals. Planning a life style is, they find, unrealistic; planning a profession is not.

Bird, Caroline. *Born Female: The High Cost of Keeping Women Down.* **New York: Pocket Books, 1972. 302p.**

Born Female first appeared in 1968. It was based on interviews and research which had been undertaken two years earlier and which described the status of American women, particularly in the professional work force. The revised edition contains a new final chapter which summarizes relevant activities of the first two years of the women's liberation movement. The result is that Bird offers a credible account of ways in which women have been prevented from participating as productive workers in the American economy and the attempts made to correct the unequal distribution of power and wealth.

Like Betty Friedan, Caroline Bird is concerned primarily with educated, middle-class women. But where Friedan's exposure of the ''feminine mystique'' led her to criticize broad areas of American culture, Bird is concerned with the institutions of employment which treat women in stereotyped ways, and offer them ''jobs'' rather than ''careers.'' An important distinction that Bird makes between herself and Friedan is that Friedan puts the burden for change on women, whereas she believes that institutions themselves must change.

In presenting the evidence, Bird is far more convincing in showing the obstacles facing women than in offering hope for the future. She describes many cases involving prejudice, unfair practices, myths and downright lies about women: women are not offered jobs because men save them for other men; women are not taken seriously as workers; nepotism keeps equally well-trained women out of the academic posts which their husbands enjoy; in spite of labor statistics which point out the contrary, women are suspected of controlling most of the wealth in America; although they often head their own households and support their children, women's jobs are viewed as second incomes. In a chapter on what she calls "loop-hole women" Bird describes the attitudes of women who have made it to the top. They often fail to recognize or acknowledge prejudice against women, even though they have had to work twice as hard and twice as competently as men. However, one candid interviewee did say that she was looking forward to the day when a mediocre woman could go as far as a mediocre man.

To support her optimism, Bird refers to the transition that occurred between 1966 and 1970 when the women's movement was creating a sense of revolutionary change. At issue now is whether or not the movement has succeeded in manifesting the changes Bird talks about, changes which would give women freedom from sex-role stereotyping. Certainly the climate of opinion has altered so that women are freer to examine their options. But whether those in power will relinquish their hold enough to treat women fairly is still an open question.

Epstein, Cynthia Fuchs. *Woman's Place*. Berkeley: University of California Press, 1970. 221p.

At a time when sex discrimination suits were beginning to be filed against corporations and universities, Cynthia Epstein in *Woman's Place* provided additional explanations for professional women's limited career achievement. She brings the tools of the sociologist to bear on the dilemmas facing contemporary women. By pulling together pertinent research data from Jessie Bernard, Alice Rossi, Robert Merton and others, as well as material from her own dissertation on women lawyers, Epstein provides an analysis of what problems for women exist within the professional scene and how they can overcome them.

Epstein is interested not only in women's failures in the professional world, but also in some women's successes in a society which has insisted that women's place is in the home. It is in the examination of some of the prejudices against working women that Epstein's insights seem relevant to all women.

She examines a variety of role models and images that have created particular pressures on women who look outside the home for fulfillment. One of the outside influences she describes are behavioral scientists, particularly Freudians who have used their skills to persuade women to find their rightful place, meaning a domestic role. The concepts of "penis envy" and "castrating women" have had oppressive effects on women with ambition. Pervasive throughout the society is the way in which the career woman has been portrayed in literature and popular culture. If unmarried, she is at the very least frustrated, often becoming "the other woman," and if she is married and committed to some outside work, she is ultimately made to realize that true happiness can only be found in serving her family.

There are still other causes for the lack of significant numbers of women in "men's professions." Epstein points out, for instance, that so strong is the expectation to marry that fewer gifted women than gifted men enter college; and once they do, their tendency is to major in liberal arts programs rather than in more specific training. Epstein uses the phrase "the pattern of revocability," to refer to the fact that American women have cultural approval for dropping out of a profession without losing face; by the same token, a man who drops out is considered a failure.

In one of the best chapters in her book, Epstein deals with the obstacles facing women with families and professional lives who are suffering from what Epstein calls "role-strain." She offers suggestions for the resolution of some of the conflicts that inevitably occur between home and work responsibilities. Choosing friends who also work, delegating household responsibilities, and being selective in community involvements are a few of the ways in which a woman can operate with a minimum of criticism and with the greatest potential for functioning well.

For growing numbers of women re-examining their own aims in life, and for mothers thinking about their daughters' lives in other than traditional terms, *Woman's Place* is a book that can help to sort out problems and deal with them intelligently. Although the book addresses itself to an educated if not professional audience, the truths that Epstein reveals about conditioning and role-conflict inherent in the society apply to all women.

Kundsin, Ruth, ed. *Women & Success: The Anatomy of Achievement.* New York: William Morrow, 1974. 256p.

Much of the recent literature about women and careers discusses married women's failure to achieve professional goals, but the editor of this book has brought together essays which describe how many such women have succeeded. The conflicts that have always bedeviled the average married, childbearing woman have also affected the lives of successful women. The question under investigation then becomes why some women succeed where others fail? And as a measure of "success," Kundsin suggests we ask whether or not people are able to perform what they perceive as their work.

In her opening essay in this collection, Kundsin raises the following questions about women and success: "What is the source of their motivation? What factors influence their performance? How do these women look at themselves with regard to the traditional female roles of wife and mother? How are they able to achieve — and how do they feel about their achievement — in the context of an ambivalent and often hostile environment?"

The answers to these questions are provided by twelve biographical essays written by women who have achieved successful careers in the sciences.

They describe their family situations, how they chose their fields, what their obstacles have been and how they manage to get around them. The statements are honest, and have obviously been selected because the women tell their stories without pretending that they have had no problems. Some even suggest that they would have made different choices in planning their futures, given the difficulties they have had to work through. The phenomenon of the academic jet-setter is, for instance, a relatively new and inconvenient style of life that has come about since women have become resigned to taking jobs in places geographically distant from their husbands.

Essays by social scientists follow the biographies. They examine the influences that consistently appear — family background, education, problems of marriage and motherhood, and societal attitudes toward working women. Among these analyses is an essay by Matina Horner whose work on women and the motive to avoid success is germane to studies of achieving women. Other well known contributors include Mary Calderone, Esther Peterson and Mary I. Bunting.

This book presents important issues about successful professional lives for women and suggests still others. It offers conclusions from studies showing that women who desire to pursue careers are more content than those who feel such goals cannot be combined with marriage. What is suggested, however, is that successful women may possess levels of energy that exceed the average and that their records of achievement may be unobtainable to the majority. Material from the biographies also suggests that the fast-paced life resulting from combined job and domestic responsibilities may not be desirable for some women.

*   *   *

Arbanel, Karin and Connie McClung Siegel. *Woman's Work Book.* **New York: Praeger, 1975. 327p.**

Recognizing the difficulties that face women seeking employment in the 1970's, the authors have put together a guidebook giving specific information for women who want to match their skills to the job market. Geared to educated women, the book offers suggestions for writing resumés, finding jobs and being interviewed. It includes a directory of occupational organizations, career-counseling services and women's centers.

Baker, Elizabeth Faulkner. *Technology and Woman's Work.* **New York: Columbia University Press, 1964. 460p.**

A major study written by a professor of economics, this book describes the impact of technology on the employment patterns of women. More than one out of every three women was employed outside the home when this book was written, and that number is growing. Baker's study shows that World War II caused both government and industry to encourage married women to enter the labor market on a large scale, and that many remained there, those with more education more likely to be working outside the home than those with less education.

Benét, Mary Kathleen. *The Secretarial Ghetto.* **New York: McGraw-Hill, 1972. 181p.**

Benét views the masses of women in low-paying white collar office jobs as the proletariat with the male boss as the capitalist. She believes that the low status of female office workers will never be improved by waiting for men to rectify injustice, but that women will have to find their own direct and aggressive ways of improving their situations.

Bird, Caroline. *Everything a Woman Needs to Know to Get Paid What She's Worth.* **New York: David McKay, 1973. 304p.**

Like Benét, Bird views most women's areas of employment as a ghetto. In this book she supplies practical information for women seeking improvement — tactics for job-hunting, promotion and self-employment, ways to anticipate and avoid discrimination.

Cole, Doris. *From Tipi to Skyscraper: A History of Women in Architecture.* **Boston: I Press, 1973. 136p.**

The author, an architect, points out that only two percent of the architects practicing today are women, and that less than half of the women who have earned architectural degrees are registered architects. It is Cole's contention that this falling off of women from the profession is a contemporary phenomenon, since women have traditionally had an important place within the field. She refers to the Shakers and their Utopian communes and to the designs implemented by Catharine Beecher as nineteenth-century examples. It is only in the modern period with its corporate structure of architectural firms, and the exclusion of women from schools that have assured their departure from the field. Cole's book is a unique study, abetted by fine photographs that clarify her case.

Fidell, Linda S. and John DeLamater, eds. *Women in the Professions: What's All the Fuss About?* **Beverly Hills: Sage, 1971. 144p.**

Some interesting conclusions about job discrimination come out of the discussion in this collection about women in the professions: that low self esteem causes low status for women; that women tend not to complain about discrimination in situations where male peers report its existence.

Garson, Barbara. *All the Livelong Day: The Meaning and Demeaning of Routine Work.* **Garden City, New York: Doubleday, 1975. 221p.**

Garson spent two years examining the way people cope with routine, monotonous work. Although not specifically addressing her investigation to women, she is in fact exploring the work lives of numbers of women. For example, she interviewed women who spent their day stacking ping-pong paddles into groups of fifty. She found that the workers humanized their situations by inventing games to prevent themselves from turning into robots. She concludes that people passionately want to work and will find ingenious ways to measure their accomplishments.

Golde, Peggy, ed. *Women in the Field: Anthropological Experiences.* Chicago: Aldine, 1970. 343p.

The twelve women anthropologists contributing to this volume describe not only their memorable field trips, but also the subjective impact of these experiences. They discuss how they felt as women working in a foreign culture.

Gordon, Francine E. and Myra H. Strober, eds. *Bringing Women into Management.* New York: McGraw-Hill, 1975. 168p.

Based on a conference held at the Stanford Business School, this book is intended to encourage and assist top management in bringing women into the upper echelons of the corporate world. It contains discussions by top women academics, and provides practical information on how to implement change.

Gregory, Chester W. *Women in Defense Work During World War II: An Analysis of the Labor Problems and Women's Rights.* New York: Exposition, 1974. 243p.

The war brought several million women into positions that were unfamiliar to them. Women employed in the defense plants demonstrated such skill that a new social, economic and psychological equality between men and women developed. Gregory feels that as a result of the war crisis, women were able to emancipate themselves to a greater degree than ever before.

Hoffman, Lois Wladis and F. Ivan Nye. *Working Mothers.* San Francisco: Jossey-Bass, 1974. 272p.

This volume pulls together the available sociological and psychological research on the effects of the working mother on the family and on the woman herself. One of the authors' aims is to indicate where further research in this broad area is needed, and they provide an extensive bibliography which will be important to scholars engaged in this area of investigation.

Holmstrom, Lynda Lytle. *The Two-Career Family.* Cambridge, Mass.: Schenkman, 1972. 203p.

With more women aspiring to careers rather than jobs, new problems are facing more couples who both have demanding outside commitments. Holmstrom has done a detailed analysis of the living patterns of twenty-seven couples and found that in the two-career family certain barriers were encountered: "the rigid structure of the professions, the isolation of the small modern family, and the current equation of masculinity with superiority." She describes in her book how couples organized their lives to meet these challenges.

Kreps, Juanita. *Sex in the Marketplace: American Women at Work.* Baltimore: Johns Hopkins University Press, 1971. 117p.

This is a survey of the literature on the subject of the activity of women in the labor force, addressing itself to such questions as when women work, at what jobs, and under what arrangement.

Kane, Paula. *Sex Objects in the Sky.* **Chicago: Follett, 1974. 159p.**

Next to the Playboy Bunny, the airline stewardess has symbolized the most sexually available ''working-girl'' in America. Paula Kane writes an exposé of the life on that job, a life she rejected with the help of the Stewardesses for Women's Rights organization. She notes the changes brought about by that group, including the right of stewardesses to marry and have children.

Lloyd, Cynthia B., ed. *Sex, Discrimination, and the Division of Labor.* **New York: Columbia University Press, 1975. 431p.**

Since economics scholarship has traditionally focused only on the male, this book is valuable as a resource for students who need an overview of the economic picture for women. Aside from essays, the book contains helpful notes and a good bibliography.

Lyle, Jerolyn R. *Women in Industry: Employment Patterns of Women in Corporate America.* **Lexington, Mass.: D.C. Heath, 1973. 164p.**

Written for other economists, this book describes economic discrimination in technical terms. Among Lyle's findings, for instance, is the fact that among non-industrial firms, those with more diversification in output and with suburban locations exhibit less discrimination than do the very specialized firms in cities.

Lynch, Edith M. *The Executive Suite — Feminine Style.* **New York: AMACOM, 1973. 258p.**

Edith Lynch, herself a business executive, writes honestly about the role of women in management, and provides a helpful description of how women can achieve careers in the business world.

Loeser, Herta. *Women, Work, and Volunteering.* **Boston: Beacon Press, 1974. 254p.**

Acknowledging that volunteer work is viewed with suspicion by feminists, Loeser still maintains that paid employment is not for everyone. She considers that many women are involved in life patterns where they move from full responsibilities as housewives and mothers to outside work. Her view is that with proper counseling, such women can acquire training and confidence as volunteers, and acquire skills that can lead them to paid work. Loeser views volunteer work as potentially more interesting and fulfilling than many paid jobs, and has a Utopian dream that larger proportions of society — not just middle and upper class women — will find reward by working within their communities as volunteers. This is a handbook filled with information for women who are seeking intelligent ways to bridge their passage from domestic life to the outside world.

Lopata, Helena Z. *Occupation Housewife.* New York: Oxford University Press, 1971. 387p.

This sociological study of a group of Chicago-area women finds that the role of housewife in America has low status in spite of the complex activities and responsibilities of women who carry out these duties.

Lopate, Carol. *Women in Medicine.* Baltimore: Johns Hopkins University Press, 1968. 204p.

Lopate's study focuses on the under-utilization of women in the medical profession. It is addressed to educators, counselors and social scientists as well as to M.D.'s. In the spirit of the 1960's, Lopate speaks of the waste of the potential of women who have been educated but socialized not to choose demanding professions. She offers suggestions for the future, including ways to combine a commitment to work with marriage and children.

Loring, Rosalind and Theodora Wells. *Breakthrough: Women into Management.* New York: Van Nostrand Reinhold, 1972. 213p.

This is a practical discussion of how women can enter higher management positions. Directed to those who hold hiring power in organizations, the book indicates how and why the admission of more women into the managerial ranks will ensure greater productivity for organizations.

Madden, Janice Fanning. *The Economics of Sex Discrimination.* Lexington, Mass.: D.C. Heath, 1973. 140p.

Written for the professional economist, this book provides an economic analysis of discrimination against women in the labor market.

Marks, Geoffrey and William K. Beatty. *Women in White.* New York: Scribner's, 1972. 239p.

The authors present a survey of the relationship of women to the field of medicine, and provide biographical sketches of some of the most important women doctors in history. These include Elizabeth Blackwell, Mary Putnam Jacobi and Alice Hamilton.

Oakley, Ann. *The Sociology of Housework.* New York: Pantheon, 1974. 242p.

This is a sociological study of housework, an occupation that has been neglected by scholars who either study women in outside work or else in relationship to other members of their families. But here Oakley examines such areas as women's attitudes about themselves as housewives and their attitudes about the work itself.

————. *Woman's Work: The Housewife, Past and Present.* New York: Pantheon, 1974. 275p.

The author, a British sociologist, questions the history and the nature of women's unpaid work in the home. Oakley thinks that the division of "real" work (men's work) from housework is a phenomenon that began with the industrial revolution. Women, she feels, should refuse to be put into a designated role. Her study includes four detailed interviews with housewifes.

O'Neill, William. *Women at Work: Including the Long Day, the Story of a Working Girl* by Dorothy Richardson and *Inside the New York Telephone Company* by Elinor Langer. Chicago: Quadrangle, 1972. 360p.

O'Neill has brought together reprints of two descriptions of working women, the first a description of factory life at the beginning of the century, and the other, the telephone company in 1970. O'Neill draws some interesting conclusions in the introduction showing that women are still exploited, even though their standards of living have improved over the years.

Osen, Lynn M. *Women in Mathematics.* Cambridge, Mass.: MIT Press, 1974. 185p.

In general, great mathematicians are not lionized like their counterparts in music, literature or science. Even less is known about women who have made contributions in the field. Osen's book is an effort to "trace the impact women have had on the development of mathematical thought, to profile the lives of these women, and to explore the social context within which they worked."

O'Sullivan, Judith. *Workers and Allies: Female Participation in the American Trade Union Movement, 1824-1976.* Washington, D.C.: Smithsonian Institution, 1975. 96p.

The Smithsonian Institution sponsored a Traveling Exhibition about the participation of women in the labor movement, and this book is a guide to that collection. It contains photographs and biographical information about the many women whose activities are just being recognized.

Samuels, Catherine. *The Forgotten Five Million, Women in Public Employment: A Guide to Eliminating Sex Discrimination.* New York: Women's Action Alliance, 1975. 298p.

The Women's Action Alliance, a national non-profit organization, is a clearinghouse of resources and information to assist women in overcoming social barriers. In this spirit, they have developed this "how to" publication to aid women in analyzing their jobs as public employees and, if necessary, to organize affirmative action plans.

Schneiderman, Rose with Lucy Goldthwaite. *All for One.* New York: Paul Eriksson, 1967. 264p.

Rose Schneiderman came up through the ranks of the American Labor Movement to become the president of the New York Women's Trade Union League. She helped organize the International Ladies Garment Workers Union, worked for suffrage, and became the only woman on the Labor Advisory Board of the National Recovery Act. In *All For One* she tells the story of her growing commitment to the labor movement, and gives glimpses into her personal friendships with such American women as Eleanor Roosevelt and Mary Dreir. Though the theme of the immigrant boy making good in America is familiar, stories about successful immigrant women are rare. Rose Schneiderman's story is an important corrective.

Schwartz, Eleanor Brantley. *The Sex Barrier in Business.* Atlanta: Georgia State University Press, 1971. 116p.

Based on a questionnaire answered by almost 300 men and women in top management positions, this study discusses the problems of women gaining executive positions in business organizations. It offers recommendations for bringing equality to big business.

Seed, Suzanne. *Saturday's Child: 36 Women Talk about Their Jobs.* New York: Bantam, 1974. 159p.

Taking its title from the well known nursery rhyme that begins and ends: "Monday's child is fair of face ... Saturday's child worked hard for a living," Seed's book is a collection of brief statements by women who are working in diverse fields such as sportswriting, TV reporting, the sciences, trades and government service.

Spradley, James P. and Brenda J. Mann. *The Cocktail Waitress: Woman's Work in a Man's World.* New York: Wiley, 1975. 154p.

The authors of this study are urban anthropologists who studied the ordinary activities of a neighborhood bar to gather data about female identity in American culture. By observing the division of labor, social structure, the division of territory, and the use of language within the typical bar, they documented male dominance in everyday situations. That the particular bar they studied was a male sanctuary was startling to the investigators because the clientele were young college students and not working-class men. This is a gem of a book which points out the need for further research on the social interaction between men and women in ordinary settings.

Strainchamps, Ethel, ed. *Rooms with No View: A Woman's Guide to the Man's World of the Media.* Compiled by the Media Women's Association. New York: Harper and Row, 1974. 333p.

Exposés of what goes on behind the scenes in the publishing world are always fascinating, and this is true of this book written by women employed in the mass communications industry. Realizing the responsibility of the media for influencing popular thought, the women insist on the importance of companies hiring women for top jobs where decisions are made. Instead, women are in the lowest, poorest paid jobs throughout the industry.

Teitz, Joyce. *What's a Nice Girl Like You Doing in a Place Like This?* New York: Coward, McCann and Geoghegan, 1972. 285p.

The title aside, this book contains serious biographical essays on young women who have managed successfully to combine marriage with ambitious careers.

The eleven subjects include lawyer Marian Wright Edelman and writer Susan Edmiston. The book is a popular discussion of the issues presented in the scholarly *Women and Success* edited by Ruth Kundsin.

Theodore, Athena, ed. *The Professional Woman.* **Cambridge, Mass.: Schenkman, 1971. 769p.**

Athena Theodore has brought together in this collection research about the status of professional women in America. As a sociologist, Theodore is interested in exploring the role of the professional woman within a sociological framework; as a feminist she is interested in pointing out the obstacles that obstruct women who have career ambitions.

Warrior, Betsy and Lisa Leghorn. *Houseworker's Handbook.* **Cambridge, Mass.: Women's Center, 1975. 109p.**

The authors present a feminist view of issues relating to women as housewives — the controversy over doing unpaid work, the situation of battered wives — and provide reasons for housewives to organize and fight for recognition as people doing valuable and important work.

Appendix

Since 1975 books about American women have been appearing at an even more prodigious rate than they did during the first half of the decade. To some extent this output is the result of the efforts of trade publishers to capitalize on what they perceive as a passing fad. But the work itself is largely the result of the phenomenon of the women's studies movement, the academic arm of the women's movement that has placed feminist issues within the structure of intellectual inquiry.

Academic courses about women came about when feminist instructors and their students realized that the inequities apparent in contemporary society were only a continuation of what historically had been true for women. Typically, women had been left out of most academic disciplines—absent from history, ignored by the social sciences, and overlooked in literature and the arts. The mission of the women's studies movement is to correct the male bias of the curriculum that exists at most institutions of higher learning. Until the time when standard courses provide an integrated view of the perceptions and contributions of both men and women, courses focusing on women will continue to be necessary.

These courses present a woman-centered perspective that asks new questions within the disciplines; merely tacking on a few books about women to a standard curriculum is hardly sufficient, for that results in intellectual tokenism of a particularly condescending type.

The support and development of women's studies programs vary among institutions. Traditional academics raise questions about its methodology, in particular expressing uneasiness about its interdisciplinary nature. Even more obstructive to its widespread implementation has been the inability of traditionalists to acknowledge that the prevailing notion of woman as "other" has distorted knowledge. Perhaps this is a truth that must be felt if it is to be accepted. While some would argue that not only women, but certain men are effective champions of feminism, the more interesting question is why numbers of women still resist it. Feminist awareness is a discomforting process. It requires a willingness to examine the past to see how women in general have been denigrated and to scrutinze the details of one's own life for evidence of hostile treatment and missed opportunities. For white middle- and upper-class women, viewing the self as disadvantaged requires courage and emotional honesty, for it invites having to deal with such negative feelings as anger, frustration, and regret. Racial minorities and the poor have had less protection against these emotions.

The authors of most of the books considered here, though they differ in areas of interest and degrees of intensity, share the belief that feminist awareness leads to an intellectually enriched and more politically just way of looking at the world. The development of new topics of inquiry and the expansion of others since 1975 are impressive evidence of the growing strength and imaginativeness of feminist thought in America. Writers are investigating every discipline outside of the physical sciences for new information about the experiences and perceptions of women and for insights about how women have been viewed in the past and are perceived today. Some painful subjects are being addressed by authors in their attempt to understand problems inherent in the relationship between men and women. All of the violence issues— woman-abuse, incest, pornography, sexual mutilation, and rape—are receiving feminist analyses today, whereas in 1975 only rape was being discussed within the context of sexual politics. Lesbianism was narrowly defined previously by heterosexuals as sexual preference alone, but is now being self-defined by lesbians as a feminist position with a complex philosophical and political view of life.

The work within such areas as history, literary criticism, and art history, all subjects of intense concern to women's studies scholars since the beginning of the movement, has grown not only in quantity but also in sophistication. In general, authors' analyses seem more considered and self-assured. Scholars are less driven to produce all at once a tightly constructed methodology to package women's history, or feminist literary or art criticism. They see themselves as contributors to a process, an evolving level of theory that grows more refined each year. These signs all indicate that the future of feminist thought in America will be even richer and more comprehensive.

Abortion

Unlike books written before 1973, which were mainly abstract debates over the morality of abortion, the current literature deals with the practical realities. The 1973 Supreme Court decision to allow abortion and the subsequent cutting off of Medicaid funds by the federal government have led to new themes. The arguments center around the question of whose rights should have the higher priority: those of the unborn or those of women?

In *Abortion in America,* James C. Mohr places the argument within a historic and legal perspective. Most surprising, he reports that laws against abortion did not exist at the beginning of the nineteenth century. Such laws came into being throughout the century largely by members of the medical profession in their efforts to take control of an area they perceived to be strictly medical business.

Two outspoken opponents of the legalization of abortion are John T. Noonan, Jr., author of *A Private Choice,* and Dr. Bernard N. Nathanson, author of *Aborting America.* Noonan, who is consistent in his opposition, having written against legalization in 1970, now argues for an amendment to the Constitution to protect the lives of the unborn. He wishes to return to the community the power to defend the family structure centered on the child. His philosophical position insists that abortion cannot be a private choice. Unlike Noonan, Nathanson has recently switched sides on the issue. As a co-founder in 1969 of the National Association for Repeal of Abortion Laws (later renamed the National Abortion Rights Action League), he was at the forefront of the repeal movement. His book is an explantion of why he now takes an anti-abortion stand. Like Noonan, Nathanson centers his argument on the plight of the fetus, never complicating his discussion by considering the plight of women.

To the unsympathetic, the choice of women to abort their unborn is perceived as a callous decision. However, the common theme of two books written by women who underwent abortions is that the decision is painful and ambivalent. In her book, *In Necessity and Sorrow,* Magda Denes writes: "Abortion is an abomination unless it is experienced as a human event of great sorrow and terrible necessity." Her book, an exploration of the complicated feelings of the patients, staff, and physicians at one particular hospital, is a long statement of the personal anguish involved in the abortion decision. In *The Ambivalence of Abortion,* Linda Bird Francke stresses that before abortion was legal, the energy of most counselors went into expediting safe abortions for women, and not into helping couples work through the decision-making process. Francke feels that to the detriment of both men and women the responsibility for all things concerning reproduction is placed on women. This burden leads to unresolved feelings about abortion that do not go away.

What is clear to both these authors and to Ellen Franfort, author of *Rosie:*

The Investigation of a Wrongful Death, is that whether legal or not, abortions will continue to be sought by women. Rosaura Jimenez died in 1977 from infection resulting from an illegal abortion. After investigating this death, Frankfort proves that had Medicaid funding not been cut off by the federal government, Jimenez would never have resorted to the dangerous and ultimately fatal procedure that she underwent at the hands of an unlicensed practitioner.

Denes, Magda. *In Necessity and Sorrow: Life and Death in an Abortion Hospital.* New York: Basic Books, 1976. 247p.

Francke, Linda Bird. *The Ambivalance of Abortion.* New York: Random House, 1978. 267p.

Frankfort, Ellen. *Rosie: The Investigation of a Wrongful Death.* New York: Dial Press, 1979. 173p.

Mohr, James C. *Abortion in America: The Origins and Evolution of National Policy, 1800–1900.* New York: Oxford University Press, 1978. 331p.

Nathanson, Bernard N. *Aborting America.* Garden City, N.Y.: Doubleday, 1979. 320p.

Noonan, John T., Jr. *A Private Choice: Abortion in America in the Seventies.* New York: The Free Press, 1979. 244p.

Black and Other Minority Women

Minority women suffer all of the discrimination facing white women in the society plus the additional burden of being part of a racial minority in a racist society. Unlike white women who often improve their status through marriage to upwardly mobile white males, minority women have had little help in improving their situations. The feminist movement initially held little appeal for black and other minority women who justifiably feared dividing their communities and isolating themselves. However, in recent years a black feminist movement, which celebrates the collective experience of black women, has appeared. Members of this movement see as their priority the support of other black women; therefore, their relationship to the white feminist movement is necessarily of less concern to them.

Just as the strongest writing during the earliest period of the women's movement appeared as articles and poetry, the most powerful black feminist writing is presently in short form and is found in journals. *Conditions: Five,* a special issue of a periodical devoted to black women's experiences, is a particularly fine example.

Black women's search for their own history is a theme that permeates all feminist writing. The absence of black women from traditional American historiography is the particular concern of Sharon Harley and Rosalyn Terborg-Penn, editors of *The Afro-American Woman.* This collection of nine historical essays includes articles on black women in the early days of the republic, discrimination against black women in the woman suffrage movement, and the history of black women's education, among other topics. *Beautiful, Also, Are the Souls of My Black Sisters* by Jeanne Noble, an impassioned book celebrating black women, is based mainly on secondary sources. The material on twentieth-century writers and singers is particularly good.

A concern for the historic record is one of the themes of Michele Wallace's *Black Macho and the Myth of the Superwoman.* She observes, for example, that black women have been written out of the history of the civil rights movement. However, Wallace's major concern is that black men and women hold distorted views of one another. Because the black militant movement advocated power for men, Wallace feels that a "black macho mystique," which ignores the needs of women, was created. And at the same time, she feels that the myth of the black superwoman—a view of all black women as powerful and resilient—has been created by whites. Wallace has been criticized by black reviewers for her lack of a feminist analysis of the relationship between black men and women.

The recovery of women writers, a leitmotif of the women's movement as a whole, is a priority for black feminists. The works of Zora Neale Hurston are being reprinted, and a fine biography, *Zora Neale Hurston* by Robert Hemenway, has appeared. A student of Franz Boas, Hurston was already a published writer before she studied anthropology at Columbia. Her fiction and the folklore she collected were celebrations of black people. Alice Walker, who wrote the foreword to Hemenway's book, says that Hurston's work contains: "racial health—a sense of black people as complete, complex, undiminished human beings."

Books with some feminist perspective about other minority women are just beginning to appear. Beatrice Medicine's *The Native American Woman* is a good introductory book that offers insights about how to pursue research on native American women. Medicine warns that most anthropological works ignore native women or at best present them as drudges. Histories are even worse, for they consistently denigrate women by emphasizing only the bizarre aspects of their lives. As Medicine illustrates with the excerpts she includes in her book: "One must simply set about examining a great many ethnological studies of Indian tribes to glean information about the diverse role of women in Native cultures."

In *Daughters of the Earth*, Carolyn Niethammer attempts to construct a narrative of tribal life from the female perspective by pulling together information from interviews, fables, songs, and incantations. Jane Katz's collection, *I Am the Fire of Time*, offers almost ninety examples of songs, poetry, prose, prayer, and oral history of the voices of native American women. Many of the writings are a moving testimony to the central position of these women within their cultures.

Considering that a sexist ideology permeates Latin American and Puerto Rican cultures, one could reasonably expect to see a flood of feminist books to appear in reaction. So far, however, there is only a trickle. *The Puerto Rican Woman*, edited by Edna Acosta-Belén, provides an overview of women's place in Puerto Rican history and society, indicating the difficulties confronting women who struggle for their rights. *La Chicana*, an important new study by Alfredo Mirandé and Evangelina Enriquez, provides a historic overview and a contemporary analysis of the lives of Mexican-American women. The authors perceive Chicanas as experiencing multiple forms of oppression: "as women, as members of a colonized group, and as members of a culture perceived to be dominated by males."

Acosta-Belén, Edna, ed. *The Puerto Rican Woman*. New York: Praeger, 1979. 169p.

Conditions: Five. (P.O. Box 56, Van Brunt Station, Brooklyn, N.Y. 11215).

Harley, Sharon, and Rosalyn Terborg-Penn, eds. *The Afro-American Woman: Struggles and Images*. Port Washington, N.Y.: National University Publications, 1978. 137p.

Hemenway, Robert E. *Zora Neale Hurston: A Literary Biography*. Urbana: University of Illinois Press, 1977. 432p.

Katz, Jane B., ed. *I Am the Fire of Time: The Voices of Native American Women.* New York: E. P. Dutton, 1977. 201p.

Medicine, Beatrice. *The Native American Woman: A Perspective.* Las Cruces, N.M.: ERIC/CRESS: for sale by National Educational Laboratory Publishers, Austin, Tex., 1978. 107p.

Mirandé, Alfredo, and Evangelina Enriquez. *La Chicana: The Mexican-American Woman.* Chicago: University of Chicago Press, 1979. 283p.

Niethammer, Carolyn. *Daughers of the Earth: The Lives and Legends of American Indian Women.* New York: Collier Books, 1977. 281p.

Noble, Jeanne L. *Beautiful, Also, Are the Souls of My Black Sisters.* Englewood Cliffs, N.J.: Prentice-Hall, 1978. 346p.

Wallace, Michele. *Black Macho and the Myth of the Superwoman.* New York: Dial, 1978. 182p.

Crime and Imprisonment

The notion of women as the "forgotten offenders" is no longer the central theme for scholars working in the area of women and crime, for significant work has begun. Carol Smart, a British sociologist, explores in *Women, Crime and Criminology* the possibilities for creating a feminist intellectual framework within which to study the woman criminal. Her examination of standard literature in her field reveals two commonly held views: a male-oriented ideology that assumes that any rejection of the female role—as in criminal behavior—is an indication of personality disorder; and the absence of women as subjects of analysis, the implication being that they are insignificant members of society and not worthy of study. Smart points out that women have been ignored not only as criminals, but until recently, as victims of crime. And no work has yet been done on the effect of the imprisonment of women on their families.

In discussing the possibilities for a feminist approach to criminology, Smart brings up a point that concerns most feminist theorists: that by keeping the study of women separate from the study of men, one runs the risk of ghettoizing the field. In effect this could maintain the double standard, the very situation feminists are trying to overcome. Although Smart offers no solution to this problem, she does insist that future studies of female criminality should consider the wider question of women's roles in the society-at-large. This approach will expose underlying assumptions about women held by the justice system.

In their collection of essays, *The Criminology of Deviant Women*, editors Freda Adler and Rita James Simon bring together "contemporary issues in female criminality and their solution by the criminal justice system with an historical and cross-cultural emphasis representing all the theoretical schools of thought." The editors point out the need for further research to collect original data for an analysis of the relationship between the social status of criminals and the kinds of crimes they commit and to know more about women who commit larceny, embezzlement, or fraud, since comparatively more is already known about those involved in homicide, prostitution, and shoplifting.

In another anthology, *The Female Offender*, edited by Laura Crites, contributors point out that although women have been treated more leniently within the judicial system, the "pedestal factor" has seldom operated to their advantage, just as it has not for women in the larger society. They find the current laws against prostitution hypocritical and unfair, and argue for decriminalization rather than legalization, which would have controls.

In her study, *Women, Crime, and the Criminal Justice System*, Lee Bowker describes that system as "a behemoth dominated by men and male ways of looking at the world" and says that it represents "the most formal development of cross-sex social controls in human society." And in her monograph, *Easy Time: Female Inmates on Temporary Release,* Belinda McCarthy describes the effect of home furlough programs on female inmates. She looks at their perceptions of freedom and at their attempts to manage the demands of independence. She found that inmates enjoyed their freedom and—unlike expectations—managed their stress very well. Such unexpected findings underlie the need for more work on specific aspects of women offenders.

Adler, Freda, and Rita James Simon, eds. *The Criminology of Deviant Women.* Boston: Houghton Mifflin, 1979. 425p.

Bowker, Lee H. *Women, Crime, and the Criminal Justice System.* Lexington, Mass.: Lexington Books, 1978. 286p.

Crites, Laura, ed. *The Female Offender.* Lexington, Mass.: Lexington Books, 1976. 230p.

McCarthy, Belinda Rodgers. *Easy Time: Female Inmates on Temporary Release.* Lexington, Mass.: Lexington Books, 1979. 214p.

Smart, Carol. *Women, Crime and Criminology: A Feminist Critique.* Boston: Routledge & Kegan Paul, 1977. 208p.

Education

Feminists continue to be intensely concerned with the subject of education, for it is rightly perceived as a process that can either perpetuate injustices to women or lead the way to change. Two recent issues of the *Harvard Educational Review* (November 1979 and Feburary 1980), devoted entirely to "Women and Education," demonstrate the range of issues that fall within the subject: psychological development of females, women's status in higher education and as school administrators, feminist reflections on the social sciences, philosophy, and socialism, commentary on sexism in teacher education texts, perspectives on the history of women's education, and issues in women's studies. All of these topics are featured in principal essays in these journals, and many are the subject of recent books.

Sex Bias in the Schools, edited by Janice Pottker and Andrew Fishel, is a compilation of forty-one selections that describe and measure sexism as it occurs throughout the educational experience of girls and women. The unavoidable conclusion of the editors is that "the schools, acting as agents for the existing social order, contribute to the maintenance of a society where sex rather than ability determines the limits of a person's accomplishment." In *Undoing Sex Stereotypes,* a team of researchers headed by Marcia Guttentag and Helen Bray describe the degree of sexism found in the attitudes of the 400 children they studied. The authors explain how nonstereotyped views can be introduced into schools and provide resources for doing so.

Other writers are pointing out that the initiative to change this social order must come from parents and counselors as well as from teachers within formal classrooms. Two books, *Right from the Start* by Selma Greenberg and *Non-Sexist Childraising* by Carrie Carmichael, offer practical advice to parents attuned to feminist issues who aspire to raise children free from tradition-stereotyped roles. According to both authors, this accomplishment will affect every aspect of family life and will call for a redefinition of motherhood and fatherhood. *Perspectives on Non-Sexist Early Childhood Education,* edited by Barbara Sprung, is a collection of papers from the first National Conference on Non-Sexist Education sponsored in 1976 by The Women's Action Alliance. The contributors trace the problem beyond the classroom to a myriad of social attitudes that reflect built-in biases against women. These attitudes turn up in the prevailing educational counseling as Michael Harway and Helen S. Astin show in *Sex Discrimination in Career Counseling and Education.* They point out how females are routinely and unmindfully channeled into socially prescribed occupational slots.

To understand why the problems that beset women in educational institutions have taken their present form, scholars are pursuing historic inquiries into the purpose and nature of women's education. In *Better than Rubies,* Phyllis Stock charts the course of women's education in the Western world from the Renaissance to the present. She examines the types of education available to women in the past, what the social conditions have been, and how women's education related to the social order and to women's relationships with men. In her study, *Women at Cornell*, Charlotte Conable takes a hard look at the realities that faced women who attended the first major institution in the East to adopt coeducation. She provides evidence showing that although Cornell appeared to be committed to educating women, in reality the University concentrated on the educational, professional, and athletic needs of men. All of the differences imposed by the society-at-large were played out in the Cornell setting: women were treated as a privileged, protected group, restricted to specific parts of the University, and were thereby kept in their place.

Several current books examine the history of the Seven Sister colleges for evidence of their role in the shaping of women's education in America. In *I'm Radcliffe! Fly Me!* Liva Baker accuses the prestigious women's colleges of failure. By emulating male colleges and by accepting the subordinate role of women in society, the schools have institutionalized a timidity that "has resulted in an historical failure of the Seven Sisters to assume responsibility for serious women's education, which in turn has helped to perpetuate the ancillary role of women." Although she covers the same ground as Baker, Elaine Kendall in *"Peculiar Institutions"* presents an uncritical, informal history of the Seven Sister colleges. Most striking are her revelations about the dissimilarity in the origins of the various schools. Radcliffe and Barnard were ancillary to key male institutions, while Smith, Vassar, Wellesley, and Bryn Mawr were independently established by wealthy benefactors who were not particularly knowledgeable about the educational needs of women. Mount Holyoke's founder, Mary Lyon, was notable in that she had educational ideals. In *Collegiate Women*, Roberta Frankfort offers the thesis that after the first generation of women college graduates, the women's colleges gave up the commitment to educate women for leadership. Instead, they used their influence to convince women that education was an important enhancement to their key role within the domestic setting.

The current women's studies movement takes on a new meaning in the light of these histories of women's education in America. Women are saying not only that the traditional educational system is failing them now but also that it has always failed them. Innovative education designed for the interests of women has been slow to come and has met resistance; however, its need becomes most clear when historians point out that the need has always been there and that it has never before been met.

Joan Roberts's intention in *Beyond Intellectual Sexism* is to grasp the underlying ideas within specific academic disciplines that have led to sex discrimination in academia and the professions. She brings together essays written from a variety of perspectives by feminist scholars from the University of Wisconsin, Madison. Chapters about education include essays on public schools, higher education, physical education, the status of home economics, and the status of women. Other chapters explore literary criticism, psychology, biology, and law. *The Study of Women,* edited by Eloise Snyder, is another anthology that deals with the deficiencies of traditional higher education curricula by pointing out established intellectual biases against women. In a thoughtful foreword and afterword, Jessie Bernard explains the necessity and the challenge of women's studies as a corrective.

Women's Studies, edited by Kathleen Blumhagen and Walter Johnson, is an anthology that goes beyond justifying the need for women's studies, by providing some history of the field, a discussion of current issues and problems facing it, and examples of the methodology of research in women's studies. *Seven Years Later* by Florence Howe is a report of the structures and effectiveness of fifteen women's studies programs across the nation. Although her study is a survey rather than an evaluation, Howe does provide the first systematic approach to reviewing past accomplishments and future needs of responsible programs in the field.

Although most of the books about women's studies are concerned with higher education, *Women's Studies* by Gail McLure and John McLure explores the ways in which women's studies can be introduced into elementary and secondary education. In chapters about traditional school subjects, they indicate how an enlightened approach to information and attitudes about women can effectively change standard school curricula.

Baker, Liva. *I'm Radcliffe! Fly Me! The Seven Sisters and the Failure of Women's Education.* New York: Macmillan, 1976. 246p.

Blumhagen, Kathleen O'Connor, and Walter D. Johnson, eds. *Women's Studies: An Interdisciplinary Collection.* Westport, Conn.: Greenwood Press, 1978. 142p.

Carmichael, Carrie. *Non-Sexist Childraising.* Boston: Beacon Press, 1977. 162p.

Conable, Charlotte Williams. *Women at Cornell: The Myth of Equal Education.* Ithaca, N.Y.: Cornell University Press, 1977. 211p.

Frankfort, Roberta. *Collegiate Women: Domesticity and Career in Turn-of-the-Century America.* New York: New York University Press, 1977. 121p.

Greenberg, Selma. *Right from the Start: A Guide to Nonsexist Child Rearing.* Boston: Houghton Mifflin, 1978. 242p.

Guttentag, Marcia, and Helen Bray. *Undoing Sex Stereotypes: Research and Resources for Educators.* New York: McGraw-Hill, 1976. 342p.

Harway, Michael, and Helen S. Astin. *Sex Discrimination in Career Counseling and Education.* New York: Praeger, 1977. 154p.

Howe, Florence. *Seven Years Later: Women's Studies Programs in 1976.* Washington, D.C.: National Advisory Council on Women's Educational Programs, 1977. 104p.

Kendall, Elaine. *"Peculiar Institutions": An Informal History of the Seven Sister Colleges.* New York: G. P. Putnam's Sons, 1976. 272p.

McLure, Gail Thomas, and John W. McLure, *Women's Studies.* Washington, D.C.: National Education Association, 1977. 80p.

Pottker, Janice, and Andrew Fishel, eds. *Sex Bias in the Schools. The Research Evidence.* Cranbury, N.J.: Associated University Presses, 1977. 571p.

Roberts, Joan I., ed. *Beyond Intellectual Sexism: A New Woman, A New Reality.* New York: David McKay, 1976. 386p.

Synder, Eloise C., ed. *The Study of Women: Enlarging Perspectives of Social Reality.* New York: Harper & Row, 1979. 379p.

Sprung, Barbara, ed. *Perspectives on Non-Sexist Early Childhood Education.* New York: Teachers College Press, 1978. 192p.

Stock, Phyllis. *Better than Rubies: A History of Women's Education.* New York: G. P. Putnam's Sons, 1978. 252p.

Feminism

In the late 1970s feminist writers produced books that provide a retrospective of their development as activists and writers along with their current views on feminist issues. Adrienne Rich presents in *On Lies, Secrets, and Silence* a collection of prose written between 1966 and 1978, which traces the ever-expanding consciousness of a gifted artist and feminist theorist. Her astonishing versatility is exhibited as she moves through such subjects as history, language, poetry, racism, lesbianism, motherhood, and the uses of scholarship as they affect the lives of women. Her concern throughout is to sharpen her readers' awareness of the hostility to women inherent within the culture, and above all, to help them resist colluding in their own oppression by urging changes in female patterns of passivity and silence.

Going Too Far is a collection of articles, speeches, letters, and other writings that chronicle Robin Morgan's growth as a feminist activist and as a woman. Her incipient feminism is evident in letters written in the mid-1960s that secretly recorded grievances about her marriage. She grows up during the 1960s and 1970s, turning away from the radical left—an event crystallized in her famous essay, "Goodbye to All That," and goes on to become an effective and energetic leader in the women's movement.

There is a deep humaneness present in *Dreamers & Dealers*, Leah Fritz's personal account of a decade of feminism. Her vision of a better world insists on an end to factionalism among groups of women, and she is clearly grieved by a lesbian separatist movement that at times has cut her off from productive feminist involvement. Vivian Gornick's *Essays in Feminism*, a collection of articles written mainly for the *Village Voice* during a period of nine years, is a summation of her "political apprenticeship" and "self-education" as a feminist. She writes with great verve about whatever happens to interest her: why men hate women, why women fear success, women and money, and the conflict between love and work. And finally there is Betty Friedan's collection, *It Changed My Life*, a title that refers to the effect of *The Feminine Mystique* on her readers and herself. The book is organized around her developing identity as a spokeswoman for feminism and includes letters from readers of *The Feminine Mystique*, documents relating to the founding of the National Organization for Women, excerpts from her *McCall's* column, and articles about her meetings with Pope Paul VI, Indira Ghandi, and Simone de Beauvoir.

The blending of the personal and the political has been a trademark of feminist style, affecting great numbers of women through consciousness-raising, which served to convince women that perceived individual problems were in fact shared by a community of women. The use of autobiographical detail is also effective in the writings of feminist theorists who reach conclusions about themselves that apply to women generally. By analyzing her own experiences as an "outsider" (a Jew, a feminist, one of a tiny minority of tenured female faculty at Columbia), Carolyn Heilbrun in *Reinventing Womanhood* attempts to understand "the forces which operate upon a woman acting against the current of her time." She believes that the male monopoly on human history has inhibited women to the extent that they are unable to imagine themselves as both ambitious and female. Heilbrun makes her point by exploring current psychological theory and by examining women's fiction, claiming that women have been so handicapped that they are unable to invent autonomous female characters. To reinvent themselves, she says, women will have to resist the temptation to enter the male mainstream and will have to form supportive bonds among themselves.

In *Of Woman Born*, Adrienne Rich says about herself: "When I first became pregnant I set my heart on a son . . . I wanted to give birth, at twenty-five, to my unborn self . . . someone independent, actively willing, original." Rich pushes beyond the personal as she examines the patriarchal forces that had informed her earlier attitudes. By viewing motherhood as an institution, she perceives how history and ideology have created a misogyny that has shaped women's lives.

Mary Daly's use of language is brilliant and outrageous as she indicts patriarchal institutions in *Gyn/Ecology,* a radical feminist guidebook for women's journey toward self. Daly has moved irreconcilably away from any notion of finding space for feminists within the existing male-dominated structure, a world she views as "death-oriented." Instead, she encourages women to move beyond the culture, to reserve their life-affirming energy for themselves and for one another. Poet Susan Griffin shows the connections between feminism and ecology by indicating how the patriarchy has controlled both women and nature. Her book, *Woman and Nature,* is innovative in form and totally unlike any other kind of writing. Through brief essays and by rendering a parody of the patriarchal voice, she indicts such spoilers of nature as strip-miners and such violators of women as gynecological surgeons.

Innovative style and strength of language are perhaps as important in the writings of feminist authors as the urgent messages they present. The intensity and force of Andrea Dworkin's *Our Blood* are partly explained by the fact that the essays originally appeared as speeches delivered at college campuses in the mid-1970s. Declarative sentences spill out, one after the other: "I want to talk to you about rape . . . what it is, who does it, to whom it is done, how it is done, and what to do about it so that it will not be done any more." Her feminism is hard-line radical, and she is uncompromising in her hatred and contempt for all forces that conspire against women.

Daly, Mary. *Gyn/Ecology: The Metaethics of Radical Feminism.* Boston: Beacon Press, 1978. 485p.

Dworkin, Andrea. *Our Blood: Prophecies and Discourses on Sexual Politics.* New York: Harper & Row, 1976. 118p.

Friedan, Betty. *It Changed My Life; Writings on the Women's Movement.* New York: Random House, 1976. 388p.

Fritz, Leah. *Dreamers & Dealers: An Intimate Appraisal of the Women's Movement.* Boston: Beacon Press, 1979. 293p.

Gornick, Vivian. *Essays in Feminism.* New York: Harper & Row, 1978. 234p.

Griffin, Susan. *Woman and Nature: The Roaring Inside Her.* New York: Harper & Row, 1979. 263p.

Heilbrun, Carolyn G. *Reinventing Womanhood.* New York: Norton, 1979. 244p.

Morgan, Robin. *Going Too Far: The Personal Chronicle of a Feminist.* New York: Random House, 1977. 333p.

Rich, Adrienne. *Of Women Born: Motherhood as Experience and Institution.* New York: Norton, 1976. 318p.

Rich, Adrienne. *On Lies, Secrets, and Silence: Selected Prose, 1966–1978.* New York: Norton, 1979. 310p.

Health

At the end of the 1960s, when modern feminists began to challenge a whole range of sexist attitudes within society, the women's health movement emerged as a response to a national system that ignored the needs of women's health care. Groups of women began to question a system that profits from illness and treats as disease the normal function of childbirth. In its early period these groups fought for the repeal of laws against abortion. They are now addressing issues such as the dangers of oral contraceptives, intrauterine devices, and hormone therapy; inhumane practices in childbirth; and unnecessary surgery on women's breasts and reproductive organs.

The Women's Health Movement by Sheryl Ruzek is a scholarly study of that movement within the context of social movement theory. Ruzek writes: "In the initial stages of a social movement, considerable attention goes to amassing tales of the inhumanity of a group's adversaries. In the women's health movement, this account involved documenting medical misogyny and sexism in science. Laywomen, health professionals, and academics wrote critiques for a wide range of audiences. To raise discontent, stir people to action, and create a potential membership base, a shared perspective must be generated. To do this, an effective communication network is essential." For the purpose of her study, Ruzek investigated the conventional settings of hospitals and clinics and alternative settings such as women's health collectives and health centers.

In *Seizing Our Bodies,* Claudia Dreifus provides a veritable handbook of women's health issues in this anthology that includes articles by major feminist writers. At the center of their concern is the propensity of male physicians to organize the care of female patients around their reproductive organs. Historians, journalists, and health care specialists all voice complaints against organized medicine. For Dreifus, "The great success of the women's health movement has come with the creation of a new, aggressively informed class of consumer."

In *The Hidden Malpractice,* another general book that indicts the treatment of women by the medical establishment, Gena Corea looks not only at women as patients but also as professionals who suffer poor treatment by men. She reviews past and present discrimination against women by hospitals and medical schools and provides an overview of the effect of medical misogyny within chapters on venereal disease, birth control, contraception, abortion, sterilization, and childbirth.

Barbara Seaman, who has been writing about women's health issues since the beginning of the health movement, coauthored with her husband, Gideon, a book deploring the indiscriminate use of hormones prescribed for women by the medical profession. In *Women and the Crisis in Sex Hormones,* the authors describe the dangers of oral contraceptives, DES, and estrogen therapy for menopause and offer suggestions for safe alternatives. For contraception they advise the intelligent use of diaphragms, and for the treatment of menopause symptoms they suggest sound nutrition and vitamin supplements.

Some recent books discuss health problems such as alcoholism from a woman-centered perspective or examine health problems specific to women such as anorexia nervosa. Jean Kirkpatrick, founder of Women for Sobriety, an alternative to Alcoholics Anonymous, describes in *Turnabout* her personal fight to survive what might have been a terminal disease. Kirkpatrick is convinced that women alcoholics have needs that differ from those of men because society treats women with suspicion if they are successful and with rejection if they are unskilled. Furthermore, women alcoholics suffer the stigma of being "unladylike" and are scorned. The aim of the Women for Sobriety program is to affirm the value and worth of each woman. *The Drinking Woman* by Edith Hornik and *A Dangerous Pleasure* by Geraldine Youcha are descriptions of the problems of women alcoholics by writers who, though not alcoholic themselves, understand the special problems facing women alcoholics. Hornik points out that the reaction to a drinking woman is: "How could she do this to her family," while the male alcoholic is said to be "driven to drink."

Although the condition of anorexia nervosa certainly existed before feminists began to take notice, only recently has it been recognized as an ailment particularly affecting adolescent girls. It is an eating disorder that leads to severe malnutrition and sometimes death. Its victims, typically high-achieving girls from successful families, starve themselves and put themselves through vigorous regimens of exercise. In describing her own experience in *Solitaire,* Aimee Liu indicates that by taking total control over her own body she was compensating for the lack of control she felt within her family and in the world at large.

As in so many other topics in women's studies, historians are providing documentation and interpretations that explain why certain attitudes about women have evolved. Several important studies relating to women and health have appeared in recent years. In *The Horrors of the Half-Known Life,* G. J. Barker-Benfield sets out to explain nineteenth-century male views on women and sexuality. He analyzes de Tocqueville's observation "of the uniquely extreme separation of the sexes in America"; examines the victory of male obstetricians over midwives and their subsequent control over reproduction; discusses the work of the Reverend John Todd, who wrote popular books of advice for young men; and traces the influence of Augustus Kinsley Gardner, an obstetrician and gynecologist with social and political views about reproduction. Barker-Benfield makes the point that "hostility toward women and competition among men were the conditions for the rise of modern gynecology."

Barbara Ehrenreich and Deirdre English, who have collaborated before on the subject of women and health, feel that women have too willingly accepted the authority of science. Their book, *For Her Own Good,* traces the diminution of women's past role as healers to the present state of professional medicine, which is dominated by men. A mystique about science has also interfered with women's functions in child-rearing and in household management. A social milieu in which women have been set apart as different and special—a sexual romanticism about them according to Ehrenreich and English—has just about run its course. The time has come, they feel, for a new and rational ordering of society in which women will be on an equal footing with men.

The shared faith by doctors and their women patients in the practical science of medicine is the reason why childbirth has moved into the hospital setting and away from the more humane setting of the home. Richard Wertz and Dorothy Wertz, authors of *Lying-In: A History of Childbirth in America,* provide a chronicle of 350 years of changing attitudes and theories about birth in America. An uncritical belief in the efficacy of science has led to the contemporary situation in which birthing mothers have been placed in isolation, drugged, and promptly separated from their newborn. The authors say: "What had begun in the 1920s as a pursuit of safety, comfort and efficiency, a shared effort by doctors and patients to have the 'best' for birth, had become by the 1950s and 1960s an unpleasant and alienating experience for many women." Since the 1970s women, in their effort to take control of their own bodies, have reinstituted childbirth at home and have rediscovered the midwife.

It is hard to believe that midwives assisted at 50 percent of all births in the United States until about 1910. The reasons for their disappearance are the subject of two recent histories: *Women and Men Midwives* by Jane Donegan, which describes developments between the sixteenth and nineteenth centuries; and *American Midwives: 1860 to the Present* by Judy Barrett Litoff.

Two recent books approach the history of birth control from widely differing points of view. In *From Private Vice to Public Virtue,* James Reed traces the careers of three prominent leaders—Margaret Sanger, Robert Dickinson, and Clarence Gamble—and describes how they influenced and finally won the support of the medical establishment. In contrast, Linda Gordon, who writes from a Marxist feminist perspective, sees Sanger as "part of a movement, not its inventor." In *Woman's Body, Woman's Right,* she argues that birth control has always been a political rather than a technological matter, for methods of birth control have been known since antiquity. The issue only became controversial when modern sexual repression inhibited its distribution and use.

Barker-Benfield, G. J. *The Horrors of the Half-Known Life: Male Attitudes toward Women and Sexuality in Nineteenth-Century America.* New York: Harper & Row, 1976. 352p.
Corea, Gena. *The Hidden Malpractice: How American Medicine Treats Wo-*

men as Patients and Professionals. New York: William Morrow, 1977. 309p.

Donegan, Jane B. *Women and Men Midwives: Medicine, Morality, and Misogyny in Early America.* Westport, Conn.: Greenwood Press, 1978. 316p.

Dreifus, Claudia, ed. *Seizing Our Bodies: The Politics of Women's Health.* New York: Vintage Books, 1977. 321p.

Ehrenreich, Barbara, and Deirdre English. *For Her Own Good: 150 Years of the Experts' Advice to Women.* Garden City, N.Y.: Anchor Press, 1978. 325p.

Gordon, Linda. *Woman's Body, Woman's Right: A Social History of Birth Control in America.* New York: Grossman, 1976. 479p.

Hornik, Edith Lynn. *The Drinking Woman.* New York: Association Press, 1977. 191p.

Kirkpatrick, Jean. *Turnabout: Help for a New Life.* Garden City, N.Y.: Doubleday, 1978. 183p.

Litoff, Judy Barrett. *American Midwives: 1860 to the Present.* Westport, Conn.: Greenwood Press, 1978. 197p.

Liu, Aimee. *Solitaire.* New York: Harper & Row, 1979. 215p.

Reed, James. *From Private Vice to Public Virtue: The Birth Control Movement and American Society Since 1830.* New York: Basic Books, 1978. 456p.

Ruzek, Sheryl Burt. *The Women's Health Movement: Feminist Alternatives to Medical Control.* New York: Praeger, 1978. 351p.

Seaman, Barbara, and Gideon Seaman. *Women and the Crisis in Sex Hormones.* New York: Rawson Associates, 1977. 502p.

Wertz, Richard W., and Dorothy C. Wertz. *Lying-In: A History of Childbirth in America.* New York: Free Press, 1977. 260p.

Youcha, Geraldine. *A Dangerous Pleasure.* New York: Hawthorn Books, 1978. 251p.

History

GENERAL STUDIES

Within the women's studies movement, the study of women's history is absorbing students of literature, the arts, and the social sciences, most of whom are learning the history of their respective fields only to learn that women have been left out. In the process they have come to realize that women have been ignored in general history as well. Having received their impetus from the women's movement, historians of women are now providing social history studies that illuminate the present. They are examining women's political involvement, issues about employment, health, sexuality, family responsibilities, and, most recently, the characteristics of female culture.

As the purposeful ambiguity of Nancy Cott's title would suggest, *The Bonds of Womanhood* is a study that interprets how women's separate sphere served both to tie women down as well as together. Specifically, she investigates the period between 1780 and 1835 in New England to understand the place of middle-class women in society and to see how the substance of their experience was a precondition for the emergence of the nineteenth-century feminist movement. In discussing the importance of that movement in her book, *Feminism and Suffrage,* Ellen DuBois argues that the suffrage movement, along with the black liberation and labor movements, was one of the major democratic reform efforts in American history. She focuses on the earlier years of the movement—1848–69—and traces the political strategies of Elizabeth Cady Stanton and Susan B. Anthony, who broke with abolitionism and sought an alliance with labor reformers before organizing an independent movement for women's rights. In *The Remembered Gate,* Barbara Berg refutes the traditional belief that nineteenth-century feminism grew out of abolitionism, a view held by Blanche Hersh in *The Slavery of Sex.* Instead, Berg sees the movement as an outgrowth of women's urban experience as they gained organizational skills and political awareness through working in voluntary benevolent associations on behalf of women.

While most feminist historians are attempting to demonstrate the positive aspects of female culture, Ann Douglas describes how nineteenth-century American women caught up in a socially defined identity had a deleterious effect on the culture. In *The Feminization of American Culture,* Douglas documents how two disenfranchised groups, middle-class women and Protestant clergymen, formed an alliance that ultimately led to vapid moralizing and the sentimentalization of culture. Through an examination of sources such as popular magazines, contemporary novels, and religious tracts, Douglas portrays aspects of Victorian life that she believes were the origins of modern mass culture. Through the examination of another kind of imaginative source, the records of the Lydia Pinkham Medicine Company, Sarah Stage presents in *Female Complaints* an analysis of a cultural phenomenon that sheds light on changing attitudes toward female sexuality and on the place of women in

American society. In *Women and Men on the Overland Trail,* John Faragher examines the gender cultures of the men and women who participated in the movement West between 1843 and 1870. He finds that while opportunities for women's employment outside the home were increasing in the East, "the move West called upon people not to change but to transfer old sexual roles to a new but altogether familiar environment."

For the most part, the new studies in women's history are narrowly focused and cover a brief period. But *Woman's Proper Place* by Sheila Rothman is a far ranging study that examines the period of 1870 to the present to trace changing ideas of women's proper roles and how these models have affected social policy. In a final chapter on the politics of women's liberation, Rothman finds that the issues of equal employment, day-care, and women's health have led to improvements for middle-class women while the problems of the poor have remained unchanged. In *A History of Women in America,* Carol Hymowitz and Michaele Weissman have organized a comprehensive survey of women's history based mainly on secondary sources and aimed for a popular audience. The authors' feminist perspective consistently informs the narrative they construct.

The history and politics of the women's liberation movement are the subjects of Sara Evans's *Personal Politics,* a narrative of that period told within the context of the author's own involvement. She traces the development of an independent women's movement in the 1960s from its origins in the civil rights and New Left movements.

Berg, Barbara J. *The Remembered Gate: Origins of American Feminism, The Woman and the City, 1800–1860.* New York: Oxford University Press, 1978. 334p.

Cott, Nancy F. *The Bonds of Womanhood: "Woman's Sphere" in New England, 1780–1835.* New Haven, Conn.: Yale University Press, 1977. 225p.

Douglas, Ann. *The Feminization of American Culture.* New York: Knopf, 1977. 403p.

DuBois, Ellen Carol. *Feminism and Suffrage: The Emergence of an Independent Women's Movement in America, 1848–1869.* Ithaca, N.Y.: Cornell University Press, 1978. 220p.

Evans, Sara. *Personal Politics: The Roots of Women's Liberation in the Civil Rights Movement and the New Left.* New York: Knopf, 1979. 274p.

Faragher, John Mack. *Women and Men on the Overland Trail.* New Haven, Conn.: Yale University Press, 1979. 281p.

Hersh, Blanche Glassman. *The Slavery of Sex: Feminist-Abolitionists in America.* Urbana: University of Illinois Press, 1978. 280p.

Hymowitz, Carol, and Michaele Weissman. *A History of Women in America.* New York: Bantam, 1978. 400p.

Rothman, Sheila M. *Woman's Proper Place: A History of Changing Ideals and Practices, 1870 to the Present.* New York: Basic Books, 1978. 322p.

Stage, Sarah. *Female Complaints: Lydia Pinkham and the Business of Women's Medicine.* New York: Norton, 1979. 304p.

ANTHOLOGY

Anthologies in women's history are serving important needs within classrooms, for they provide a useful tool for surveying the social history of American women. Until a comprehensive synthesis based on the new scholarship in women's history is written, collections of essays are essential.

In *The Female Experience,* Gerda Lerner documents the history of American women through excerpts from primary sources. The organization of the book is imaginative, as materials are arranged around the life cycle of women and include the experiences of ordinary women as well as the famous.

Lerner's more recent anthology, *The Majority Finds Its Past,* is a collection of her historiographical essays written between 1969 and 1979, many of which are now classics. One of the benefits of this book is that it provides a historic perspective on the development of the methodology of women's history through Lerner's pioneering and ardent scholarship. Barbara Welter's now famous essay, "The Cult of True Womanhood," appears in *Dimity Convictions,* a collection of nine of her essays on nineteenth-century American women. Welter's vast knowledge of popular literature is evident in most of these pieces and is put to particularly creative use in an essay about Anna Katharine Green, writer of the first truly American detective story.

Women of America, edited by Carol Berkin and Mary Beth Norton, offers both original documents and new essays in historiography, while *Liberating Women's History,* edited by Berenice Carroll, provides theoretical and critical essays that examine historiography, issues of sex, race, and class, and the new methodology of women's history.

In *A Heritage of Her Own,* Nancy F. Cott and Elizabeth H. Pleck provide a thoughtful collection of recent essays on the social history of American women. Articles are arranged chronologically to provide as comprehensive a view as possible of the range of scholarship now available in the field, and the editors provide an important overview in their introductory essay. *Woman's Being, Woman's Place,* edited by Mary Kelley, is a collection of articles based mainly on papers given at the Conference on the History of Women held in St. Paul in 1977. The essays are organized around the topics of sources and methodology and the themes of identity and vocation.

Berkin, Carol Ruth, and Mary Beth Norton. *Women of America: A History.* Boston: Houghton Mifflin, 1979. 442p.

Carroll, Berenice A., ed. *Liberating Women's History: Theoretical and Critical Essays.* Urbana: University of Illinois Press, 1976. 434p.

Cott, Nancy F., and Elizabeth H. Pleck. *A Heritage of Her Own: Toward a New Social History of American Women.* New York: Simon and Schuster, 1979. 608p.

Kelley, Mary, ed. *Woman's Being, Woman's Place: Female Identity and Vocation in American History.* Boston: G. K. Hall, 1979. 372p.

Lerner, Gerda, ed. *The Female Experience: An American Documentary.* Indianapolis: Bobbs-Merrill, 1977. 449p.

Lerner, Gerda. *The Majority Finds Its Past.* New York: Oxford University Press, 1979. 217p.

Welter, Barbara. *Dimity Convictions: The American Woman in the Nineteenth Century.* Athens: Ohio University Press, 1976. 230p.

BIOGRAPHY

We are not yet seeing many of what might be called "new biographies of women," that is, interpretations of women's lives that give emphasis to the conflicts they endured because they were women: the strain between professional and private roles; psychological needs; relationships to family members and to lovers. Two reasons can perhaps explain the absence of such books. First, the genre of biography is out of fashion with social historians who are concerned with the experiences of large numbers of women and not with the sensibilities of a select few. And the other reason is that first-rate biographies take a very long time to write. The biographer is committed not only to an analysis of the subject's life but also must understand the historical context of that life, an achievement that can involve years of research. It may well be that significant numbers of books will appear in the next few years.

However, a significant historical biography that does bring a woman-centered perspective to the subject is *Margaret Fuller* by Paula Blanchard, who undertook "an attempt to view Margaret Fuller's life through the eyes of another woman, living in the 1970s with an awareness of the questions raised about women in the past decade." A major task for Blanchard was to correct harsh misconceptions about Fuller that had originated with her contemporaries and had prevailed for over a century. What Blanchard achieves is a sympathetic portrait of a woman whose intellectual power is not perceived to be incompatible with her sexuality.

Bell Gale Chevigny's *The Woman and the Myth,* partly biography, mostly an anthology of Fuller's writing, also provides a generous and feminist view of Fuller's life and work. A contemporary and admirer of Margaret Fuller, the writer Julia Ward Howe is best known as the author of "The Battle Hymn of the Republic." But in *Mine Eyes Have Seen the Glory,* Deborah P. Clifford provides a full biography that examines Howe's long life and points out the strictures of mid-nineteenth–century American life on aspiring women. Ann Lane's *Mary Ritter Beard* is a collection of excerpts from Beard's writings prefaced by a long biographical essay. Beard is generally considered to be the founder of the new field of women's history and before World War II led a zealous but unsuccessful mission to establish an international archives to preserve women's records. Most astonishing to the reader, therefore, is Lane's disclosure that Beard had destroyed her own records, thereby insuring that a full-scale biography would be difficult if not impossible to execute.

A kind of book that has been appearing with regularity is the collective biography. Since they are often about unknown women and in turn reveal information on additional numbers of anonymous women, these books are compatible with the current social history trend. For example, *Let Them Speak for Themselves,* edited by Christiana Fischer, contains excerpts from diaries, letters, reminiscences, and journals of twenty-five women who lived in the American West. The cumulative effect of the book is to shatter romantic notions about frontier life. Having reluctantly left their home in the East, these frontier women were lonely, homesick, and anxious and were victimized by an ideology that obliged them to keep to their homes. The themes of isolation, sense of loss, and the need for the companionship of other women recur throughout this collection.

On a very different subject, but with the emphasis still on the experiences of unknown women, *From Parlor to Prison,* edited by Sherna Gluck, is the oral history testimony of five suffragists. From a distance of sixty years, these women—one of them is 104—recall their experiences from multiple vantage points: Greenwich Village radical, Midwestern activist in the birth control movement, newspaperwoman, federal lobbyist, advertising executive, and clubwoman.

Another collection of firsthand feminist accounts, *These Modern Women,* contains autobiographical essays by seventeen women that appeared originally in *The Nation* in 1926–27. Elaine Showalter, who edited the book, writes an excellent introduction pointing out the differences between these women and the nineteenth-century feminists who did not attempt to combine marriage with an independent life. At the same time, Showalter underlines the similarities between women in the 1920s and the 1970s, both periods in which issues such as job discrimination, sex-role conditioning, marriage contracts, and birth control have been raised and debated.

Blanchard, Paula. *Margaret Fuller: From Transcendentalism to Revolution.* New York: Delacorte Press, 1978. 364p.

Chevigny, Bell Gale. *The Woman and the Myth: Margaret Fuller's Life and Writings.* Old Westbury, N.Y.: Feminist Press, 1976. 501p.

Clifford, Deborah Pickman. *Mine Eyes Have Seen the Glory: A Biography of Julia Ward Howe.* Boston: Little, Brown, 1979. 313p.

Fischer, Christiana, ed. *Let Them Speak for Themselves: Women in the American West, 1849–1900.* Hamden, Conn.: Archon Books, 1977. 346p.

Gluck, Sherna, ed. *From Parlor to Prison: Five American Suffragists Talk about Their Lives.* New York: Vintage, 1976. 285p.

Lane, Ann J., ed. *Mary Ritter Beard: A Sourcebook.* New York: Schocken Books, 1977. 252p.

Showalter, Elaine, ed. *These Modern Women: Autobiographical Essays from the Twenties.* Old Westbury, N.Y.: Feminist Press, 1978. 147p.

Law and Politics

It comes as no surprise that the number of women holding public office has increased only slightly in the last decade. While there were 2.5 percent in 1968, by 1978 the number had crept up to only 8 percent. Political power remains a male prerogative, and traditional work in political science has ignored the role of women. However, in the light of the women's movement and its fundamental concern for equality, the reasons for the shocking under-representation of women in politics have come under analysis.

A Portrait of Marginality, edited by Marianne Githens and Jewel L. Prestage, is a comprehensive collection of essays on the political behavior of American women. Contributors discuss the problems created by female socialization for aspiring office-seekers, barriers to female involvement, the performance of women in the political arena, and the special problems of black women in politics. The editors point out that current work on women in politics has been mainly descriptive, centering on the distinctive characteristics of those few women who have participated in active politics. In constructing a useful framework for analyzing why women are largely absent from professional politics, Githens and Prestage refer to the "marginal man" theory. They explain that women who enter political life find themselves cut off from the world to which they have been socialized yet never feel at home in the world of elite politics. Such a position creates strains that serve to inhibit women from aspiring to political careers.

In the same format as her 1968 book *Few Are Chosen,* which contained interviews with ten successful political women, Peggy Lamson presents portraits of six prominent women in *In the Vanguard.* Her interviews with leaders such as Millicent Fenwick and Elizabeth Holtzman focus on seeking out those qualities that have contributed to their success against great odds. In *The Making of Political Women,* Rita Mae Kelly and Mary Boutilier are also interested in trying to explain why certain women are able to achieve political prominence. They contrast the unusual lives of thirty-six famous women with the more typical lives of political wives to reveal unique aspects of the childhoods and adult lives of women with their own careers. In her study, *Sex Roles in the State House,* Irene Diamond examines the involvement of women as state legislators and concludes that unless fundamental institutions in the larger society are restructured, women will not gain political equality. Kirsten Amundsen's *A New Look at the Silenced Majority* is an update of her earlier book, *The Silenced Majority.* Her gloomy conclusions are that women have made only token advances in the last few years and that until they gain political power, the effect of the women's movement will remain superficial.

In *Women in Western Political Thought,* Susan Okin brings a historical as well as a philosophical perspective to her analysis of the acute political disadvantages of women. She presents a systematic examination of the writings on women of such classical political philosophers as Plato, Aristotle, and Rousseau. Okin finds that these philosophers considered women only in light of their roles in families and never as individuals, the equal of men. Furthermore, she argues that a functionalist view of women continues to this day and is reflected in current laws.

Sexism and the Law by Albie Sachs and Joan Hoff Wilson focuses on the impact of sexism on the thinking and structure of the legal profession and the judiciary. The unconscious paternalism that pervades the American legal system is traced in a historical essay that reviews the legal status of women from colonial times to the present. The authors also indicate how male biases can negatively affect female lawyers and their clients.

The importance to feminists of the passage of the Equal Rights Amendment is reflected in two recent books dealing with women and the law. *Women's Rights and the Law,* written by a group of feminist attorneys connected with The Women's Law Project, describes the potential impact of ERA on state laws. *Impact ERA: Limitations and Possibilities,* edited by the Equal Rights Amendment Project of the California Commission on the Status of Women, is a collection of essays that describe the economic, social, and psychological impact implicit in the amendment.

No problem was more vexing to the new wave of proponents of ERA in the early 1970s than the opposition of labor leaders who had fought for protective legislation for women at a time when it was needed. Although the Civil Rights Act of 1964 and the Equal Pay Act of 1963 have been interpreted to invalidate most protective legislation, Judith Baer still finds the issue significant for feminists. In *The Chains of Protection,* she traces the history of protective laws and sees them as a microcosm for "assumptions and logical fallacies which have characterized our thinking about sex equality." Baer is also concerned here with the implications of the tensions between protection and restriction in the law and between women's rights and the rights of the society in general.

Amundsen, Kirsten. *A New Look at the Silenced Majority: Women and American Democracy.* Englewood Cliffs, N.J.: Prentice-Hall, 1977. 172p.

Baer, Judith A. *The Chains of Protection: The Judicial Response to Women's Labor Legislation.* Westport, Conn.: Greenwood Press, 1978. 238p.

Brown, Barbara A., et al. *Women's Rights and the Law: The Impact of the ERA on State Laws.* New York: Praeger, 1977. 432p.

California. Equal Rights Amendment Project. *Impact ERA: Limitations and Possibilities.* Edited by the Equal Rights Amendment Project of the California Commission on the Status of Women. Millbrae, Calif.: Les Femmes, 1976. 287p.

Diamond, Irene. *Sex Roles in the State House.* New Haven, Conn.: Yale University Press, 1977. 214p.

Githens, Marianne, and Jewel L. Prestage, eds. *A Portrait of Marginality: The Political Behavior of the American Woman.* New York: David McKay, 1977. 428p.

Kelly, Rita Mae, and Mary Boutilier. *The Making of Political Women: A Study of Socialization and Role Conflict.* Chicago: Nelson-Hall, 1977. 376p.

Lamson, Peggy. *In the Vanguard: Six American Women in Public Life.* Boston: Houghton Mifflin, 1979. 233p.

Okin, Susan Moller. *Women in Western Political Thought.* Princeton, N.J.: Princeton University Press, 1979. 371p.

Sachs, Albie, and Joan Hoff Wilson. *Sexism and the Law: A Study of Male Beliefs and Legal Bias in Britain and the United States.* New York: Free Press, 1978. 257p.

Lesbian/Feminism

Lesbian/feminism is much more than a sexual choice. Janice Raymond defines it as "a total perspective on life in a patriarchal society representing a primal commitment to women on all levels of existence and challenging the bulwark of a sexist society—that is, heterosexism." While heterosexual feminists are reformist in that they put their energy into the long and difficult job of trying to create equity between men and women, lesbian/feminists begin at a different place. By rejecting close relationships with men, they circumvent the possibility of male dominance, thus reserving their energy for themselves and for other women. Mary Daly and Adrienne Rich consistently write brilliant critiques of the institution of heterosexuality and are influential proponents of the lesbian/feminist position.

Like other feminist writing, contemporary works by lesbians reflect an intense need to reclaim and celebrate a history. Adrienne Rich describes the condition of lost history as "cultural imperialism—the decision made by one group of people that another group shall be cut off from their past, shall be kept from the power of memory, context, continuity." *Lesbian Lives* and *The Lavender Herring,* both edited by Barbara Grier and Coletta Reid, are collections of essays from *The Ladder,* a unique lesbian publication, which appeared from 1956 to 1972. *Lesbian Lives* brings together all of the biographical essays that appeared in the journal, and *The Lavender Herring* is a selection of nonfiction on topics such as rape and medical sadism, issues that only later became primary to all feminists. Both anthologies are significant contributions to lesbian history. And lesbians and gay men are currently recording their own history. *The Gay Report* by Karla Jay and Allen Young gives the results of the first comprehensive survey of the homosexual community based on 5,000 copies of a questionnaire. Participants gave information about their childhood, sexual experiences, politics, and ambitions.

Jonathan Katz's *Gay American History* is an impressively researched collection of documents that span 400 years of the experiences of lesbians and gay men. Katz is sensitive to the particular problems of lesbians, understanding that their persecution is closely associated with the oppression of all women. In a chapter on women who passed themselves off as men, he provides a feminist analysis by noting that although these women may have rejected their assigned female role, they all too quickly embraced the socially defined male role. While earlier writing focused on homosexuality as a purely psychological phenomenon, Katz's and other recent books are evidence that gay men and lesbians are now defining themselves.

The growth of lesbian identity has led to a sense of community among women who, until recently, felt isolated as outsiders. Resource books that provide essential information to homosexuals are now appearing. *Our Right to Love,* edited by Ginny Vida and produced in cooperation with women of

The National Gay Task Force, is a comprehensive collection of articles on such topics as health, politics, the law, and the media, and includes personal testimonies by lesbians of varying ages. *Positively Gay,* edited by Betty Berzon and Robert Leighton, is a book of essays designed to aid members of the gay community develop positive attitudes about themselves. Experts present gay and lesbian perspectives on family relationships, religion, professional life, job security, aging, and gay parenting. The book includes an excellent foreword by Evelyn Hooker, a heteroxesual psychologist who was instrumental in formulating principles underlying the gay rights movement of the 1970s.

The problems of lesbian mothers are receiving increasing attention. *The Lesbian* by Bernice Goodman, a psychotherapist and one of the founders of The Institute for Human Identity, contains essays that explode the myths and explore the avenues of help for lesbian mothers who are viciously misunderstood in the society. *By Her Own Admission* by Gifford Gibson and Mary Jo Risher is the painful account of one mother's losing battle for the custody of her child because of her lesbian life-style.

Berzon, Betty, and Robert Leighton, eds. *Positively Gay.* Millbrae, Calif.: Celestial Arts, 1979. 219p.

Gibson, Gifford Guy, and Mary Jo Risher. *By Her Own Admission: A Lesbian Mother's Fight to Keep Her Son.* Garden City, N.Y.: Doubleday, 1977. 276p.

Goodman, Bernice. *The Lesbian: A Celebration of Difference.* Brooklyn, N.Y.: Out & Out Books, 1977. 69p.

Grier, Barbara, and Coletta Reid, eds. *The Lavender Herring: Lesbian Essays from The Ladder.* Baltimore: Diana Press, 1976. 357p.

Grier, Barbara, and Coletta Reid. *Lesbian Lives: Biographies of Women from The Ladder.* Oakland, Calif.: Diana Press, 1976. 432p.

Jay, Karla, and Allen Young. *The Gay Report: Lesbians and Gay Men Speak Out about Sexual Experiences and Lifestyles.* New York: Summit Books, 1979. 816p.

Katz, Jonathan. *Gay American History: Lesbians and Gay Men in the U.S.A.* New York: Thomas Y. Crowell, 1976. 690p.

Vida, Ginny, ed. *Our Right to Love: A Lesbian Resource Book.* Englewood Cliffs, N.J.: Prentice-Hall, 1978. 318p.

Life Styles

Certain nonfiction books provide descriptions of the texture and milieu of women's lives not often found outside of fiction. Susan Sheehan's *A Welfare Mother* takes the reader through the daily life of Carmen Santana, a Puerto Rican woman living in New York. Through a spare writing style and with a keen eye, Sheehan describes the endless round of poverty that keeps Santana living only for the moment and never planning for the future, a cycle that will inevitably be repeated by the next generation. The lack of social or economic improvement throughout six generations of an American family is the most sobering observation drawn by Dorothy Gallagher from her impressive *Hannah's Daughters,* an unromanticized oral history of working-class women. Gallagher interviewed five generations of Lambertsons, beginning with the ninety-eight-year-old Hannah, who lived alone on welfare, and ending with Lisa, a twenty-year-old mother married to an unskilled worker. To her surprise, Gallagher learned that within the family new generations were never urged to obtain more education; family members had never involved themselves in organized labor; and most of the women had experienced several failed marriages. The women's oral testimonies also revealed the inability of mothers to express love to daughters, a way of being that no doubt began when Hannah was deprived of her mother when she was three years old.

In *Women of Crisis,* Robert Coles and Jane Coles present portraits of five women: a migrant farm worker, a resident of Harlan County, Appalachia, a Chicana of San Antonio, an Eskimo of Alaska, and a maid from Cambridge, Massachusetts. Their lives are made difficult by the compound problems of class, race, and sex, factors emphasized by the Coleses in their astute commentaries that are interwoven among the direct quotations from the women themselves. Although they describe lives of utter hardship, the Coleses find the dignity that is present in these women and are ever mindful of the sad unfairness of life that separates the poor from the privileged.

Lillian Rubin's intention in *Worlds of Pain* is similar to the Coleses' in that she investigates the lives of ordinary women to see how they cope. She interviewed fifty white working-class families and, for the purposes of comparison, twenty-five professional, middle-class families. Rubin is concerned with the contrast between the myth of the American dream, which promises affluence for all who are willing to work for it, and the realities of the static quality of working-class life in an inflationary economy. She looks at the dynamics of family life and how her subjects respond to the forces that are creating change within familiar institutions. In *Nobody Speaks for Me!* Nancy Seifer is interested in seeing how the last decade of social change has influenced some traditional working-class women to take on roles as activists. Seifer sees the women's movement "as the most significant movement for social change in our history [the success of which] will depend to a great extent upon the involvement of working-class women and upon our ability to relate communalism to feminist goals." The ten women portrayed in the oral histories presented here found their political voices by working on behalf of their immediate communities.

Jessie Bernard's *Self-Portrait of a Family* introduces a range of women's issues different from questions of class and race. Bernard faced problems as a single parent of three (her husband died when the youngest child was less than one year old), trying to manage a professional life while raising and guiding her family. Her book includes letters written during the 1960s, a tumultuous period for everybody, but particularly difficult for adolescents trying to find their way. Bernard's skill as a sociologist and her feminist convictions add special dimensions to this rich account of family life.

Bernard, Jessie. *Self-Portrait of a Family: Letters by Jessie, Dorothy Lee, Claude and David Bernard.* Boston: Beacon Press, 1978. 344p.

Coles, Robert, and Jane Hallowell Coles. *Women of Crisis: Lives of Struggle and Hope.* New York: Delacorte Press/S. Lawrence, 1978. 291p.

Gallagher, Dorothy. *Hannah's Daughers: Six Generations of an American Family: 1876–1976.* New York: Thomas Y. Crowell, 1976. 343p.

Rubin, Lillian B. *Worlds of Pain: Life in the Working-Class Family.* New York: Basic Books, 1976. 268p.

Seifer, Nancy. *Nobody Speaks for Me! Self-Portraits of American Working Class Women.* New York: Simon and Schuster, 1976. 477p.

Sheehan, Susan. *A Welfare Mother.* Boston: Houghton Mifflin, 1976. 109p.

Literature and the Fine Arts

LITERARY CRITICISM

Feminist books about women and literature have proliferated in the last few years. According to the analysis of one major feminist critic (see Annette Kolodny's "Dancing through the Minefield: Some Observations on the Theory, Practice and Politics of a Feminist Literary Criticism" in *Feminist Studies,* Spring 1980), feminist critics have been discovering lost women writers and their works and at the same time have been subjecting male writing to feminist scrutiny. The result of this work has not been a unified school of feminist literary criticism but instead, according to Kolodny, "an acute and impassioned attentiveness to the ways in which primarily male structures of power are inscribed . . . in our literary inheritance; the consequences of that encoding and, with that, a shared analytic concern for the implications of that encoding not only for a better understanding of the past, but also for an improved reordering of the present and future as well." Kolodny defends pluralism in feminist approaches to literature because she finds it to be consistent with the current status of the women's movement, which is full of debate, espousing no one single cause.

In the past, most students of literature found acceptable the dictum that to write "like a woman" was a subliterary exercise to be avoided in oneself and scorned in others. Now scholars are finding rich female traditions in the writings of women. In *A Literature of Their Own,* Elaine Showalter provides interesting social and literary commentary by placing well-known novelists such as the Brontës, George Eliot, Virginia Woolf, and Doris Lessing within the context of their unknown female contemporaries. The intent of Ellen Moers's *Literary Women* is to suggest that the experiences of women have led them to special traditions that appear in their writings. In *Communities of Women,* Nina Auerbach describes a strong and positive tradition of sisterhood among characters in the novels of Jane Austen, Louisa May Alcott, and others.

The most ambitious study to date that analyzes female traditions in literature is *The Madwoman in the Attic* by Sandra M. Gilbert and Susan Gubar. In the first of six parts of the book, "Toward a Feminist Poetics," the authors show that despite "anxiety of authorship," women began in the eighteenth century to write books that contained "fictional worlds in which patriarchal images and conventions were severely, radically revised." Other parts of the book are about specific nineteenth-century women writers. The "madwoman" of the title refers to Rochester's demented wife in *Jane Eyre,* but symbolizes the alter egos of many nineteenth-century heroines and their female creators who felt trapped by patriarchal convention. Barbara Rigney, whose approach in *Madness and Sexual Politics in the Feminist Novel* is psychoanalytic, discusses madness in Virginia Woolf's *Mrs. Dalloway,* Doris Lessing's *The Four-Gated City,* and Margaret Atwood's *Surfacing* as well as in Charlotte Brontë's

Jane Eyre. Rigney uses R. D. Laing's interpretation of madness as a coping device to describe the plight of feminist characters in conflict with society.

Recent studies are examining traditions within American literature. In *Woman's Fiction*, Nina Baym analyzes popular fiction of the nineteenth century and suggests that within the restrictions of Victorian life women writers urged their women readers to take responsibility for their own lives. Although Baym is cautious in her literary claims for these novels, she is convinced of their significance as social history. Two studies, *The Faces of Eve* by Judith Fryer and *The Resisting Reader* by Judith Fetterley, apply a feminist perspective to male writing. Fryer looks at the myth of America as Garden of Eden and points out that although the American Adam in literature has been widely studied, Eve has been ignored. She looks at the portrayal of women by major writers such as Hawthorne, Melville, James, and Howells. Like Fryer, Fetterley scrutinizes the treatment of women by male writers, but applies her analysis to twentieth-century writers as well as to the nineteenth-century giants.

In a highly readable collection of essays, *Sex, Class, and Culture,* Lillian Robinson provides both theoretical essays in criticism and selections that put her criticism to use. She is equally comfortable whether setting out theory of high art or gauging the significance of popular television shows or trashy novels. In setting up criteria for feminist criticism she says, "To be effective, feminist criticism cannot become bourgeois criticism in drag. It must be ideological and moral criticism; it must be revolutionary." Two other important collections, *Feminist Criticism* edited by Cheryl Brown and Karen Olson and *The Authority of Experience* edited by Arlyn Diamond and Lee Edwards, bring together an eclectic array of writings by a number of feminist critics.

Auerbach, Nina. *Communities of Women: An Idea in Fiction.* Cambridge, Mass.: Harvard University Press, 1978. 222p.

Baym, Nina. *Woman's Fiction: A Guide to Novels by and about Women in America, 1820–1870.* Ithaca, N.Y.: Cornell University Press, 1978. 320p.

Brown, Cheryl, and Karen Olson, eds. *Feminist Criticism: Essays on Theory, Poetry, and Prose.* Metuchen, N.J.: Scarecrow Press, 1978. 369p.

Diamond, Arlyn, and Lee R. Edwards, eds. *The Authority of Experience: Essays in Feminist Criticism.* Amherst: University of Massachusetts Press, 1977. 304p.

Fetterley, Judith. *The Resisting Reader: A Feminist Approach to American Fiction.* Bloomington: Indiana University Press, 1978. 198p.

Fryer, Judith. *The Faces of Eve: Women in the Nineteenth-Century American Novel.* New York: Oxford University Press, 1976. 294p.

Gilbert, Sandra M., and Susan Gubar. *The Madwoman in the Attic: The Woman Writer and the Nineteenth-Century Literary Imagination.* New Haven, Conn.: Yale University Press, 1979. 719p.

Moers, Ellen. *Literary Women.* Garden City, N.Y.: Doubleday, 1976. 336p.

Rigney, Barbara Hill. *Madness and Sexual Politics in the Feminist Novel.* Madison: University of Wisconsin Press, 1978. 148p.

Robinson, Lilliam S. *Sex, Class, and Culture.* Bloomington: Indiana University Press, 1978. 349p.

Showalter, Elaine. *A Literature of Their Own: British Women Novelists from Brontë to Lessing.* Princeton, N.J.: Princeton University Press, 1977. 378p.

BIOGRAPHY

Martha Saxton's biography of Louisa May Alcott, *Louisa May,* has a feminist perspective in that Saxton views Alcott's life within the context of her assigned female role as it was played out as dutiful daughter, devoted sister, spinster, and successful writer. Saxton uses *Little Women* as a central metaphor to explain how Alcott dealt with the moral pressure imposed by her highly principled parents who had great expectations for all their children. Saxton interprets the novel as an imaginative acceptance of the moral prescription imposed by Bronson Alcott. Like her creator, Jo must fight to control her anger and spunkiness, and she must take responsibility for the survival of the March family. Saxton contrasts that novel with Alcott's fiction written under a pseudonym, work that exhibits the darker side of her imagination. In it her characters deal with sexuality and other strong passions.

Although she is not seriously read today, Edna Ferber was an immensely popular novelist in her own time. In this first biography, *Ferber,* oddly presented in reverse chronology, Julie Gilbert offers a vivid portrait that captures her great-aunt's volatile personality. Most interesting were her complicated relationships with her mother and sister, whom she financially supported. Their disappointing marriages had brought little reward, and Ferber, who had never married, seems to have despised them for their failure and dependence.

Edith Wharton, whose novels earned considerable money and critical acclaim when they first appeared, has been consistently admired as a major American writer. Now the appearance of two recent biographies, *Edith Wharton* By R. W. B. Lewis and *A Feast of Words* by Cynthia Wolff, has created interest in her life as well as her art. In his preface Lewis writes: "Wharton's writings are quiet, continuing testimony to the female experience under modern historical and social conditions, to the modes of entrapment, betrayal, and exclusion devised for women in the first decades of the American and European twentieth century." His biography is aimed at balancing the facts of Wharton's life against the time in which she lived, and in indicating how her experiences became absorbed into her fiction. Wolff concerns herself with the question of how it was possible for a woman of Wharton's background and emotional makeup to become a successful novelist. To explain this creative process, Wolff makes judicious use of psychological theory, her focus always on how Wharton's experiences affected her fiction.

The appearance of *The Habit of Being,* the letters of Flannery O'Connor, was hailed as a literary event because they reveal the integrity and spirit of a woman whose short stories are considered masterpieces. When failing health confined her to her home in the South under the care of her mother, most of O'Connor's communication with the world transpired through her writing— in her literature and in these letters. Her relationship with her mother was obviously the key one in her life, a connection that is being explored in a forthcoming biography by Sally Fitzgerald, the editor of this volume.

Anne Sexton's letters, edited by Linda Gray Sexton and Lois Ames, reveal a personality that contrasts sharply with O'Connor's. Thoroughly modern in the literary sense of the term, Sexton's intensity focused on herself and led to anxiety and feelings of alienation that drove her to mental illness and eventual suicide. Her emotions are the subject of her often moving poetry.

Gilbert, Julie Goldsmith. *Ferber: A Biography.* Garden City, N.Y.: Doubleday, 1978. 445p.

Lewis, Richard Warrington Baldwin. *Edith Wharton: A Biography.* New York: Harper & Row, 1975. 592p.

O'Connor, Flannery. *The Habit of Being.* Letters edited and with an introduction by Sally Fitzgerald. New York: Farrar Straus & Giroux, 1979. 617p.

Saxton, Martha. *Louisa May: A Modern Biography of Louisa May Alcott.* Boston: Houghton Mifflin, 1977. 428p.

Sexton, Anne. *Anne Sexton: A Self-Portrait in Letters,* edited by Linda Gray Sexton and Lois Ames. Boston: Houghton Mifflin, 1977. 433p.

Wolff, Cynthia Griffin. *A Feast of Words: The Triumph of Edith Wharton.* New York: Oxford University Press, 1977. 453p.

FINE ARTS

Feminist art historians are bringing up issues that are as richly complex as those being addressed by feminist literary critics. Challenges to the male-dominated art world go beyond a concern for the establishment of a female aesthetic and include a feminist reappraisal of art and art history; re-examinations of art, artists, and society; restructuring of art education; and the creation of changes within institutions. *Feminist Collage,* edited by Judy Loeb, is a collection of essays that treats all of these topics in an attempt to educate women in the visual arts. Lucy Lippard, an established art critic and a feminist, defines in *From the Center* her personal development as a feminist and applies her new awareness to the works of women artists. She makes no claim for establishing a new feminist criticism, but instead hopes that her contributions will help to develop one.

As in literature, the search for lost artists is a consistent theme in books about women and art. *Women and Creativity* by Joelynn Snyder-Ott explores differences between male and female experiences as exhibited in art and describes how women's contributions have been neglected and misunderstood.

In 1977 art historians Ann Sutherland Harris and Linda Nochlin organized an international exhibition of art by women for the Los Angeles County Museum of Art, an exhibit that traveled to Austin, Pittsburgh, and Brooklyn. *Women Artists 1550–1950* is the catalog of this exhibit, which included the work of eighty-five women painters. Illustrations of the paintings accompanied by detailed commentaries about each artist, her work, and the context of her time make up the major part of the book. Harris and Nochlin offer a long introductory essay to this groundbreaking exhibit. Three books, *Women Artists* by Karen Petersen and J. J. Wilson, *Women and Art* by Elsa Honig Fine, and *The Obstacle Race* by Germaine Greer, cover hundreds of years of the history of women and art in these authors' attempts to set right the historic neglect of women artists. Petersen and Wilson include Chinese art, while Fine confines her study to European and American work, including American folk art. Greer's intention is "to shown women artists not as a string of overrated individuals but as members of a group having much in common, tormented by . . . the obstacles both external and surmountable, internal and insurmountable of the race for achievement." Her text is replete with social commentary and amusing remarks. However, her conclusion is most serious, for her analysis of women's art leads her to believe that there have been no female daVincis because the society has conditioned women to be self-destructive. And a damaged ego does not create great art.

While most of the re-examination of women's place in art focuses on professional painters, some recent books are looking at women's contributions to folk art and to crafts. *Artists in Aprons* by C. Kurt Dewhurst, Betty MacDowell, and Marsha MacDowell, based on a show organized by the authors, illustrates how untrained women exceeded traditional expectations and produced beautiful art. In keeping with their prescribed roles, women folk artists created works to decorate their own homes, including embroideries, drawings, watercolors, and oils. This book examines traditions in folk art and places the work within the context of its period. The arts and crafts movement, which started in England as a reaction to industrialization and the dread of shoddy workmanship, has not credited women with their contributions. In *Women Artists of the Arts and Crafts Movement,* Anthea Callen identifies four distinct groups who were involved: working-class women, who were trained and employed in traditional rural crafts; aristocratic women, who organized training for destitute gentlewomen; destitute gentlewomen, who worked for wages in their homes; educated middle-class women, usually related to men who were in the vanguard of the movement. Callen describes these women's lives and their art, amply illustrating what they created. While women gained creative satisfaction and financial rewards, the movement remained in the hands of men who until now have received all the credit.

Judy Chicago's *The Dinner Party,* is undoubtedly the best known example of feminist art today. Her book tells the story behind the creation of what is described as a "monumental sculpture," consisting of thirty-nine china-painted plates, elaborately embroidered runners covering an open triangular table, and a "Heritage Floor" made of 2,300 porcelain tiles bearing the names of 999 historically significant women. Chicago looked to traditional women's folk art for inspiration and ideas for executing her massive tribute to women.

Where most of the recent books on women and art involve a historic quest for neglected artists and their work, Eleanor Munro's *Originals* approaches contemporary women artists who have already received recognition. She interviewed forty women for clues on the source of their creativity. She learns, for instance, that an identification with nature is common to women artists and is the basis of their images, while for men the female nude form is a fundamental source of images. More than a series of interviews, Munro's book is a learned and sensitive examination of art and women and, most important, confronts the question of whether there is a "woman's art."

Callen, Anthea. *Women Artists of the Arts and Crafts Movement, 1870–1914.* New York: Pantheon, 1979. 282p.

Chicago, Judy. *The Dinner Party: A Symbol of Our Heritage.* New York: Anchor Press/Doubleday, 1979. 255p.

Dewhurst, C. Kurt, Betty MacDowell, and Marsha MacDowell. *Artists in Aprons: Folk Art by American Women.* New York: E. P. Dutton in association with the Museum of American Folk Art, 1979. 202p.

Fine, Elsa Honig. *Women and Art: A History of Women Painters and Sculptors from the Renaissance to the 20th Century.* Montclair, N.J.: Allanheld & Schram/Prior, 1978. 240p.

Greer, Germaine. *The Obstacle Race: The Fortunes of Women Painters and Their Work.* New York: Farrar Straus & Giroux, 1979. 373p.

Harris, Ann Sutherland, and Linda Nochlin. *Women Artists, 1550–1950.* Los Angeles: Los Angeles County Museum of Art; New York: Knopf, 1977. 367p.

Lippard, Lucy R. *From the Center: Feminist Essays on Women's Art.* New York: E. P. Dutton, 1976. 314p.

Loeb, Judy, ed. *Feminist Collage: Educating Women in the Visual Arts.* New York: Teachers College Press, 1979. 317p.

Munro, Eleanor. *Originals: American Women Artists.* New York: Simon and Schuster, 1979. 528p.

Petersen, Karen, and J. J. Wilson. *Women Artists: Recognition and Reappraisal from the Early Middle Ages to the Twentieth Century.* New York: Harper & Row, 1976. 212p.

Snyder-Ott, Joelynn. *Women and Creativity.* Millbrae, Calif.: Les Femmes, 1978. 144p.

Marriage

Changing expectations of and attitudes about women's roles in marriage have been basic themes in feminist literature since the beginning of the women's movement. Older women who are already committed to traditional marriage but at the same time attracted to feminist ideology are finding themselves with new sets of problems as they attempt to change rules that have been implicit in their relationships. Angela McBride describes this dilemma in *A Married Feminist*. Younger women who have not yet been restricted by old conventions are being advised about new options. *For Better, For Worse* by Jennifer Baker Fleming and Carolyn Washburne is a book about marriage and other choices for contemporary living. At the heart of the authors' advice is the assumption that women must never place themselves in situations of complete dependence, but must instead maintain a degree of emotional and economic independence. Although marriage and motherhood are still the choice of many young women, Fleming and Washburne point out other possibilities: marriage without children, living together without marrying, the single life, lesbian relationships, and group living. The authors bring up other issues, such as conflicts of motherhood, violence in marriage, wages for housework, and discrimination against women in the workplace. The problems facing women who are combining motherhood with careers is the focus of *The Balancing Act* edited by Sydelle Kramer, in which five young women describe the style of their marriages and how they cope in trying to balance career, husband, child, and self.

Single life is no longer considered to be a deviant or temporary condition. In *Single Blessedness*, Margaret Adams, who considers herself happily unmarried, takes issue with the notion that single people lead lonely "half-lives." Adams believes that her insights, which are based on her own experiences and on interviews with other single people, have significance in that "an honest exploration of the role and status of single women . . . can add to feminist literature a hitherto untapped wealth of facts, ideas, and philosophical perspectives that will broaden understanding of women's position in general." Lucia Bequaert in *Single Women, Alone and Together* looks at the range of women who are single—widows, divorced women, never-married women, lesbians—in an analysis of the texture of their lives. She finds that a large number of these women aspire to a future that includes a long-term relationship with a man. Bequaert advocates women bonding together to help one another lead productive lives not dependent on old norms.

Many women are seeking identities as single women only after having gone through the trauma of a divorce. They often approach divorce not only in emotional confusion but also in ignorance of their legal options. In *Dissolution*, Riane Eisler demystifies the ramifications of changing divorce laws as they affect women's lives, especially the economic effects of the no-fault divorce laws. Two books provide journal-like narratives of the divorce experience. Nancy Wilkins's *Divorced* is a sober, often anguished, account of her passage from a standard middle-class housewife and mother to a self-reliant single parent and provider. Although the essential facts of Erica Abeel's story are the same as Wilkins's, *Only When I Laugh* is written with an irony and wit that overlays the pain and anger that are described. Abeel's literary imagination gives her some perspective on her plight as a ditched wife and mother of two.

Anna Demeter's *Legal Kidnaping* begins as a classic account of a woman breaking out of a marriage made impossible by a violent and controlling husband. However, when the enraged husband steals the couple's two young children and disappears, the experience takes on profound significance, for it raises questions about the rights of parents over children. As Demeter learned, fathers have "rights of access to their children, exactly as if they were pieces of property." In contrast, a mother's right to her children is based on an examination of the nature of the relationship. As other unfortunate women are finding out, the kidnaping of children by vengeful fathers is a growing problem, and mothers are discovering that the law offers virtually no protection.

Abeel, Erica. *Only When I Laugh.* New York: William Morrow, 1978. 336p.

Adams, Margaret. *Single Blessedness: Observations on the Single Status in Married Society.* New York: Basic Books, 1976. 264p.

Bequaert, Lucia H. *Single Women, Alone and Together.* Boston: Beacon Press, 1976. 256p.

Demeter, Anna. *Legal Kidnaping: What Happens to a Family When the Father Kidnaps Two Children.* Boston: Beacon Press, 1977. 148p.

Eisler, Riane Tennenhaus. *Dissolution: No-Fault Divorce, Marriage, and the Future of Women.* New York: McGraw-Hill, 1977. 279p.

Fleming, Jennifer Baker, and Carolyn Kott Washburne. *For Better, For Worse: A Feminist Handbook on Marriage and Other Options.* New York: Scribner's, 1977. 406p.

Kramer, Sydelle, ed. *The Balancing Act.* Chicago: Chicago Review Press/Swallow Press, 1976. 217p.

McBride, Angela Barron. *A Married Feminist.* New York: Harper & Row, 1976. 244p.

Wilkins, Nancy, with Mary Ellen Reese. *Divorced.* New York: Wyden Books, 1977. 217p.

Prostitution

Although few books about prostitution have appeared recently, those that have are of particular value because authors are approaching the subject from a serious and woman-centered point of view. In the introduction to their comprehensive *Prostitution: An Illustrated Social History,* Vern Bullough and Bonnie Bullough state that "prostitution is the ultimate sign of the inequality of the sexes, and as long as women are subordinate and live in a society where there is a double standard, we will have prostitution." The Bulloughs have amassed a compendium of information from antiquity to the present, using foreign language treatises and literary sources as well as standard English language studies. In discussing contemporary American attitudes about prostitution, they point out inconsistencies and hypocrisies inherent in a society that is both uninformed about the problem and punitive to women in its laws. The Bulloughs feel that decriminalization of sexual activities between consenting adults is a rational objective for this country.

In *The Madam as Entrepreneur,* sociologist Barbara Heyl presents a life history of Ann, a former prostitute and madam, as she moves away from a deviant toward a respectable world. Whereas other studies usually take up the theme of why women turn to a life of prostitution, Heyl asks how they do it. She is concerned with process: "What are the steps the woman takes as she moves into the illegal occupation? What are the psychological turning points in that process? What experiences significantly increase the chances that she will become a prostitute, and what experiences diminish those chances? How does she learn to work in her new occupation, and how does she adapt to its accompanying life-style?" Heyl presents extraordinary data. For instance, she had at her disposal the teaching tapes used by the madam to train inexperienced prostitutes. While direct statements by the prostitutes are always interesting, Heyl's frequent reference-laden sociological analyses can be wearing. Nevertheless, the book provides new information and insights about prostitutes.

In contrast to Heyl's book, which is a life history in the sociological sense, with attention to corroborating data, *The Maimie Papers* provides an autobiographical account of a former prostitute through her letters. From 1910 to 1922, Maimie Pinzer corresponded with Fanny Quincy Howe, a high-born Bostonian. The two had met through a social worker, and Howe's unlikely involvement grew out of a highly developed social consciousness and a responsiveness to Maimie's gift for expression. This book chronicles Maimie's half of the correspondence. Maimie made keen observations about herself and others, vividly describing past hardships and everyday problems. "Respectability too often means a cheap room with cheap surroundings," she comments, offering readers an insight into why she had preferred prostitution to factory work. Her early life was filled with bitter family fights, struggles against venereal disease that led to the loss of an eye, and a winning battle against morphine addiction. By the time she met Howe, Maimie was trying to lead a respectable life, an aspiration to which she ultimately succeeded.

Female Sexual Slavery is an account of the sexual exploitation of women written with an intensity and anger reminiscent of Susan Brownmiller's *Against Our Will*, a study of rape. Its author, Kathleen Barry, set out to prove that "sadistic violence and sexual enslavement are not isolated or remote phenomena." She describes and documents the modern day international traffic in women, the savagery of pimps, and the obscenity of pornography. Barry shares with Brownmiller the conviction that all women are potential victims in a society in which men routinely abuse women.

Barry, Kathleen. *Female Sexual Slavery.* Englewood Cliffs, N.J.: Prentice-Hall, 1979. 274p.

Bullough, Vern, and Bonnie Bullough. *Prostitution: An Illustrated Social History.* New York: Crown, 1978. 336p.

Heyl, Barbara Sherman. *The Madam as Entrepreneur: Career Management in House Prostitution.* New Brunswick, N.J.: Transaction Books, 1979. 276p.

Pinzer, Maimie. *The Maimie Papers.* Old Westbury, N.Y.: Feminist Press, 1977. 439p.

Psychology

The issue of difference between men and women is a continuous theme in the literature about women. Sociobiologists believe that inherent differences exist and account for the social organization that traditionally has existed between the sexes. In contrast, most feminists believe that—apart from the obvious genital differences—men and women are essentially the same and that society has constructed roles for women that narrowly define their expectations and behavior. Writing from the perspective of a multiple of disciplines, feminists point out how social institutions systematically inhibit the development of autonomy for women. However, more complex views of how to think about difference has emerged recently in literature on the psychology of women.

Nancy Chodorow rejects the usual social learning explanation accepted by most feminists who believe that females begin to learn their role when they are handed their first doll. Although she certainly agrees that society reinforces stereotyped behavior, Chodorow looks to psychoanalytic theory to explain the source of the sexual division of labor. *The Reproduction of Mothering* is a closely argued account of how the motive to mother is reproduced across generations. She sees "the contemporary reproduction of mothering as a central and constituting element in the social organization and reproduction of gender" and argues that "the contemporary reproduction of mothering occurs through social structurally induced psychological processes. It is neither a product of biology nor of intentional role-training. I draw on the psychoanalytic account of female and male personality development to demonstrate that women's mothering reproduces itself cyclically. Women, as mothers, produce daughters with mothering capacities and the desire to mother." Though the book is devoted mainly to developing and supporting her argument, Chodorow is also concerned with social change. In her view, the sharing of primary child-care responsibilities between women and men will not only lead to autonomy for women, but will reverse the psychological dynamic that causes men to devalue women.

Dorothy Dinnerstein makes the same point in *The Mermaid and the Minotaur* and also undertakes an analysis of why both men and women resist changing the fixed psychological complementarity that has dominated relations between the sexes. At the root of what she calls "human malaise," a description of this stagnant arrangement, is the fear of female will, a fear carried over from everyone's infancy when women held all power over the young. To explain male dominance, Dinnerstein says, "The essential fact about paternal authority, the fact that makes both sexes accept it as a model for the ruling of the world, is that it is under prevailing conditions a sanctuary from maternal authority." Dinnerstein arrives at her insights not only from her training as a psychologist, but also through intuition and a literary imagination. She uses the terms "mermaid" and "minotaur" to symbolize "the pernicious prevailing forms of collaboration between the sexes" in which "both men and women will remain semi-human, monstrous." She predicts dire consequences for a society that continues to distort and undervalue its human potential, for she concludes that women's lack of participation in history is ultimately life-rejecting.

Jean Baker Miller is also concerned with the issue of difference in *Toward a New Psychology of Women,* a book more suggestive than definitive in its intent. Miller explains that her overall attempt "is to look toward a more accurate understanding of women's psychology as it arises out of women's life experiences rather than as it has been perceived by those who do not have that experience." She effectively examines what she perceives to be women's strengths, qualities generally undervalued in the society: to create and nurture human life, to be able to admit to feelings of weakness and vulnerability, to give and to serve others, and to affiliate with others. She urges women to seek self-definition and self-determination rather than autonomy, a concept that does not encompass women's ability to relate to others. Miller has, in effect, laid the groundwork for a feminist humanism, a world she envisions in which life-affirming qualities will take precedence over old definitions of power and conflict.

Two general books on the psychology of women offer feminist perspectives on a wide range of topics. Juanita Williams's *Psychology of Women* is a basic introductory text that describes myths and stereotypes about women in a historical context, presents early psychoanalytic views of women, and discusses the two extreme schools that attempt to explain women's behavior: biological determinism and sociocultural learning. Other chapters, organized around woman's life cycle, treat topics such as sexuality, birth control, and aging. In *Women: Psychology's Puzzle,* Joanna Rohrbaugh examines research in five key areas of female psychology—biology, personality, social roles, bodily functions, and mental health—and compares what she finds with women's own opinions and findings. With erudition and wit she criticizes conclusions about women that have gone unchallenged. Of the biological determinists she says, "Each researcher tends to concentrate on a species whose behaviors support that researcher's underlying assumptions and attitude about sex difference."

Chodorow, Nancy. *The Reproduction of Mothering: Psychoanalysis and the Sociology of Gender.* Berkeley: University of California Press, 1978. 263p.

Dinnerstein, Dorothy. *The Mermaid and the Minotaur: Sexual Arrangements and Human Malaise.* New York: Harper & Row, 1976. 288p.

Miller, Jean Baker. *Toward a New Psychology of Women.* Boston: Beacon Press, 1976. 143p.

Rohrbaugh, Joanna Bunker. *Women: Psychology's Puzzle.* New York: Basic Books, 1979. 505p.

Williams, Juanita H. *Psychology of Women: Behavior in a Biosocial Context.* New York: Norton, 1977. 444p.

Rape and Other Violence against Women

By 1975 rape had become a central issue for feminists who see the act or the threat of rape as a means by which women are kept subjugated. In the last few years other violent acts against women—battering, incest, sexual mutilation, and pornography—have been gaining attention. They are issues that have been ignored by a society which correctly views them as repellent. Ridding themselves of the taboos against talking about these atrocities, feminists are now finding and reporting pertinent data and offering important interpretations.

Susan Griffin, who wrote a landmark essay on rape in 1971 which first appeared in *Ramparts,* includes that essay and three others in her book, *Rape: The Power of Consciousness.* In a summary of how she now has come to think about the subject, she writes: "But I am no longer impassioned to argue with anyone that women do not seek pain, that we do not want to be raped; that we do not cause our own rapes. Because in this last eight years . . . we have created another culture for ourselves—a refuge in which women's words are believed."

In a vivid narrative describing her own desperate experience as a rape victim, Jennifer Barr conveys in *Within a Dark Wood* the trauma of victimization not only during the assult, but for months after. The young mother of a new baby, Barr had been attacked in her own suburban community during a morning walk. In addition to the terror and humiliation of the assault itself, there was the legacy of having to deal with repressed anger and grief. Barr could not understand how nature and God could have allowed this to happen. She was prevented from taking solitary walks and otherwise enjoying life. With the help of a support group made up of other rape victims, Barr eventually moved out of her deep depression and toward a better understanding of herself. She also gained a better understanding of the harshness of a world where men can dominate women by sheer brute force.

The importance of institutional support of rape victims is the substance of *The Victim of Rape: Institutional Reactions* by Lynda L. Holmstrom and Ann W. Burgess. The authors, a sociologist and a psychiatric nurse, collaborated on an earlier book, *Rape: Victims of Crises,* which describes the need for rape crises intervention services. In their recent book they make policy recommendations for the institutional responses to rape victims, calling for the need for programs for victims, the need to sensitize professionals, including those connected with the criminal justice system, and a system for compensating victims.

Diana E. H. Russell, a feminist sociologist, who also wrote an earlier book on rape, has co-edited with Nicole Van de Van *Crimes against Women: Proceedings of the International Tribunal.* In 1976, over 2,000 women from forty countries met to denounce crimes against women. Their list includes forced motherhood, crimes perpetuated by the medical profession, persecution of lesbians, economic crimes, and violence against women (rape, woman battering, and the atrocities of genital mutilation—clitoridectomy, excision, and infibulation).

The growing international network among feminists is reflected in Betsy Warrior's work, *Working on Wife Abuse.* The book is a guide to information about services and sources of funding for individuals and groups personally or professionally concerned with the problem. Among her many insights, Warrior points out that while women have been battered uninterruptedly for centuries, the rights and safety of men cause continuing concern (i.e., the worry over police who are endangered in cases involving domestic crises).

Questions about why men abuse their wives and why the victims stay around to be repeatedly brutalized are examined by Del Martin in *Battered Wives.* Wife-beating, she says, "has roots in historical attitudes towards women, the institution of marriage, the economy, the intricacies of criminal and civil law, and the delivery system of social service agencies." Women stay in violent situations because they become locked in a role, unable to imagine themselves living any other way. Battered women who are trapped by economic needs, the lack of child care, and no job training suffer from a paralysis of will and become unable to deal with the world. This syndrome is described as "learned helplessness" by psychologist Lenore E. Walker in her book, *The Battered Woman.* She identifies a three-stage battering cycle: "The slow tense escalation of violence; the violent battering episode; the period of reconciliation in which the assaulter becomes contrite, affectionate, and promises never to do it again." After all this, the whole cycle begins again. In looking for a solution, Walker concludes that only when true equality between men and women exists can the society be free from domestic violence.

In *Family Violence,* sociologist Richard Gelles points out that violent crimes are more likely to occur within the domestic setting that anywhere else in our society. He offers the startling fact that violence toward pregnant wives is a regular phenomenon. And in her book, *Battered Women,* editor Maria Roy explains the cyclical pattern whereby children repeat their parents' behavior.

Terry Davidson writes about her own experiences as the child of a wife-beating clergyman in *Conjugal Crime.* Her father's abuse of her mother was the family secret, and Davidson indicates how his sordid violence negatively affected the children in the family, jeopardizing normal relationships with people.

Incest, a problem of increasing social concern, is finally being discussed by professionals and victims from a feminist point of view. Two recent books written by women who had been victimized are *Kiss Daddy Goodnight* by Louise Armstrong and *Father's Days* by Katherine Brady. In preparation for her study, Armstrong advertised for respondents who would discuss their experiences with the author. She talked to 183 women and presents here seventeen accounts including her own. Of her own experience, Brady writes: "I tell my story now with the hope that other incest victims will hear in it the two things I wished most, but had to wait years to learn: You are not alone and you are not to blame." Brady endured her father's sexual abuse until she was engaged, thereby becoming the property of another man in her father's eyes.

Armstrong, Louise. *Kiss Daddy Goodnight: A Speak-Out on Incest.* New York: Hawthorn Books, 1978. 256p.

Barr, Jennifer. *Within a Dark Wood: The Personal Story of a Rape Victim.* Garden City, N.Y.: Doubleday, 1979. 284p.

Brady, Katherine. *Father's Days: A True Story of Incest.* New York: Seaview, 1979. 216p.

Davidson, Terry. *Conjugal Crime: Understanding and Changing the Wife-beating Pattern.* New York: Hawthorn Books, 1978. 274p.

Gelles, Richard J. *Family Violence.* Beverly Hills: Sage, 1979. 218p.

Griffin, Susan. *Rape: The Power of Consciousness.* New York: Harper & Row, 1979. 134p.

Holmstrom, Lynda Lytle, and Ann Wolbert Burgess. *The Victim of Rape: Institutional Reactions.* New York: John Wiley, 1978. 293p.

Martin, Del. *Battered Wives.* San Francisco: Glide, 1976. 269p.

Roy, Maria, ed. *Battered Women: A Psychosociological Study of Domestic Violence.* New York: Van Nostrand, 1977. 334p.

Russell, Diana E. H., and Nicole Van de Ven, eds. *Crimes against Women: Proceedings of the International Tribunal.* Millbrae, Calif.: Les Femmes, 1976. 298p.

Walker, Lenore E. *The Battered Woman.* New York: Harper & Row, 1979. 270p.

Warrior, Betsy. *Working on Wife Abuse,* 6th ed. Cambridge, Mass.: Privately printed (46 Pleasant St.), 1978. 110p.

Religion

To the unenlightened, feminist activity in religion is thought to be confined to the comings and goings of women who are either leaving convents on their way to matrimonial altars or are banging on the doors of churches demanding to be priests and ministers. As such incidents have occurred, the media have played them up as signs of our revolutionary times. However, the real revolution involving women and religion is not yet attracting public attention because it is occurring in the minds of feminist theologians who are challenging every patriarchal assumption existing in Western thought. Women's studies in religion is paradigmatic of the larger women's studies movement. It is multidisciplined, making use of the content and methodology of history, literature, classics, psychology, anthropology, and art history.

Feminists believe that traditional religions have betrayed women by passing off as "truth" a virulent sexism that has been largely responsible for women's historic subjugation. Rosemary Ruether, a highly regarded theologian, relates the sexism of Christian tradition to the dualistic and hierarchal views that originated in the classical world. Soul, spirit, rationality, and transcendence are seen as opposites of body, flesh, matter, and nature. The positive aspects of the dualism relate to God, while the negative sides relate to the material world. Ruether believes that classical dualism became the model for women's oppression when men identified the positive side of the division with themselves, and the negative with women over whom they felt entitled to rule. Furthermore, the construction of male language and imagery in traditional religion has served to shut women out from all central roles in the worship of God.

Ruether's analysis can be found in *Womanspirit Rising,* a collection of contemporary feminist essays on religion that offers a range of perspectives startling in its diversity. Editors Carol Christ and Judith Plaskow identify a major division between thinkers they call "reformist," who are trying to create radical feminist change within existing religions, and those they call "revolutionary," who are basing a feminist theology on women's unique life experiences, since they find traditional religions hopelessly sexist. Some of the "revolutionaries" are turning to the prebiblical past to construct new feminist spiritual visions and are exploring the history of goddess worship and witchcraft. Others are finding significant feminist symbols in women's literature and in dreams.

Women of Spirit, edited by Rosemary Ruether and Eleanor McLaughlin, is a collection of essays on leadership roles of women in the Jewish and Christian traditions. The content ranges from an examination of women in early Christian communities to the struggle for priesthood in contemporary times. The editors hope that women who are now gaining access to central roles of leadership will use the insights of these historic women in order to "reshape and enlarge the vision and life of the church today." *Women and Religion,* edited by Elizabeth Clark and Herbert Richardson, contains representative selections from St. Augustine, Thomas Aquinas, Martin Luther, and others that epitomize traditional negative religious attitudes toward women.

Referring to herself as a "psychologist of religion," Naomi Goldenberg writes that "when feminists succeed in changing the position of women in Christianity and Judaism, they will shake these religions at their roots." Convinced that the nature of religion lies in the symbols and images it exalts, Goldenberg argues that as women take over religious leadership, a demasculinization of God will bring an end to God. Her book, *Changing of the Gods,* is an exploration of where the new wave of religion will lead for women and men both. Goldenberg is attracted to symbols and myths that have an inward as opposed to an external reality and sees spiritual possibilities in modern feminist witchcraft. As Starhawk explains in *The Spiral Dance,* modern witchcraft should not be confused with popular notions of hags on broomsticks, or worse, with devil worship. She defines it as "not based on dogma or a set of beliefs, nor on scriptures or a sacred book revealed by a great men [but] takes its teachings from nature, and reads inspiration in the movement of the sun, moon, and stars, the flight of birds, the slow growth of trees, and the cycles of the seasons." In *When God Was a Woman*, Merlin Stone offers the thesis that thousands of years before the Old Testament a female deity reigned supreme in the ancient Near East and that women held more power and prestige in the goddess-worshipping cultures. Stone suggests that by unearthing these images of female power, women can gain a renewed sense of both female and religious possibilities.

The intransigence of the Mormon Church on feminist issues is already well documented. What Marilyn Warenski provides in *Patriarchs and Politics* is a history and analysis of Mormon attitudes toward women, pointing out that the Mormon culture is a microcosm of patriarchy. The patriarchal ways of the Jewish religion have been commented upon since the beginning of the women's movement by feminists, some of whom have formed a distinct Jewish feminist movement. *The Jewish Woman,* edited by Elizabeth Koltun, is a collection of essays that goes beyond a listing of grievances against traditional thought in an attempt to discover new roles for women and men. Contributors investigate women in history, provide insights about the life cycle of women, reinterpret biblical stories, and suggest new liturgy.

The desire of religiously committed women to be spiritual leaders, a calling never questioned in men, has been the subject of great controversy. In 1974 eleven women were ordained priests of the Episcopal Church in defiance of Church regulations that have since changed. Two of the participants, Alla Bozarth-Campbell and Carter Heyward, have written accounts that include their spiritual development before the ordination and what has happened to them since. Bozarth-Campbell's *Womanpriest* is an effusive biography that touches only briefly on the event of the ordination; Heyward's *A Priest For-*

ever, a more tightly constructed book, focuses almost entirely on that critical period of her life.

It is a sign of the times that books about nuns are no longer wrenching accounts of individual leave-taking in the mode of Monica Baldwin's *I Leap Over the Wall.* The new books are sociological studies. In her general survey *The Nuns,* British writer Marcelle Bernstein interviewed more than 500 nuns around the world, from cloistered women to executives in competitive business. Bernstein is interested in the effect of the radical religious movements on convent life and in the growing irritation with male dominance that the nuns are expressing. Sociologist Suzanne Campbell-Jones has written a scholarly study, *In Habit,* which investigates why women are drawn to religious life and measures their reactions to changes within religious orders. Lucinda SanGiovanni's *Ex-Nuns* is concerned with the 30,000 nuns who have in the last decade made the transition from religious to secular life. Her study is presented as an analysis of role passage in adult life.

Bernstein, Marcelle. *The Nuns.* Philadelphia and New York: J. B. Lippincott, 1976. 326p.

Bozarth-Campbell, Alla. *Womanpriest: A Personal Odyssey.* New York: Paulist Press, 1978. 229p.

Campbell-Jones, Suzanne. *In Habit: A Study of Working Nuns.* New York: Pantheon, 1978. 229p.

Christ, Carol P., and Judith Plaskow, eds. *Womanspirit Rising: A Feminist Reader in Religion.* New York: Harper & Row, 1979. 287p.

Clark, Elizabeth, and Herbert Richardson, eds. *Women and Religion: A Feminist Sourcebook of Christian Thought.* New York: Harper & Row, 1977. 296p.

Goldenberg, Naomi. *Changing of the Gods: Feminism and the End of Traditional Religions.* Boston: Beacon Press, 1979. 152p.

Heyward, Carter. *A Priest Forever: The Formation of a Woman and a Priest.* New York: Harper & Row, 1976. 146p.

Koltun, Elizabeth, ed. *The Jewish Woman: New Perspectives.* New York: Schocken Books, 1976. 294p.

Ruether, Rosemary, and Eleanor McLaughlin. *Women of Spirit: Female Leadership in the Jewish and Christian Traditions.* New York: Simon and Schuster, 1979. 400p.

SanGiovanni, Lucinda. *Ex-Nuns: A Study of Emergent Role Passage.* Norwood, N.J.: Ablex, 1978. 184p.

Starhawk. *The Spiral Dance: A Rebirth of the Ancient Religion of the Great Goddess.* New York: Harper & Row, 1979. 218p.

Stone, Merlin. *When God Was a Woman.* New York: Dial Press, 1976. 265p.

Warenski, Marilyn. *Patriarchs and Politics: The Plight of the Mormon Woman.* New York: McGraw-Hill, 1978. 304p.

Sex Roles

No one committed to the cause of equal rights for women still has to be convinced that sex-role socialization is damaging. The facts are in. From the start of the women's movement feminists have testified that obstacles confront the development of females in the society from the moment the first tiny pink bow is attached to a baby girl's first lock of hair. Academics are now documenting the undermining effects of sex-role stereotyping. Literary critics are identifying negative images of women in fiction; art historians are revealing the limitations that have been imposed on female artists; social historians are describing a variety of restrictions placed on women in the past; and psychologists and sociologists are providing data that describe the effects of present restrictions.

A great number of studies, textbooks, and readers that instruct about the evils of socially constructed roles for women—and for men as well—have come into existence. In *Women and Sex Roles,* a team of social psychologists provides a comprehensive review of existing research that illuminates the effects of sexism on men and women, the reasons for sex differences between men and women, and the psychological effects of traditional sex roles. Janet Giele's *Women and the Future* pulls together an impressive amount of sociological literature on changing sex roles and provides an analysis of the implications of these changes on the future. *The Longest War* by Carol Tavris and Carole Offir provides an overview and an evaluation of the best available research on sex differences from the perspectives of all of the social sciences. Although *The Second X* by Judith Long Laws is bluntly feminist in its purpose and tone, it is also a scholarly book. In chapters entitled "Woman as Worker," "Woman as Housewife," "Woman as Object," "Woman as Girl-Child," and "Woman as Androgyne," Laws sets out to expose the viciousness of socially prescribed roles, and her intention always is to help create social change. Though written for a general audience, *Beyond Sugar and Spice* by Caryl Rivers, Rosalind Barnett, and Grace Baruch is based on a wide range of data from psychology, sociology, and anthropology. The authors are concerned with the question of competence in women and describe not only the possible negative influences of parenting, the educational system, and society on young females, but also point the way to rearing daughters in an atmosphere free from socially imposed restrictions.

The most imaginative approach to the subject of sex roles that has yet appeared is Janice Raymond's *The Transsexual Empire.* Most of the people who subject themselves to sex-change operations are male, and Raymond's appraisal of what she calls the male-to-constructed-female transsexual is that such a person is not a woman at all, but a multilated victim of a sexist society. The supposition of the medical/psychiatric professionals who create transsexuals is that a stereotyped world of femaleness exists. Patients who seek entrance to such a world would be better served if they were given encouragement "to transcend cultural definitions of both masculinity and femininity, without changing [their] body."

Frieze, Irene H., et al. *Women and Sex Roles: A Social Psychological Perspective.* New York: Norton, 1978. 444p.

Giele, Janet Zollinger. *Women and the Future: Changing Sex Roles in Modern America.* New York: Free Press, 1978. 386p.

Laws, Judith Long. *The Second X: Sex Role and Social Role.* New York: Elsevier, 1979. 405p.

Raymond, Janice G. *The Transsexual Empire: The Making of the She-Male.* Boston: Beacon Press, 1979. 220p.

Rivers, Caryl, Rosalind Barnett, and Grace Baruch. *Beyond Sugar and Spice: How Women Grow, Learn, and Thrive.* New York: G. P. Putnam's Sons, 1979. 333p.

Tavris, Carol, and Carole Offir. *The Longest War: Sex Differences in Perspective.* New York: Harcourt Brace Jovanovich, 1977. 333p.

Work

The topic of work continues to be of major interest to feminist activists and to scholars writing about women from a sociological or historical perspective. The topic remains intrinsic to the study of women because it captures the problems connnected to the social changes experienced by women as they leave the context of the family for additional social roles.

While many of the current books deal with the problems of professional women—lack of advancement in business, the complexities of juggling multiple responsibilities, difficulties within the dual-career family—numbers of books are investigating the problems of working-class women.

The Managerial Woman by Margaret Hennig and Anne Jardim is an influential book that seems to have inspired a genre devoted to the subject of how women can get ahead in business. The authors are concerned with the question of female style in management and point out its deficiencies for reaching high levels of achievement. They offer the examples of twenty-five successful women to illustrate the demands of ambition and the sacrifices required to compete within a male-dominated culture. The thesis of Rosabeth Moss Kanter's *Men and Women of the Corporation* is that "forms of work organization, and the conceptions of roles and distributions of people within them, shape behavioral outcomes." Her impressive chapter on the dynamics of tokenism and its effects on blacks and women has received wide attention from feminists as well as from those concerned with corporate structure.

Alice M. Yohalem, who studied the lives of professional women in the early 1960s, takes a new look at their dilemmas in *The Careers of Professional Women.* This study centers on the extent to which women with graduate or professional training have used their skills and how they resolved conflicts between professional and traditional responsibilities. In *The Two-Paycheck Marriage,* Caroline Bird pulls together what is presently known about the impact of a wife's job on her family and on the community. Basing her information on studies, biographies, and interviews, Bird concludes that enough women are earning enough money to change the terms of both family and work. For example, she points out that by having their children in their forties after careers have been established, women will be in a position to hire people to attend to domestic responsibilities. This impact of increased numbers of working women on the quality of American life is the subject matter of *Women at Work* edited by Henry Myers. Based on a series of articles originally appearing in *The Wall Street Journal* in 1978, the book looks at such phenomena as the demise of voluntary organizations, the lack of shoppers in stores during the workday, and the growing disparity in income between traditional and two-career families—all the result of the numbers of women now in the work force.

Two books that offer more personal testimonies of the experience of women at work are *Working It Out* edited by Sara Ruddick and Pamela Daniels and *Pink Collar Workers* by Louise Kapp Howe. The first book consists of essays by well-known feminist writers and artists such as Catharine Stimpson, Tillie Olsen, and Miriam Schapiro, for whom work is creative and spiritually fulfilling. In contrast, Howe's book examines the world of women who work for little or no wages—beauticians, department store clerks, homemakers—in traditional female occupations that have not yet benefited from the attention activated by the women's movement. Office workers have fared somewhat better in that organizations such as 9 to 5 in Boston, Women Employed in Chicago, Cleveland Women Working, and Women Office Workers in New York are working toward better pay and benefits and improved working conditions for their constituents. In *Not Servants, Not Machines,* Jean Tepperman describes the origins and activities of this organized movement.

American working women are the subject of numerous recent studies by historians. Their scholarship is encompassing the preindustrial period, women's participation in manufacturing, and women as trade-unionists, as domestic workers, in white-collar jobs, and as unpaid workers in their own home.

In *We Were There,* Barbara Wertheimer provides a narrative history of working women from the precolonial period to the mid-twentieth century. She focuses on wage-earning women, leaving out the contributions of women artists, professionals, and reformers whose history has been less ignored. Most noteworthy is her material on black women in colonial times and as slaves in the nineteenth century. Philip Foner's *Women and the American Labor Movement,* based mainly on primary sources, is also concerned with the history of wage-earning women, but focuses on their participation in the organized labor movement.

The editors of *America's Working Women* have brought together documents that trace the participation of working-class women throughout American history. Beginning with native American women, selections include information about slaves, indentured servants, factory women, immigrants, and war workers and lead up to the present concerns of welfare mothers and gay workers. Since working women leave few lasting records, the compilers had to use union records, short stories, poems, songs, social workers' reports, newspaper accounts, and statistical studies. As Marxist-feminists, the editors feel that the neglect of working-class women has not been accidental but rather "part of a systematic exclusion of the working class from the history and cultural records of our country, and an attempt to dissuade the contemporary working class from imagining that it could be in control of its own destiny." This book is offered as a political act in the conviction that a restored history can lead to change.

In an historical overview of white working-class women in America, Susan Kennedy argues that "the primary characteristic which distinguishes American working-class women of the mid-1970s from their historical counterparts is the beginning of identity and recognition." Her book, *If All We Did Was to Weep at Home,* takes its title from a quotation from a Jewish immigrant woman who participated in the angry protest against the price of kosher meat in 1902. Documents about that protest can be found in *America's Working Women.*

In a study limited to the period between 1870 and 1920, David Katzman examines the lives of domestic servants. *Seven Days a Week* focuses on this period of rapid American industrialization and urbanization to explore why women became servants, what they thought of their jobs, and how the nature of their work changed over time. He concludes that "as long as the personalized mistress/servant relationship is retained, household labor will command low status, and unhappy mistresses and oppressed servants will persist."

Leslie Tentler, who looks at women workers in the years between 1900 and 1930, argues that working-class women were all too willing to leave the work place in exchange for the economic security of marriage. *Wage-Earning Women* concludes that the experience of work reinforced women's dependency. For women in low-paying jobs, advancement did not seem possible, and staying home became their goal.

Thomas Dublin looks at a much earlier period in history, 1820–60, in a study of the first generation of American women who entered the work force in numbers. *Women at Work* is a history of the beginning of the textile industry in Lowell, Massachusetts, and a description of the community life of the women workers who left farm for factory. By interpreting demographic as well as traditional sources, Dublin traces the decline of working conditions and wages as immigrant workers began to replace Yankee women.

Other contemporary historic accounts of women workers can be found in *Class, Sex and the Woman Worker,* edited by Milton Cantor and Bruce Laurie. This collection of essays from recent conferences applies new perspectives on labor history, ethnic history, and women's studies to the history of American women workers from the early nineteenth to the mid-twentieth century, and includes essays by Alice Kessler-Harris, Lise Vogel, Robin Jacoby Miller, and Nancy Schram Dye.

Accounts of the place of women within the development of specific occupations are providing important social history. Dee Garrison, who writes about librarians, and Mary Walsh, who is concerend with the history of women doctors, present interesting conclusions. In *Apostles of Culture* Garrison shows that as the field changed from all male in the 1850s to more than three-quarters female by 1910, women received lower wages than men and rarely advanced to higher positions. Furthermore, as the field became feminized, the status of library work declined. Conversely, as Walsh describes in *Doctors Wanted; No Women Need Apply,* after 1900 women were effectively barred from medical education by male physicians who feared that an influx of women would decrease the status of the profession, thereby reducing medical fees.

Baxandall, Rosalyn, et al., comps. *America's Working Women: A Documentary History, 1600 to the Present.* New York: Random House, 1976. 408p.

Bird, Caroline. *The Two-Paycheck Marriage.* New York: Rawson, Wade, 1979. 305p.

Cantor, Milton, and Bruce Laurie, eds. *Class, Sex and the Woman Worker.* Westport, Conn.: Greenwood Press, 1977. 253p.

Dublin, Thomas. *Women at Work: The Transformation of Work and Community in Lowell, Massachusetts, 1826–1860.* New York: Columbia University Press, 1979. 312p.

Foner, Philip S. *Women and the American Labor Movement: From Colonial Times to the Eve of World War I.* New York: Free Press, 1979. 621p.

Garrison, Dee. *Apostles of Culture: The Public Librarian and American Society, 1876–1920.* New York: Free Press, 1979. 319p.

Hennig, Margaret, and Anne Jardim. *The Managerial Woman.* Garden City, N.Y.: Doubleday, 1977. 221p.

Howe, Louise Kapp. *Pink Collar Workers: Inside the World of Women's Work.* New York: G. P. Putnam's Sons, 1977. 301p.

Kanter, Rosabeth Moss. *Men and Women of the Corporation.* New York: Basic Books, 1977. 348p.

Katzman, David M. *Seven Days a Week: Women and Domestic Service in Industrializing America.* New York: Oxford University Press, 1978. 374p.

Kennedy, Susan Estabrook. *If All We Did Was to Weep at Home: A History of White Working-Class Women in America.* Bloomington: Indiana University Press, 1979. 331p.

Myers, Henry, ed. *Women at Work: How They're Reshaping America.* Princeton, N.J.: Dow Jones Books, 1979. 236p.

Ruddick, Sara, and Pamela Daniels, eds. *Working It Out: 23 Women Writers, Artists, Scientists, and Scholars Talk about Their Lives and Work.* New York: Pantheon Books, 1977. 349p.

Tentler, Leslie Woodcock. *Wage-Earning Women: Industrial Work and Family Life in the United States, 1900–1930.* New York: Oxford University Press, 1979. 266p.

Tepperman, Jean. *Not Servants, Not Machines: Office Workers Speak Out.* Boston: Beacon Press, 1976. 188p.

Walsh, Mary Roth. *"Doctors Wanted; No Women Need Apply": Sexual Barriers in the Medical Profession, 1835–1975.* New Haven, Conn.: Yale University Press, 1977. 303p.

Wertheimer, Barbara M. *We Were There: The Story of Working Women in America.* New York: Pantheon Books, 1977. 427p.

Yohalem, Alice M. *The Careers of Professional Women: Commitment and Conflict.* Montclair, N.J.: Allanheld Osmun and Co., 1979. 224p.

Index

247

A Note on the Author

Barbara Haber is the curator of printed books at the Arthur and Elizabeth Schlesinger Library on the History of Women in America at Radcliffe College. She is also an advisory editor in women's studies for G. K. Hall & Co., Boston, and is presently working on a series, *Women in American History,* for Twayne, a division of G. K. Hall. Born and reared in Milwaukee, Wisconsin. Ms. Haber has a B.S. from the University of Wisconsin, a M.A. from the University of Chicago, and a M.L.S. from Simmons College. In 1979 she was designated special Radcliffe Scholar.